JOHN FORREST.

EXPLORATIONS

IN

AUSTRALIA:

I.—EXPLORATIONS IN SEARCH OF DR. LEICHARDT AND PARTY.

II.—FROM PERTH TO ADELAIDE, AROUND THE GREAT
AUSTRALIAN BIGHT.

III.—FROM CHAMPION BAY, ACROSS THE DESERT TO THE
TELEGRAPH AND TO ADELAIDE.

WITH AN APPENDIX ON THE CONDITION OF

WESTERN AUSTRALIA.

By JOHN FORREST, F.R.G.S.

ILLUSTRATIONS BY G. F. ANGAS.

GREENWOOD PRESS, PUBLISHERS
NEW YORK

Originally published in 1875
by Sampson Low, Marston, Low, & Searle

First Greenwood Reprinting 1969

Library of Congress Catalogue Card Number 68-55225

SBN 8371-1648-1

PRINTED IN UNITED STATES OF AMERICA

TO HIS EXCELLENCY

FREDERICK ALOYSIUS WELD, ESQ., C.M.G.,

GOVERNOR OF TASMANIA,

LATE GOVERNOR AND COMMANDER-IN-CHIEF OF WESTERN AUSTRALIA.

———◆———

My dear Governor Weld,

It was during your administration of the Government of Western Australia, and chiefly owing to your zeal and support, that most of the work of exploration described in this volume was undertaken and carried out. Your encouragement revived the love of exploration which had almost died out in our colony before you arrived.

With gratitude and pleasure I ask you to accept the dedication of this volume as an expression of my appreciation of your kindness and support.

Yours very faithfully,

JOHN FORREST.

CONTENTS.

CHAPTER I.

CHAPTER II.

FIRST EXPEDITION IN SEARCH OF LEICHARDT.

CHAPTER III.

SECOND EXPEDITION.—FROM PERTH TO ADELAIDE, ROUND THE GREAT BIGHT.

CONTENTS.

MAPS.

ILLUSTRATIONS.

EXPLORATIONS IN AUSTRALIA.

CHAPTER I.

Previous Expeditions into the Interior.—Attempts to discover a Route between South and Western Australia.—Eyre's Disastrous Journey.—Leichardt, the Lost Explorer.—The Latest Explorations.

As the history of the principal expeditions into the interior of Australia has been narrated by several able writers, I do not propose to repeat what has already been so well told. But, to make the narrative of my own journeys more intelligible, and to explain the motives for making them, it is necessary that I should briefly sketch the expeditions undertaken for the purpose of ascertaining the nature of the vast regions intervening between Western and the other Australian colonies, and determining the possibility of opening up direct overland communication.

With energetic, if at times uncertain, steps the adventurous colonists have advanced from the settlements on the eastern and southern coasts of

the vast island into the interior.   Expeditions, led
by intrepid explorers, have forced their way against
all but insurmountable difficulties into the hitherto unknown regions which lie to the north and
west of the eastern colonies.   Settlements have
been established on the shores of the Gulf of Carpentaria.   Burke and a small party crossed Australia from south to north, enduring innumerable
hardships, Burke, with two of his associates, perishing on the return journey.   About the same time
Stuart crossed farther to the west, reaching the
very centre of Australia, and telegraphic wires now
almost exactly follow his line of route, affording
communication, by way of Port Darwin, between
Adelaide and the great telegraphic systems of the
world.

The telegraph line divides Australia into two
portions, nearly equal in dimensions, but very different in character.   To the east are the busy and
rapidly advancing settlements, fertile plains, extensive ranges of grassy downs, broad rivers,
abundant vegetation; to the west a "great lone
land,"—a wilderness interspersed with salt marshes
and lakes, barren hills, and "spinifex deserts."
It is the Sahara of the south, but a Sahara
with few oases of fertility, beyond which is the
thin fringe of scattered settlements of the colony
of Western Australia.   To cross this desert, to
discover routes connecting the western territory
with South Australia and the line marked by the

telegraph, has been the ambition of later explorers. Mr. Gregory attempted, from the north, to ascend the Victoria River, but only reached the upper edge of the great desert. Dr. Leichardt, who had previously travelled from Moreton Bay, on the eastern coast, to Port Essington on the northern, attempted to cross from the eastern to the western shores, and has not since been heard of. Mr. Eyre made a journey, memorable for the misfortunes which attended it, and the sufferings he endured, from Adelaide round the head of the great bay, or Bight of Southern Australia, to Perth, the capital of Western Australia ; and much more recently Colonel Egerton Warburton succeeded in crossing from the telegraphic line to the western coast across the northern part of the great wilderness, nearly touching the farthest point reached by Mr. Gregory.

It was in the year 1840, only four years after the foundation of South Australia, that the first great attempt to discover a route from Adelaide to the settlements in Western Australia was made. There then resided in South Australia a man of great energy and restless activity, Edward John Eyre, whose name was afterwards known throughout the world in connexion with the Jamaica outbreak of 1865, and the measures which, as Governor, he adopted for repressing it. It was anticipated that a profitable trade between the colonies might be carried on if sheep and other live-stock could be transferred from one to the other in a mode less expensive than was afforded by the sea route between Adelaide and the Swan River. Eyre did not believe in the possibility of establishing a practicable route, but urged, through the press, the desirability of exploring the vast regions to the north, which he anticipated would afford a good and profitable field for adventurous enterprise. He offered to lead an expedition which should explore the country around the great salt lake lying to the north-west of the settled portion of the colony, and to which the name of Lake Torrens had been given. Very little was known of this lake, and absolutely nothing of the country beyond. The general supposition, in which Eyre shared, was that there existed a large space of barren land, most probably the bed of a sea which had at one time divided the continent into several islands ; but it was hoped that no insuperable difficulties in the way of crossing it would present themselves, and beyond might be a fertile and valuable district, offering an almost unbounded field for settlement, and with which permanent communications might without great difficulty be established. Some geographers were of opinion that an inland sea might be in existence, and, if so, of course water communication with the northern half of Australia could be effected.

Mr. Eyre's proposition found ready acceptance with the colonists. The Government granted 100*l.*

—a small sum indeed—but the colony was then young, and far from being in flourishing circumstances. Friends lent their assistance, enthusiasm was aroused, and in little more than three weeks from the time when Eyre proposed the expedition, he started on his journey. Five Europeans accompanied him, and two natives, "black boys," were attached to the party, which was provided with thirteen horses, forty sheep, and provisions for three months. Lake Torrens was reached, and then the difficulties of the expedition began. Although dignified with the name of "lake," it proved to be an enormous swamp, without surface water, and the mud coated with a thin layer of salt. The party struggled to effect a passage, and penetrated into the slime for six miles, until they were in imminent danger of sinking. The lake, or rather salt swamp, presented a barrier which Eyre considered it impossible to overcome. The party turned in a westerly direction, and reached the sea at Port Lincoln. Here a little open boat was obtained, and Mr. Scott, Eyre's courageous companion, undertook to attempt to reach Adelaide and obtain further supplies. This he successfully accomplished, returning in the "Water Witch" with stores and provisions, two more men, and some kangaroo dogs. Thus reinforced, the party reached Fowler's Bay in the great Bight of South Australia. The map shows that a journey of more than 200 miles must have been made before the

point was reached.   Thence they attempted to
make their way round the head of the Bight, but
were twice baffled by want of water.   Nothing
daunted, Eyre made a third attempt, and succeeded
in penetrating fifty miles beyond the head of the
Bight.   But the result was achieved only at a cost
which the little party could ill sustain.   Four of
the best horses perished, which deprived Eyre of
the means of carrying provisions, and he had to
decide between abandoning the expedition altogether or still further reducing the number of his
companions.   Mr. Scott and three men returned to
Adelaide, leaving behind a man named Baxter, who
had long been in Eyre's employ as an overseer or
factotum; the two natives who had first started
with him, and a boy, Wylie, who had before been
in Eyre's service, and who had been brought back
in the cutter.

Six months after Eyre had started from Adelaide,
he was left with only four companions to continue
the journey.   He had acquired considerable experience of the privations to be encountered, but
refused to comply with the wishes of Colonel
Gawler, the Governor, to abandon the expedition
as hopeless, and return to Adelaide.   Indeed,
with characteristic inflexibility—almost approaching to obstinacy—he resolved to attempt the
western route along the shore of the Great Bight
—a journey which, only a few months before, he
had himself described as impracticable.

The cutter which had been stationed at Fowler Bay, to afford assistance if required, departed on the 31st of January, 1841, and Eyre and his small party were left to their fate. He had been defeated in the attempt to push forward in a northward direction, and he resolved not to return without having accomplished something which would justify the confidence of the public in his energy and courageous spirit of adventure. If he could not reach the north, he would attempt the western route, whatever might be the result of his enterprise. After resting to recruit the strength of his party, Eyre resolutely set out, on the 25th of February, on what proved to be a journey attended by almost unexampled demands upon human endurance.

Nine horses, one pony, six sheep, and a provision of flour, tea, and sugar for nine weeks, formed the slender stores of the little party, which resolutely set forward to track an unknown path to the west. Accompanied by one of the blacks, Eyre went on in advance to find water. For five days, during which time he travelled about 140 miles, no water was obtained, and the distress endured by men and animals was extreme. It is not necessary to dwell on every incident of this terrible journey. Eyre's descriptions, animated by remembrances of past sufferings, possess a graphic vigour which cannot be successfully emulated. Sometimes it was found

necessary to divide the party, so wretched was
the country, and so difficult was it to obtain
sufficient water in even the most limited supply
for man and beast. Once Eyre was alone for
six days, with only three quarts of water, some
of which evaporated, and more was spilt. But
his indomitable determination to accomplish the
journey on which he had resolved never failed.
He knew that at least 600 miles of desert
country lay between him and the nearest settlement of Western Australia; but even that prospect, the certain privations, the probable miserable death, did not daunt him in the journey.
The horses broke down from thirst and fatigue;
the pony died; the survivors crawled languidly
about, "like dogs, looking to their masters only
for aid." After a few days, during which no
water had been obtainable, a dew fell, and Eyre
collected a little moisture with a sponge, the black
boys with pieces of rag. To their inexpressible joy,
some sand-hills were reached, and, after digging,
a supply of water was obtained for their refreshment, and for six days the party rested by the
spot to recruit their strength. The overseer and
one of the natives then went back forty-seven
miles to recover the little store of provisions they
had been compelled to abandon. Two out of the
three horses he took with him broke down, and
with great difficulty he succeeded in rejoining
Eyre. At this time the party were 650 miles from

their destination, with only three weeks' provisions, estimated on the most reduced scale.
Baxter, the overseer, wished to attempt to return ;
but, Eyre being resolute, the overseer loyally
determined to stay with him to the last. One
horse was killed for food; dysentery broke out;
the natives deserted them, but came back starving
and penitent, and were permitted to remain with
the white men. Then came the tragedy which
makes this narrative so conspicuously terrible,
even in the annals of Australian exploration.
Two of the black men shot the overseer, Baxter,
as he slept, and then ran away, perishing, it is
supposed, miserably in the desert. Eyre, when
some distance from the place where poor Baxter
rested, looking after the horses, heard the report of
the gun and hurried back, arriving just in time
to receive the pathetic look of farewell from the
murdered man, who had served him so long and
so faithfully.

Wylie, the black boy, who had been with Eyre
in Adelaide, now alone remained, and it is scarcely
possible to imagine a more appalling situation
than that in which Eyre then found himself. The
murderers had carried away nearly the whole of
the scanty stock of provisions, leaving only forty
pounds of flour, a little tea and sugar, and four
gallons of water. They had also taken the two
available guns, and nearly all the ammunition.
The body of Baxter was wrapped in a blanket—

they could not even dig a grave in the barren
rock. Left with his sole companion, Eyre sadly
resumed the march, their steps tracked by the
two blacks, who probably meditated further
murders; but, with only cowardly instincts, they
dared not approach the intrepid man, who
at length outstripped them, and they were
never heard of more. Still no water was found
for 150 miles; then a slight supply, and the two
men struggled on, daily becoming weaker, living
on horse-flesh, an occasional kangaroo, and the
few fish that were to be caught—for it must be
remembered that at no time were they far from
the coast.

On the 2nd of June, nearly four months after
they had bidden good-bye to the cutter at Fowler's
Bay, they stood on the cliffs, looking out over the
ocean, when they saw in the distance two objects
which were soon recognized as boats, and shortly
afterwards, to their unbounded joy, they discerned
the masts of a vessel on the farther side of a
small rocky island. Animated by a new life,
Eyre pushed on until he reached a point whence
he succeeded in hailing the ship, and a boat
was sent off. The vessel proved to be a French
whaler, the "Mississippi," commanded by an
Englishman, Captain Rossiter. The worn-out
travellers stayed on board for a fortnight,
experiencing the utmost kindness, and with recruited strength and food and clothing, they bade

a grateful farewell to the captain and crew, and resumed their journey.

For twenty-three days more Eyre and his attendant Wylie pursued their way. Rain fell heavily, and the cold was intense; but at length, on the 27th of July, they reached Albany, in Western Australia, and the journey was accomplished.

For more than twelve months Eyre had been engaged forcing his way from Adelaide to the Western colony; and the incidents of the journey have been dwelt upon because afterwards I passed over the same ground, though in the opposite direction, and the records of Eyre's expedition were of the greatest service to me, by at least enabling me to guard against a repetition of the terrible sufferings he endured.

It is further necessary to refer to another of the journeys of exploration which preceded my own—that of the unfortunate Leichardt. He endeavoured to cross the continent from east to west, starting from Moreton Bay, Queensland, hoping to reach the Western Australian settlements. In 1844 Leichardt had succeeded in crossing the north-western portion of the continent from Moreton Bay to Port Essington, and he conceived the gigantic project of reaching Western Australia. Towards the end of 1847, accompanied by eight men, with provisions estimated at two years' supply, he started on his journey.

He took with him an enormous number of animals —180 sheep, 270 goats, 40 bullocks, 15 horses, and 13 mules. They must have greatly encumbered his march, and the difficulty of obtaining food necessarily much impeded his movements. His original intention was first to steer north, following for some distance his previous track, and then, as opportunity offered, to strike westward and make clear across the continent. After disastrous wanderings for seven months, in the course of which they lost the whole of their cattle and sheep, the party returned.

Disappointed, but not discouraged, Leichardt resolved on another attempt to achieve the task he had set himself. With great difficulty he obtained some funds; organized a small but ill-provided party, and again started for the interior. The last ever heard of him was a letter, dated the 3rd of April, 1848. He was then in the Fitzroy Downs; he wrote in good spirits, hopefully as to his prospects :—" Seeing how much I have been favoured in my present progress, I am full of hopes that our Almighty Protector will allow me to bring my darling scheme to a successful termination."

From that day the fate of Leichardt and his companions has been involved in mystery. He was then on the Cogoon River, in Eastern Australia, at least 1500 miles from the nearest station on the western side of the continent. His last

letter gives no clue to the track he intended
to pursue. If a westerly course had been struck
he would have nearly traversed the route which
subsequently Warburton travelled; but no trace
of him has ever been discovered. Several expeditions were undertaken to ascertain his fate;
at various times expectations were aroused by
finding trees marked " L;" but Leichardt himself,
on previous journeys, had met with trees so
marked, by whom is unknown. Natives found
in the remote interior were questioned; they
told vague stories of the murder of white
men, but all investigations resulted in the conclusion that the statements were as untrust-
worthy as those generally made to explorers
who question uninformed, ignorant natives. The
white man's experience is usually that a native
only partially comprehends the question; he does
not understand what is wanted, but is anxious to
please, as he expects something to eat, and he
says what he thinks is most likely to be satisfactory.

Leichardt was certainly ill-provided for an
expedition of the magnitude he contemplated,
and it appears to be at the least as probable that
he succumbed to the hardships he encountered, or
was swept away by a flood, as that he was murdered by the blacks. Twenty-seven years have
elapsed since he disappeared in the interior; yet the
mystery attending his fate has not ceased to excite

a desire to know the fate of so daring an explorer, and ascertain something definite respecting his course—a desire which was one of the principal motives that prompted my first expedition into the unknown interior dividing the west from the east.

In 1872, Mr. Giles headed an exploring party from Melbourne, which succeeded in making known a-vast district hitherto unexplored; but his progress was stopped, when he had reached long. 129° 40', by a large salt lake, the limits of which could not be ascertained. In the following year Mr. Gosse, at the head of a party equipped by the South Australian Government, started from nearly the same point of the telegraph line, and at the same period as the Warburton expedition, but was compelled to return after eight months' absence, having reached long. 126° 59'. Gosse found the country generally poor and destitute of water. He was perhaps unfortunate in experiencing an unusually dry season; but his deliberate conclusion was, " I do not think a practicable route will ever be found between the lower part of Western Australia and the telegraph line."

At the instance of Baron Von Mueller, and assisted by a small subscription from the South Australian Government, Mr. Giles made a second attempt to penetrate westward. He reached the 125th degree of east longitude, and discovered and traversed four distinct mountain ranges, on one of which Mr. Gosse shortly afterwards found his tracks. One of his companions, Mr. Gibson, lost his way and perished in the desert, and therefore Mr. Giles turned his face eastwards, and, after an absence of twelve months, reached Adelaide. He encountered many perils, having been nine times attacked by the natives, probably in the attempt to obtain water; and on one occasion was severely wounded and nearly captured.

On the 20th March, 1874, Mr. Ross, with his son and another European, three Arabs, fourteen horses, and sixteen camels, started from the telegraph line, near the Peake station in South Australia. He was compelled to return through want of water, although, soon after starting, he had greatly reduced the number of his party by sending back three of his companions, two of the horses, and twelve of the camels.

Such, in brief, have been the results of the efforts made to cross Australia between the telegraph line and the west coast, and ascertain the probability of establishing a practicable route. I have referred to them to show how persistent has been the desire to achieve the exploit, and how little daunted by repeated failures have been Australian explorers. I now propose to relate my own experiences—the results of three journeys of exploration, conducted by myself. The first was undertaken in the hope of discovering some traces of Leichardt; the second nearly retraced the route of Eyre; the third was across the desert from Western Australia to the telegraph line in South Australia. The first journey did not result in obtaining the information sought for; the second and third journeys were successfully accomplished.

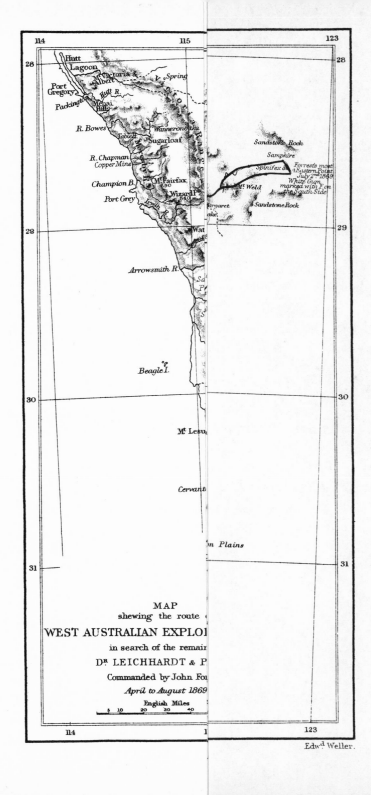

114   115   123

28   28

Hutt
Lagoon
Port   M. Victoria &
Gregory   Albert   V. Spring
Packington   Hutt R.
Menai
Hills
R. Bowes   Wanneronooka
Table H.   Sugarloaf   Sandstone Rock
R. Chapman   Samphire
Copper Mine   Spinifex   Forrests most
Eastern Point
July 2nd 1869
Champion B.   Mt Fairfax   Mt Weld   White Gum,
90   marked with F. on
Wizard P.   the South Side
Port Grey   640
Margaret   Sandstone Rock
Lake

28   29

Wat

Arrowsmith R.

Beagle I.

30   30

Mt Lesu

Cervant

n Plains

31   31

MAP
shewing the route
WEST AUSTRALIAN EXPLOI
in search of the remain
DR LEICHHARDT & P
Commanded by John Fo
April to August 1869

English Miles
5 10   20   30   40

114   1   123

Edwd Weller.

CHAPTER II.

Statements made by the Natives.—An Expedition prepared.
—Leader appointed.—Official Instructions.—The Journal.

EARLY in 1869, Dr. Von Mueller, of the Melbourne
Botanic Gardens, a botanist of high attainments,
proposed to the Government of Western Australia
that an expedition should be undertaken from
the colony for the purpose of ascertaining, if
possible, the fate of the lost explorer, Leichardt.
Reports had reached Perth of natives met with in
the eastern districts, who had stated that, about
twenty years before (a date corresponding with
that of the last authentic intelligence received
from Leichardt), a party of white men had been
murdered. This tale was repeated, but perhaps
would not have made much impression if a gentleman, Mr. J. H. Monger, when on a trip eastward
in search of sheep-runs, had not been told by his
native guide that he had been to the very spot
where the murder was committed, and had seen

the remains of the white men. His story was very circumstantial; he described the spot, which, he said, was near a large lake, so large that it looked like the sea, and that the white men were attacked and killed while making a damper—bread made of flour mixed with water, and cooked on hot ashes. So certain was he as to the exact locality, that he offered to conduct a party to the place.

This appeared like a trustworthy confirmation of the reports which had reached the colony, and created a great impression, so that the Government felt it a duty incumbent on them to make an effort to ascertain the truth of this statement, and Dr. Von Mueller's offer to lead an expedition was accepted.

I was then, as now, an officer of the Survey Department, and employed in a distant part of the colony. I was ordered to repair to head-quarters, to confer with the authorities on the subject, and was offered the appointment of second in command and navigator. This was a proposition quite in accordance with my tastes, for I had long felt a deep interest in the subject of Australian exploration, and ardently desired to take my share in the work. I at once arranged the equipment of the expedition, but, while so engaged, the mail from Melbourne brought a letter from Dr. Von Mueller, to the effect that his other engagements would not permit him to take the lead as proposed, and I was appointed to take his place in the expedition.

The Hon. Captain Roe, R.N., the Surveyor-General, who had himself been a great explorer, undertook the preparation of a set of "Instructions" for my guidance; and they so accurately describe the objects of the journey, and the best modes of carrying them out, that I transcribe the official letter :—

Survey Office, Perth,
13th April, 1869.

Sir,—His Excellency the Governor having been pleased to appoint you to lead an expedition into the interior of Western Australia for the purpose of searching for the remains of certain white men reported by the natives to have been killed by the aborigines some years ago, many miles beyond the limits of our settled country, and it being deemed probable that the white men referred to formed part of an exploring party under the command of Dr. Leichardt, endeavouring to penetrate overland from Victoria to this colony several years ago, I have been directed to furnish the following instructions for your guidance on this interesting service, and for enabling you to carry out the wishes of the Government in connexion therewith.

2. Your party will consist of six persons in the whole, well armed, and made up of Mr. George Monger as second in command, Mr. Malcolm Hamersley as third in command, a farrier blacksmith to be hired at Newcastle, and two well-known and reliable natives, Tommy Windich and Jemmy, who have already acquired considerable experience under former explorers.

3. An agreement to serve on the expedition in the above capacities has been prepared, and should be signed by each European member of the party previous to starting.

4. A saddle-horse has been provided for each member of the party, together with — pack-horses to transport such por-

tions of the outfit as cannot be carried by the former. A three-horsed cart will also accompany the expedition as far as may be found practicable through the unsettled country, and thereby relieve the pack-horses as much as possible.

5. All preparations for the journey being now complete, it is desirable that you should lose no time in starting, so as to arrive at the commencement of the unexplored country by the end of the present month, or beginning of the expected winter rains. It has been, however, already ascertained from native information that a considerable quantity of rain has recently fallen over the regions to be explored, and that no impediment may be anticipated from a scarcity of water there.

6. The route to be followed might advantageously commence at Newcastle, where some of your party and several of your horses are to be picked up, and thence proceed north-easterly to Goomaling, and 100 miles further in the same general direction, passing eastward to Mounts Chunbaren and Kenneth of Mr. Austin's, to the eastern farthest of that explorer, in 119° E. and $28\frac{3}{4}$° S. Thence the general north-easterly route of the expedition must be governed by the information afforded by your native guides as to the locality in which they have reported the remains of white men are to be found.

7. On arriving at that spot, the greatest care is to be taken to bring away all such remains as may be discovered by a diligent search of the neighbourhood. By friendly and judicious treatment of the local natives, it is also probable that several articles of European manufacture which are said to be still in their possession might be bartered from them, and serve towards identifying their former owners. The prospect of obtaining from the natives, at this remote date, anything like a journal, note-book, or map, would indeed be small ; but the greatest interest would be attached to the smallest scrap of written or printed paper, however much defaced, if only covered with legible characters. A more promising mode by which the former presence of European explorers on the spot might be detected is the marks which are generally made on the trees by travellers to record the number or reference to a halting-place, or the initials of some of the party. Thus the

letter L has in several instances been found by searching parties to have been legibly cut on trees in the interior of the eastern colonies, and in localities supposed to have been visited by the eminent explorer alluded to. It is needless to point out that metal articles, such as axes, tomahawks, gun and pistol barrels, iron-work of pack-saddles, and such like, would be far more likely to have survived through the lapse of years than articles of a more perishable nature.

8. After exhausting all conceivable means of obtaining information on the spot, and from the nature of surrounding country, an attempt should be made to follow back on the track of the unfortunate deceased, which is said to have been from the eastward and towards the settled part of this colony. Here a close and minute scrutiny of the trees might prove of great value in clearing up existing doubts, especially at and about any water-holes and springs near which explorers would be likely to bivouac.

9. After completing an exhaustive research and inquiry into this interesting and important part of your duties, the remainder of the time that may be at your disposal, with reference to your remaining stock of provisions, should be employed in exploring the surrounding country, in tracing any considerable or smaller stream it may be your good fortune to discover, and generally in rendering the service entrusted to your guidance as extensively useful and valuable to this colony as circumstances may admit.

10. Towards effecting this object, your homeward journey should, if possible, be over country not previously traversed by the outward route, or by any former explorers, and should be so regulated as to expose your party to no unnecessary risk on account of the falling short of supplies.

11. In your intercourse with the aborigines of the interior, many of whom will have no previous personal knowledge of the white man, I need scarcely commend to you a policy of kindness and forbearance mixed with watchfulness and firmness, as their future bearing towards our remote colonists may be chiefly moulded by early impressions.

12. To render the expedition as extensively useful as

possible, I would urge you, in the interests of science, to make and preserve such specimens in natural history as may come within the reach of yourself and party, especially in the departments of botany, geology, and zoology, which may be greatly enriched by productions of country not yet traversed.

13. Direct reference to minor objects, and to matters of detail, is purposely omitted, in full reliance on your judgment and discretion, and on your personal desire to render the expedition as productive as possible of benefit to the colony and to science in general.

14. In this spirit I may add that the brief instructions herein given for your general guidance are by no means intended to fetter your own judgment in carrying out the main object of the expedition in such other and different manner as may appear to you likely to lead to beneficial results. In the belief that such results will be achieved by the energy and perseverance of yourself and of those who have so nobly volunteered to join you in the enterprise, and with confident wishes for your success, in which H. E. largely participates,

I remain, Sir,

Your obedient Servant,

J. S. ROE, Surveyor-General.

John Forrest, Esq., Leader of Exploring
Expedition to the N.E.

Mr. George Monger (brother of the gentleman who gave the information), who accompanied me as second in command, had previously been on an expedition to the eastward, and Jemmy Mungaro was the black who said he had seen the spot where the remains of the white men were. His persistence in the statement encouraged me to hope that I might be the first to announce positively the fate of the lost explorer; but I had then to learn how little dependence can be placed on the testimony of Australian aborigines.

On the 15th of April, 1869, I began the journey. I was well supplied with instruments for making observations, so as to ascertain our daily position. A knowledge of at least the leading principles of the art of navigation is as necessary to the explorer as to the mariner on the ocean. Our stock of provisions consisted of 800 lbs. of flour, 270 lbs. of pork, 135 lbs. of sugar, and 17 lbs. of tea ; and we each took two suits of clothes.

The party were all in good spirits. For myself I was hopeful of success, and my white companions shared my feelings. The natives were, as they generally are, except when food is scarce, or their anger excited, on the best terms with everybody and everything, and Jemmy Mungaro, so far as could be judged from his demeanour, might have been the most veracious guide who ever led a party of white men through difficulties and dangers on an expedition of discovery.

Day by day I noted down the incidents of the journey, and that Journal I now submit to the reader.

Journal of Proceedings of an Exploring Expedition in search of the remains of the late Dr. Leichardt and party, undertaken by order of the Government of Western Australia, by John Forrest, Government Surveyor.

Sir,—In pursuance of instructions received from

you, the exploring party under my command consisted of the following persons, viz., Mr. George Monger, as second in command; Mr. Malcolm Hamersley, as third in command; probation prisoner, David Morgan, as shoeing smith, and two natives (Tommy Windich and Jemmy Mungaro). The latter native gave Mr. J. H. Monger the information respecting the murder of white men in the eastward. Reached Newcastle on the 17th and left on Monday, 19th, with a three-horse cart and teamster and thirteen horses, making a total of sixteen horses. Reached Mombekine, which is about sixteen miles E.N.E. from Newcastle.

April 20*th*.—Continued journey to Goomalling, sixteen miles, which we reached at 1 p.m., and devoted the remainder of the afternoon to weighing and packing rations, &c., for a final start.

21*st*.—Leaving Goomalling at 10.30 a.m., we travelled in a northerly direction for nine miles, and reached Walyamurra Lake; thence about E.N.E. for seven miles, we encamped at a well on north side of Kombekine Lake. The water was very bad from opossums being drowned in it, and there was hardly any feed.

22*nd*.—Hearing from a number of natives that there was no water in the direction we intended steering, viz., to Mount Churchman, we decided on changing our course and proceed there *viâ* Waddowring, in latitude 31° south and longitude 118° east. Steering about S.S.E. for eight miles, through dense scrubby thickets, which we had great difficulty in getting the cart through, we struck the road from Goomalling to Waddowring, which we followed along about east for eight miles, and camped at a well called Naaning, with hardly any feed.

23rd.—Mr. George Roe (who had come from Northam to bid us farewell) and my teamster left us this morning to return to Newcastle. Considerable delay having occurred in collecting the horses, we did not start till twelve o'clock, when we steered E.N.E. for eight miles over scrubby sand-plains, and camped at a well called Pingeperring, with very little feed for our horses.

24th.—Started at 8.50 a.m. and steered about east for seven miles over scrubby, undulating sand-plains, thence N. 50° E. mag. for two miles, thence N. 160° for one mile, and thence about N. 80° E. mag. for five miles over scrubby sand-plains. We camped at a spring called Dwartwollaking at 5 p.m. Barometer 29·45 ; thermometer 71°.

25th (Sunday).—Did not travel to-day. Took observations for time, and corrected our watches. Found camp to be in south latitude 31° 10′ by meridian altitude of sun.

26th.—Travelled in about the direction of N. 73° E. mag. for twenty-eight miles. We reached Yarraging, the farthest station to the eastward, belonging to Messrs. Ward and Adams, where we bivouacked for the night.

27*th.*—Bought some rations from Ward and Co., making our supply equal to last three months on the daily allowance of a pound and a half of flour, half a pound of pork, a quarter of a pound of sugar, and half an ounce of tea per man. Being unable to take the cart any further, and wishing to have the team horses with me, I arranged with Ward and Co. to take it to Newcastle for 2*l*. Packed up and left Yarraging with ten pack and six riding horses, and steering N. 320° E. mag. for eight miles we reached Waddowring springs in south latitude 31° and longitude 118° E.

28*th.*—Started this morning with Mr. Monger, Tommy Windich, and Dunbatch (a native of this locality) in search of water in order to shift the party. Travelling about north for eleven miles we found a native well, and by digging it out seven feet we obtained sufficient water for ourselves and horses. I therefore sent Mr. Monger back with instructions to bring the party to this spot, called Cartubing. I then proceeded in a northerly direction, and at two miles passed water in granite rocks at a spot called Inkanyinning. Shortly afterwards we passed another native well, called Yammaling, from which we steered towards a spot called Beebynyinning; but, night setting in, our guide lost his way, and we were obliged to camp for the night in a thicket without water and very little feed.

29*th.*—This morning Dunbatch brought us to

Beebynyinning, where we obtained a little water by digging. After digging a well we returned to Cartubing, where we met the party and bivouacked on a patch of green feed.

30th.—Shifted the party from Cartubing to Beebynyinning, watering our horses on the way at Inkanyinning and Yammaling, which was fortunate, as there was very little water at Beebynyinning.

May 1st.—Steering about N.E. for eight miles over grassy country, we reached and encamped at Danjinning, a small grassy spot, with native well, by deepening which about ten feet we obtained a plentiful supply of water. Mr. Austin visited Danjinning in 1854, and we could see the tracks of his horses distinctly. Barometer 29. Every appearance of rain, which we are in much want of.

2nd (*Sunday*).—Rested at Danjinning, which I found to be in south latitude 30° 34′ by meridian altitude of the sun. Read Divine Service. Jemmy shot six gnows and a wurrong to-day.

3rd.—Steering in a northerly direction for sixteen miles, we reached Yalburnunging, a small grassy spot, with water in a native well, which we deepened four feet, and procured a plentiful supply. For the first nine miles our route lay over scrubby sand-plains, after which we came into dense thickets and stunted gums.

4th.—Steering towards Mount Churchman, or Geelabbing, for about fifteen miles, we reached a grassy spot called Billeburring, and found water in a native well, probably permanent. At eight miles we passed a water-hole in some granite rocks, called Gnaragnunging. Dense acacia and cypress thickets most of the way.

5th.—Steering in a northerly direction for about twelve miles, we reached Mount Churchman, or Geelabbing, an immense bare granite hill, and camped, with plenty of feed and water. At five miles passed a spring called Coolee. Country very dense and scrubby; no feed in any of the thickets. From the summit of Mount Churchman, Ningham of Mr. Monger, or Mount Singleton of Mr. A. C. Gregory, bore N. 312° 30' E. mag. This evening a party of nine natives (friends of our native Jemmy) joined us, who state that a long time ago a party of white men and horses died at a place called Bouincabbajibimar, also that a gun and a number of other articles are there, and volunteer to accompany us to the spot.

6th.—Left Mount Churchman in company with the nine natives, and travelled about N.N.W. for ten miles to a small water-hole called Woodgine, thence in a northerly direction to a branch of Lake Moore, which we crossed without difficulty, and, following along its north shore for three miles, we bivouacked at a spring close to the lake called Cundierring, with splendid feed around the granite rocks.

7th.—Steering in a northerly direction for eleven

miles, through dense thickets of acacia and cypress, we reached some granite rocks with water on them, called Curroning, and bivouacked. Have fears that the information received from the natives relates to nine of Mr. Austin's horses that died from poison at Poison Rock. They now state they are only horses' bones, and not men's, as first stated.

8th.—Travelling in the direction of N. 30° E. for about ten miles, we reached some granite rocks, with a water-hole in them, called Coorbedar. Passed over very rough, low, quartz hills, covered with acacia thickets, &c. At four miles passed a water-hole called Yeergolling; at seven miles a small one called Gnurra; and another at eight miles called Munparra.

9th (Sunday).—Rested our horses at Coorbedar. Found camp to be in south latitude 29° 24′ 43″ by meridian altitudes of the sun and Regulus, and in longitude 118° 6′ E. From a quartz hill half a mile S.W. from Coorbedar, Mount Singleton bore N. 268° 15′ E. The supply of water from the rock having been used, I went, in company with Mr. Hamersley, to a spot one mile and a half S.S.W. from Coorbedar, called Dowgooroo, where we dug a well and procured a little water, to which I intend shifting to-morrow, as I propose staying in this vicinity for two days, so as to give me time to visit Warne, the large river spoken of by Jemmy.

10*th*.—Started this morning in company with Tommy Windich and a native boy (one of the nine who joined us at Mount Churchman) to examine the locality called Warne. Steering N. 42° E. mag. for about seven miles, we came to a grassy flat about half a mile wide, with a stream-bed trending south running through it. The natives state it to be dry in summer, but at present there is abundance of water, and in wet seasons the flat must be almost all under water. After following the flat about seven miles we returned towards camp, about five miles, and bivouacked.

11*th*.—Returned this morning to Dowgooroo and found all well. Rain, which we were much in want of, fell lightly most of the day. Barometer 28·50; thermometer 61°.

12*th*.—Steered this morning about N. 38° E. mag. for eight miles, and camped by a shallow lake of fresh water—the bivouac of the 10th. Here we met a party of twenty-five natives (friends of my native Jemmy and the nine who joined us at Mount Churchman) who had a grand corraboree in honour of the expedition. They stated that at Bouincabbajillimar there were the remains of a number of horses, but no men's bones or guns, and pointed in the direction of Poison Rock, where Mr. Austin lost nine horses. Being now satisfied that the natives were alluding to the remains of Mr. Austin's horses, I resolved to steer to the eastward, towards a spot called by the native Jemmy " Noondie," where he states he heard the remains of white men were.

13*th.*—Bidding farewell to all the natives, we steered in a south-easterly direction for fifteen miles, and camped in a rough hollow called Durkying; cypress and acacia thickets the whole way.

14*th.*—One of our horses having strayed, we did not start till 10.40 a.m., when we steered in about a S.E. direction for eight miles, and camped on an elevated grassy spot, called Mingan, with water in the granite rocks, probably permanent. The thickets were a little less dense than usual, but without any grass, except at the spots mentioned. By meridian altitudes of Mars and Regulus, we were in south latitude 29° 30′ 30″, and in longitude about 118° 30′ east.

15*th.*—Steering N.E. for four miles, and N.N.E. for seven miles, over sandy soil, with thickets of acacia and cypress, we bivouacked on an elevated grassy spot, called Earroo, with water in granite rocks.

16*th (Sunday).*—Rested at Earroo; horses enjoying good feed. By meridian altitudes of Regulus and Mars, camp at Earroo was in south latitude 29° 23′ 3″, and in longitude 118° 35′ E.; weather very cloudy; barometer 29.

17*th.*—Started 7.50 a.m., and steered N. 60° E. for about five miles; thence about N. 50° E.

for eight miles; thence N. 85° E. for five miles, to a small grassy spot called Croobenyer, with water in granite rocks. Sandy soil, thickets of cypress, acacia, &c., most of the way. Found camp to be in south latitude 29° 12′ 43″ by meridian altitudes of Regulus and Aquilæ (Altair); barometer 28·70.

18th.—Steering N. 70° E. for two miles and a half, we saw a low hill called Yeeramudder, bearing N. 62° 30′ E. mag., distant about seventeen miles, for which we steered, and camped to the north of it, on a fine patch of grass with a little rain-water on some granite rocks. At eleven miles crossed a branch of a dry salt lake, which appears to run far to the eastward.

19th.—Steering about N. 85° E. mag. for fourteen miles, attempted to cross the lake we had been leaving a little to the southward, making for a spot supposed by us to be the opposite shore, but on arriving at which was found to be an island. As we had great difficulty in reaching it, having to carry all the loads the last 200 yards, our horses saving themselves with difficulty, and, being late, I resolved to leave the loads and take the horses to another island, where there was a little feed, on reaching which we bivouacked without water, all being very tired.

20th.—On examining this immense lake I

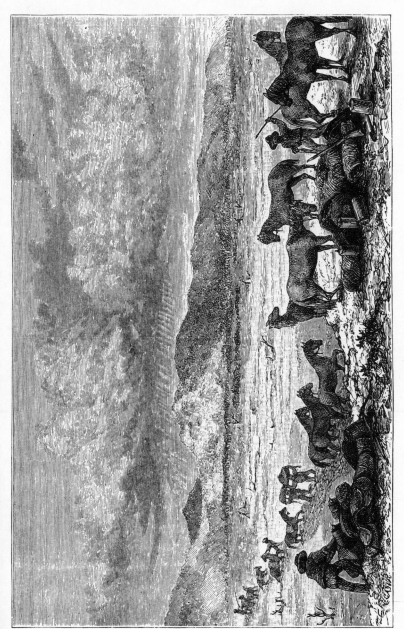

THE HORSES BOGGED IN LAKE BARLEE.

found that it was impossible to get the horses
and loads across it; I was therefore compelled
to retrace my steps to where we first entered
it, which the horses did with great difficulty
without their loads. I was very fortunate in
finding water and feed about three miles N.N.W.,
to which we took the horses and bivouacked,
leaving on the island all the loads, which we
shall have to carry at least half way, three
quarters of a mile, the route being too boggy
for the horses.

21*st.*—Went over to the lake in company
with Messrs. Monger, Hamersley, and Tommy
Windich, with four horses. Succeeded in getting
all the loads to the mainland, carrying them
about three quarters of a mile up to our knees
in mud, from which point the lake became a
little firmer, and the horses carried the loads
out. I cannot speak too highly of the manner
in which my companions assisted me on this
trying occasion. Having been obliged to work
barefooted in the mud, the soles of Mr.
Hamersley's feet were in a very bad state,
and he was hardly able to walk for a fortnight. Seeing a native fire several miles to
the southward, I intend sending Tommy Windich and Jemmy in search of the tribe to-
morrow, in order that I may question them
respecting the reported death of white men to
the eastward.

22nd.—Went over to the lake with all the horses, and brought the loads to the camp. Started Tommy and Jemmy in search of the natives. After returning to camp, overhauled all the pack bags, and dried and re-packed them, ready for a fresh start on Monday morning. Also washed the mud off the horses, who appear to be doing well, and fast recovering from the effects of the bogging. Tommy and Jemmy returned this evening, having seen some natives after dark, but were unable to get near them.

23rd (*Sunday*).—Went with Tommy Windich and Jemmy on foot to follow the tracks of the natives seen yesterday. Seeing no chance of overtaking them, as they appeared to be making off at a great rate, and were twelve hours in advance of us, we returned, after following the tracks for five miles across the lake. The camp was reached at 2 p.m., after we had walked about fifteen miles. This spot, which I named Retreat Rock, I found to be in south latitude 29° 3' 51" by meridian altitudes of Regulus and Mars, and in about longitude 119° 16' east.

24th.—Some of the horses having strayed, we were not able to start till 10.40 a.m., when we steered in about E.N.E. direction for sixteen miles, and camped on a piece of rising ground, with very little water. From this bivouac, a very remarkable peaked hill, called Woolling, which I named Mount Elain, bore N. 162° 15′ E. mag., distant about twenty miles; and two conspicuous hills, close together, called Yeadie and Bulgar, bore N. 105° E. mag. Dense thickets, acacia, cypress, &c., sandy soil with spinifex, most of the way.

25th.—Steering for Yeadie and Bulgar for five miles, and came to some granite rocks with water, where we gave drink to our thirsty horses. Leaving the party to follow, I went with Jemmy in advance to look for water, which we found in a rough stream-bed, and brought the party to it. This afternoon went with Jemmy to the summit of Yeadie, and took a round of angles. The local attraction was so great on this hill that the prismatic compass was useless; luckily I had my pocket sextant with me, by which I obtained the included angles. From the summit of Yeadie the view was very extensive. The great lake that we had already followed for forty miles ran as far as the eye could reach to the east and south, studded with numerous islands; low ranges of hills in every direction. This immense lake I named Lake Barlee, after the Colonial Secretary of Western Australia. By meridian altitudes of Mars and Regulus, camp was in south latitude, 28° 58′ 50″, and in longitude about 119° 39′ E., Yeadie bearing N. 172° E. mag., distant about two miles.

26th.—Moving in about a northerly direction for

nine miles, we turned to the eastward, rounded a branch of Lake Barlee, towards some loose granite rocks, where we encamped, but could not find water. Sent Jemmy over to another rock one mile southward, where he found a fine permanent water-hole, to which we took the horses after dark. Distance travelled to-day about eighteen miles. Tommy shot a fine emu, which was a great treat to us all.

27th.—Shifted the party over to the water found last night, one mile distant, and camped. Found camp to be in south latitude 28° 53', and in longitude about 119° 50' east. Marked a small tree with the letter F. close to the water-hole.

28th.—Some of the horses having strayed, we did not start till 9.30 a.m., when I went in advance of the party, in company with Jemmy, to look for water. After following Lake Barlee for nine miles, it turned to the southward. Then scouring the country in every direction for water without success, we reached the tracks of the party (who had passed on), and, following them over plains of spinifex and stunted gums, found them encamped with plenty of water, which they had luckily discovered at sundown. Distance travelled eighteen miles about true east. By meridian altitude of Bootes (Arcturus), this bivouac is in south latitude 28° 53' 34", and longitude about 120° 9' east.

29th.—Started in company with Tommy and Jemmy to explore the country eastward, leaving the party to take off the horses' shoes for their relief. Travelling in an easterly direction for eight miles over sandy soil and spinifex, we reached the summit of a high hill, supposed by Jemmy to be "Noondie," which I named Mount Alexander, from which we saw another range about eleven miles distant, bearing N. 82° 15′ E. mag., to which we proceeded, and found water in some granite rocks. None of these hills, however, agreed with the description given by Jemmy; and the expectations were at an end that he would succeed in showing us the spot where the remains of white men were. Returning to camp, seven miles, bivouacked on a grassy flat, without water or food.

30th (Sunday).—Started at dawn, with the saddles and rugs on our backs, in search of the horses, and, after travelling a mile and a half on their tracks, found them at a small water-hole passed by us yesterday. Saddled up and reached camp at eleven o'clock, and found all well. Yesterday morning the dogs caught an emu, off which we made a first-rate breakfast, not having had anything to eat since the previous morning. Barometer 28·44.

31st.—Started this morning in company with Mr. Monger and Jemmy in search of natives, leaving Mr. Hamersley in charge, with in-

structions to proceed eastward about twenty-two
miles, to where I found water on the 29th.
After starting the party we steered in a S.S.E.
direction towards a high range of hills, which
I named Mount Bivou, about twelve miles distant. To the westward of the range we found a
fine water-hole in some granite rocks, where we
rested an hour to allow the horses to feed.
Continuing in about the same direction for five
miles, we ascended a rough range to have a
view of the country. We descried a large fire
to the westward seven miles, towards which we
proceeded, in the hope of finding natives. When
we were within half a mile we could hear hal-
looing and shouting; and it was very evident
there was a great muster (certainly not less than
100) of natives, corrobberying, making a dreadful
noise, the dogs joining in chorus. Having
stripped Jemmy, I told him to go and speak
to them, which he started to do in very good
spirits. He soon beckoned us to follow, and
asked us to keep close behind him, as the natives
were what he called like " sheep flock." He
appeared very nervous, trembling from head to
foot. After reassuring him, we tied up our
horses, and advanced through the thicket towards
them. When getting in sight of them, Jemmy
commenced " *co-oey-ing*," and was answered by the
natives; after which he advanced and showed
himself. As soon as they saw him, the blood-

thirsty villains rushed at him, and threw three dowaks, which he luckily dodged; when fortunately one of the natives recognized him (having seen Jemmy at Mount Elain when a little boy), and called to the others not to harm him. Seeing Jemmy running towards the horses, Mr. Monger and I thought it was time to retire, as we saw the mistake we had made in leaving the horses. The thickets being dense, we had difficulty in finding the horses quickly. On reaching them Mr. Monger found he had dropped his revolver. Had not Jemmy been recognized, I feel sure we should have had bloodshed, and might probably have lost our lives. Mounting the horses, we advanced towards the natives, and had a short talk with one of them who came to speak to Jemmy. There was a guard of eight natives, with spears stripped, and dowaks in readiness, should we prove hostile. Although I assured them we were friends, and asked them to put down their spears, they took no notice of what was said. One native told us not to sleep here, but to go away and not return, or the natives would kill and eat us, after which he turned away as if he did not wish to have any more words with us. It being now dark, we took his advice, and retreated towards where we had dinner, five miles off. Camped in a thicket without water, and tied up our horses, keeping watch all night.

June 1st.—At daybreak saddled up our tired and hungry horses, and proceeded to where we had dinner yesterday. After giving our horses two hours' grazing and having had breakfast, started back towards the natives' camp, as I wished to question them respecting the reported death of white men in this neighbourhood. When we approached the natives' bivouac, we saw where they had been following up our tracks in every direction, and Jemmy found the place where they had picked up Mr. Monger's revolver. While Jemmy was away looking for the revolver, Mr. Monger saw two natives following up our trail, and within fifty yards of us. We both wheeled round and had our guns in readiness, but, soon perceived they were the same as were friendly last night, and I called Jemmy to speak to them. At my request they went and brought us Mr. Monger's revolver, which they stated they had been warming near the fire! Fortunately for them, it did not go off. On being questioned by Jemmy, they stated that the place Noondie (where Jemmy stated he heard the remains of the white men were) was two days' journey N.W. from this spot; that there were the remains of horses, but not of men, and they volunteered to show us the spot. Being now 1 p.m., and having to meet the party to-night at a place about twenty-three miles distant, we started at once, leaving the natives, who did not wish to move to-day, but who apparently sincerely promised to come to our camp to-mor-row. Reached camp at the spot arranged an hour after dark, and found all well.

2nd.—Rested our horses at the place, which I called the Two-spring Bivouac, there being two small springs here. Re-stuffed with grass all the pack-saddles, as some of the horses were getting sore backs. By meridian altitude of sun found the camp to be in south latitude 28° 51' 45", and in longitude about 120° 30' east. I was very much annoyed at the natives not putting in appearance as promised.

3rd.—No sign of the natives this morning. I decided to steer in the direction pointed out by them, and travelling about N. 306° E. mag. for fifteen miles, we found water in some granite rocks, with very good feed around, cypress and acacia thickets, light red loamy soil, destitute of grass.

4th.—Steering in about W.N.W. direction for sixteen miles, the first six of which were studded with granite rocks, good feed around them, after which through poor sandy country, covered with spinifex. We bivouacked in a thicket without water or feed, and tied up our horses. Saw a natives' fire, but was unable to get near it. Barometer 28·52; fine.

5th.—After travelling in a northerly direction for seven miles without finding water, and without seeing any hill answering the description given by

Jemmy, I struck about east for sixteen miles, and camped at a fine spring near some granite rocks, with splendid feed around them. This is the first good spring since leaving the settled districts. At 8 p.m., barometer 28·44; thermometer 72°.

6th (Sunday).—Rested at camp, which I called Depôt Spring, and found to be in south latitude 28° 36′ 31″ by meridian altitude of sun. Barometer at 8 a.m. 28·38; thermometer 57°; at 5 p.m., barometer 28·30 ; thermometer 77°.

7th.—Started this morning, in company with Mr. Hamersley and Jemmy, to explore the country to the northward, where we had seen a peaked hill. Went in that direction about thirty miles, the first twenty of which were studded with granite rocks, with fine feed around them. At twenty-seven miles crossed a salt marsh, about one mile wide, and, continuing three miles farther, reached the peaked hill, which was composed of granite, capped with immense blocks, giving it a very remarkable appearance. Bivouacked on N.W. side of hill, at a small water-hole.

8th.—This morning, after saddling up, we ascended the conical hill (which I named Mount Holmes) and took a round of angles from it, after which we struck N. 81° E. mag. to a granite range about eight miles distant, where we found two fine water-holes, and rested an hour. Thence in about a S.S.E. direction for twelve miles, we bivouacked without water on a small patch of feed.

The day was very fine, and the rainy appearance cleared off, much to our grief.

9th.—At daybreak, no sound of horses' bells, and anticipating they had made off in search of water, we put our saddles, guns, and rugs on our backs, and started on their tracks. After following the tracks for nine miles we came to a water-hole and had breakfast; afterwards we succeeded in overtaking the horses in a grassy flat, about thirteen miles S.S.E. from our last night's bivouac. The last few miles our troublesome load became very awkward and heavy. One of the horses had broken his hobbles. Continuing in about the same course for six miles, we struck about W.S.W. for ten miles, and reached camp, where we found all well, at 6 p.m. Barometer 28·64; cloudy.

10th.—Started again this morning in company with Mr. Monger and Jemmy, to explore the country to the eastward, leaving Mr. Hamersley to shift the party to our bivouac of the 2nd inst., about twenty-four miles S.E. from here. After travelling E.N.E. for six miles, we came upon a very old native at a fire in the thicket. Jemmy could not understand what he said, but he thought that he meant that there were a number of armed natives about. He was very frightened, howled the whole time we stayed, and was apparently in his dotage, hardly able to walk. Continuing our journey, we camped at a small water-hole in some granite rocks, with good feed

around them, about sixteen miles E.N.E. from
Depôt Spring.

11*th*.—Started at sunrise, and steered about
E.N.E. over lightly-grassed country; and on our
" way " came upon a middle-aged native with two
small children. We were within twenty yards
of him before he saw us. He appeared very
frightened, and trembled from head to foot.
Jemmy could understand this native a little, and
ascertained from him that he had never seen or
heard anything about white men or horses being
killed or having died in this vicinity. Did not
know any place named Noondie; but pointed to
water a little way eastward. Jemmy then asked him
all manner of questions, but to no purpose, as he
stated he knew nothing about the business. Jemmy
asked him if he had ever heard of any horses
being eaten; he answered *No,* but that the natives
had just eaten his brother! I have no doubt
parents have great difficulty in saving their children
from these inhuman wretches. Then the old
man tried to cry, and ended by saying he had
two women at his hut, a little westward. After
travelling ten miles from our last night's bivouac,
and not finding water, we struck N. 204° E. mag.
for about twenty miles, through scrubby thickets,
without feed, and arrived at the bivouac of
the 2nd, where the party will meet us to-morrow.
Reached the water at the Two Springs half an
hour after dark.

12th.—Explored the country around camp in search of a better place for feed, but could not find water. Mr. Hamersley and party joined us at 4 p.m., all well. Tommy shot a red kangaroo, which was a great treat, after living so long on salt pork. Barometer 28·60 ; fine ; cold wind from the east all day.

13th (Sunday).—Rested at camp. Intend taking a trip to the southward to-morrow. Barometer 28·76.

14th.—Started this morning, in company with Morgan and Jemmy, to examine the country to the southward. Travelled in a south-westerly direction for twenty-five miles, and camped at the spot where we had the encounter with the natives on May 31. We found they had left, and there was no water on the rocks. Luckily our horses had water six miles back.

15th.—Saddled up at daybreak, and steered about S.E. towards a high range of hills about ten miles distant. I named it Mount Ida, and from the summit I took a round of angles with my pocket sextant. On all the hills in this neighbourhood the local attraction is so great that the prismatic compass is useless. Found a fine spring of water on south side of Mount Ida, in an almost inaccessible spot. After giving the horses two hours' rest we continued our journey N. 154° E. mag. for eight miles to a granite range, where, after a diligent search, I found two water-holes, and bivouacked, with good feed around the rocks.

16*th*.—Saddled up at sunrise, and steered to some trap ranges, N. 124° E., about seven miles distant, from which I could see an immense lake running as far as the eye could reach to the eastward, and westerly and northerly, most probably joining Lake Barlee. Not being able to proceed farther southward, on account of the lake, I steered in a northerly direction for twenty miles, but, discovering neither feed nor water, bivouacked in a thicket, and tied up our horses.

17*th*.—At dawn, found that my horse Sugar, after breaking his bridle, had made off towards our bivouac of the 15th. Placing my saddle on Jemmy's horse, we followed on the track for six miles, when we came to a few granite rocks, with a little water on them, from rain that had fallen during the night. At this place Morgan was left with the horses and our guns, while Jemmy and I followed on Sugar's tracks, taking only a revolver with us. After travelling on the tracks for two miles we overtook him, and with a little trouble managed to catch him. On reaching the spot where we had left Morgan, we found him with the three double-barrelled guns on full cock, together with his revolver, in readiness. On being asked what was the matter, he stated "Nothing," but he was ready to give the natives

what he called "a warm attachment." After
having breakfast we steered N.N.W. for about
twenty miles, and reached camp at 5 p.m., and
found all well. Rained a little during the
day.

18th.—Having thus made an exhaustive search
in the neighbourhood where Jemmy expected to
find the remains of the white men, by travelling
over nearly the whole of the country between
latitude 28° and 29° 30′ south, and longitude 120°
and 121° east, I determined to make the most of
the little time at my disposal, and carry out the
instruction that I was to attempt to proceed as
far eastward as possible. Accordingly, after collecting the horses, steered about E.N.E. for nine
miles, to a low quartz range, over tolerably grassy
country, not very dense. From this range I saw
some bare granite rocks bearing about N. 120°
E. mag. For these we steered, and luckily, after
travelling six miles over a plain, which in severe
winters must be nearly all under water, found a
fine pool in a clay-pan, and bivouacked. There
was a little rain during the night.

19th.—The horses having strayed back on our
tracks, we did not start till 12 o'clock, when the
journey was continued towards the granite range
seen yesterday, about ten miles distant. We
camped on west side of N., with plenty of water
from the recent rain on the granite rocks, but
with very little feed. At five miles crossed a dry

stream-bed, eighteen yards wide, sandy bottom; thickets most of the way, but not very dense.

20*th* (*Sunday*).—Rested at camp. Jemmy shot four rock kangaroos to-day. Took a round of angles from a bare granite hill, N. 50° E. mag., about one mile from camp, which I found to be in south latitude 28° 57′ by meridian altitudes of Bootes (Arcturus) and α Pegasi (Markab); and in longitude about 120° 55′ E. Saw a high hill bearing N. 81° 30′ E. mag., about twenty-five miles distant, which I named Mount Lenora; and another bearing N. 67° E. mag., about twenty-five miles distant, which I named Mount George. Intend proceeding to Mount Lenora to-morrow. Marked a small tree (ordnance-tree of Mr. Austin) with the letter F at our bivouac.

21*st*.—Steering towards Mount Lenora over some tolerably grassy country, we reached it at sundown, and, not finding any water, camped without it, with very good feed. In south latitude 28° 53′ by meridian altitudes of Lyræ (Vega) and Aquilæ (Altair), and in longitude about 121° 20′ E.

22*nd*.—After making every search in the vicinity of the bivouac for water, and the country ahead appearing very unpromising, I decided to return ten miles on our tracks, where we found a fine pool of water in a brook, and camped. To-morrow I intend taking a flying trip in search of water.

23*rd.*—Started this morning, in company with
Tommy Windich, to explore the country to the
eastward for water, &c. After travelling three
miles towards Mount Lenora, saw a natives' fire
bearing N.E. about three miles, to which we
proceeded, and surprised a middle-aged native.
Upon seeing us he ran off shouting, and decamped
with a number of his companions, who were at a
little distance. The horse I was riding—Tur-
pin, an old police-horse from Northam—evidently well understood running down a native,
and between us we soon overtook our black
friend and brought him to bay. We could not
make him understand anything we said; but,
after looking at us a moment, and seeing no
chance of escape, he dropped his two dowaks and
wooden dish, and climbed up a small tree about
twelve feet high. After securing the dowaks, I
tried every means to tempt him to come down;
fired my revolver twice, and showed him the
effect it had on the tree. The report had the
effect also of frightening all the natives that were
about, who no doubt made off at a great rate. I
began to climb up after him, but he pelted me
with sticks, and was more like a wild beast than a
man. After discovering we did not like to be hit,
he became bolder and threw more sticks at us,
and one hitting Tommy, he was nearly shooting
him, when I called on him to desist. I then
offered him a piece of damper, showing him it was

good by eating some myself and giving some to
Tommy. He would not look at it, and when I
threw it close to him he dashed it away as
if it was poison. The only way of getting him
down from the tree was force, and, after considering a moment, I decided to leave him where
he was. We accordingly laid down his dowaks
and dish, and bade him farewell in as kindly a
manner as possible. Continuing our course,
passing Mount Lenora, we steered N. 81° 15′ E.
mag. to a table hill, which I ascended and took
a round of angles. This hill I named Mount
Malcolm, after my friend and companion, Mr.
M. Hamersley. Saw a remarkable peak bearing
N. 65° E. mag., distant about twenty miles,
towards which we proceeded, and at six miles
came upon a small gully, in which we found a
little water, and bivouacked.

24*th*.—Started early this morning, and steered
E.N.E. for six miles to some low stony ranges,
lightly grassed; thence N. 61° 30′ E. mag. to the
remarkable peak, which I named Mount Flora,
distant about nine miles from the stony ranges,
ascending which, I obtained a round of bearings
and angles. Saw a high range bearing about
N. 106° 15′ E. mag., apparently about sixteen
miles distant, towards which we travelled till after
dark, searching for feed and water on our way
without success, and there bivouacked and tied
up our horses.

25th.—Saddled at dawn, and proceeded to the range, which bore N. 93° 30′ E. mag., about five miles distant, on reaching which I ascended the highest peak, and named it Mount Margaret. Took a round of angles and bearings. From the summit of Mount Margaret the view was very extensive. There was a large dry salt lake to the southward, as far as the eye could reach, while to the east and north-east there were low trap ranges, lightly grassed. A high table hill bore N. 73° E. mag.

Being now about sixty miles from camp, and not having had any water since yesterday morning, I decided to return. Steering about west for eight miles, we struck a brook trending south-east, in which we found a small quantity of water in a clay-pan. After resting an hour, in order to make a damper and give the horses a little of the feed, which only grew sparingly on the banks of the brook, we continued our journey towards camp. Passing Mount Flora, we camped about eight miles farther onwards, near a small patch of feed, without water, about a mile north of our outward track.

26th—Started at dawn, and reached our bivouac of the 23rd. There obtained just sufficient water for ourselves and the horses. Continuing, we found a fine pool of rain-water in a brook a mile and a half west of Mount Malcolm, and, reaching camp an hour after dark, found all well. On our

way Tommy Windich shot a red kangaroo, which
we carried to camp.

27th (*Sunday*).—Rested at camp. Found it to
be in south latitude 28° 55' by meridian altitudes
of sun, Aquilæ (Altair), and Lyra, and in longitude
about 121° 10' E. Although we had great difficulty in procuring water in our last trip, I was
reluctant to return without making another
effort, especially as, from the appearance of the
country east of the farthest point, I had hope of a
change, and therefore concluded to shift the party
to the water found yesterday near Mount Malcolm,
and make another attempt to proceed farther east.

28th.—Steering about N. 81° deg. E. mag.,
over lightly-grassed country, thinly wooded for
sixteen miles, we camped a mile and a half west
of Mount Malcolm, in south latitude 28° 51' 19"
by meridian altitude of Aquilæ (Altair), and in
longitude about 121° 27' E.

29th.—Started this morning, in company with
Tommy Windich, with seven days' provisions,
leaving instructions for Mr. Monger to shift the
party back to our last camp, where the feed was
much better, in latitude 28° 55' S., and longitude
121° 10' E. Travelled about east for thirty miles
towards Mount Margaret, our farthest point last
trip. We camped in a thicket, without water, on
a small patch of feed.

30th.—Saddled up at dawn, and proceeded
towards Mount Margaret, obtaining a little water

at the spot where we found water on our former trip. Continuing, we came to a fine pool of
water in a brook, and rested an hour, Mount
Margaret being north-east about two miles and a
half. Hardly any feed near the water. Resuming, we passed Mount Margaret and started
towards the table hill seen previously, bearing
N. 73° E. mag., apparently about eighteen
miles distant, over a series of dry salt marshes,
with sandy country and spinifex intervening.
After travelling eight miles, we bivouacked
without water on a small patch of feed. With
the pocket sextant I found this spot to be in
south latitude about 28° 50', and longitude about
122° 11' E.

July 1*st.*—After journeying towards the table
hill seen yesterday for six miles, crossed a large
brook heading south-west, in which we found a
small pool of rain-water, and rested an hour to
breakfast. Resuming for about six miles, reached
the table hill, which I ascended and took a round
of angles. I have since named this hill Mount
Weld, being the farthest hill seen eastward
by us. Continuing about N. 77° E. mag. for
fifteen miles, through dense thickets—no grass
except spinifex—we bivouacked, without water
or feed, and then tied up our horses. I found
this spot to be in south latitude 28° 41' by meridian altitude of Bootes (Arcturus), and in longitude about 122° 37' E.

2nd.—Started at dawn, and steered about east, searching on our way for water, which our horses and ourselves were beginning to want much. At six miles we found a small hole in some rocks, apparently empty, but on sounding with a stick I found it to contain a little water. The mouth of the hole being too small to admit a pannican, and having used my hat with very little success, I at last thought of my gum-bucket, with which we procured about two quarts of something between mud and water, which, after straining through my pocket-handkerchief, we pronounced first-rate. Continuing for six miles over clear, open sand-plains, with spinifex and large white gums,—the only large trees and clear country seen since leaving the settled districts,—we climbed up a white gum to have a view of the country eastward. Some rough sandstone cliffs bore N. 127° E. mag., about six miles distant. The country eastward was almost level, with sandstone cliffs here and there, apparently thickly wooded with white gums, and other trees; spinifex everywhere, but no prospects of water. More to the north, a narrow line of samphire flats appeared, with cypress and stunted gums on its edges—all barren and desolate —so much so, indeed, that for the last twenty-five miles there has been no grass seen at all save spinifex. After taking a few bearings from the top of the tree (which I marked with the letter F on the south side), which is in south latitude

about 28° 41′, and longitude about 122° 50
E., I decided to return to our last watering-
place, nearly thirty-one miles distant, as we were
now over 100 miles from camp, and the horses
had been without water or feed since yesterday
morning. Therefore, keeping a little to the
north of the outward track, we travelled nearly
two hours after dark, and camped without water
or feed, and tied up the horses.

3rd.—Saddled up early, and steered westerly
towards our last watering-place, about fourteen
miles distant; but, after travelling nearly seven
miles, came to a small pool of water (at the head
of the brook where we found water on the 1st),
and rested two hours to allow our horses to feed,
as they had neither eaten nor drunk for the
last forty-eight hours. Resuming our journey
along the brook (which I named Windich Brook,
after my companion, Tommy Windich) for ten
miles, in which we found several pools of water,
but destitute of feed, camped without water about
two miles east of our bivouac of the 30th June.

4th.—Travelling about W.S.W. for twelve miles,
we reached the pool of water found on our outward track on the 30th June, two miles and
a half S.W. from Mount Margaret. There we
rested an hour. Resuming, we travelled nearly
along our outward track for eighteen miles, and
camped without water on a small patch of feed.
Tommy shot two wurrongs to-day.

5th.—Started at daybreak, and, continuing nearly along our outward track for twenty-five miles, we reached the water close to Mount Malcolm, where we left the party, they having shifted, as instructed, seventeen miles farther back. There we rested an hour; but, having finished our provisions, we roasted two wurrongs and made a first-rate dinner. Tommy also shot an emu that came to water, and which we carried to camp. Reached there at 6 p.m. and found all well, having been absent seven days, every night being without water, during which time we travelled over 200 miles.

6th.—Weighed all the rations, and found we had 283 lbs. flour, 31 lbs. bacon, 28 lbs. sugar, and 4 lbs. tea,—equal to thirty-two days' allowance of flour, ten days' bacon, nineteen days' sugar, and twenty-one days' tea on a full ration. Thereupon concluded to return to Perth as quickly as possible, and reduce the allowance of tea and sugar to last thirty days—bacon to be done without. By that time I hope to reach Clarke's homestead, Victoria Plains, and intend to return by Mount Kenneth, Nanjajetty, Ningham, or Mount Singleton, and thence to Damparwar and Clarke's homestead, thus fixing a few points that will be useful to the Survey Office.

7th.—At 6.30 a.m., barometer 28 86, thermometer 34°. Started on the return, and followed along our outward tracks for sixteen miles. Camped on east side of granite range, in south latitude 28° 57′, and east longitude 120° 55′.

8th.—Travelling nearly along our eastward track, and passing our bivouac of the 19th June, we reached the Two Springs bivouac.

9th.—Travelled twenty-two miles, and reached our bivouac of 30th May—129° 9′ E.

10th.—Reached the bivouac of May 27th. On our way I ascended a very high range, which I named Mount Alfred, and took a fine round of angles—Mount Alexander, Mount Bivou, Mount Ida, Mount Elvire, and Yeadie and Bulgar being visible.

11th (Sunday).—Plotted up our track.

12th.—Travelled for twenty-five miles and camped on a splendid patch of feed, with a little water on some granite rocks about two miles west of our bivouac of the 24th. This I found to be in south latitude 28° 57′ 48″ by meridian altitudes of Bootes (Arcturus) and Pegasi (Markab), and in longitude about 119° 28′ east; Mount Elvire bearing N. 154° E. mag., distant about twenty-one miles.

13th.—Leaving the party in charge of Mr. Monger, with instructions to proceed to Retreat Rock—our bivouac of May 23rd—I started with Mr. Hamersley and Jemmy to attempt to cross Lake Barlee, in order to explore the country on its south side, near Mount Elvire, as well as to try and find natives, Jemmy being acquainted with these tribes. Steering N. 154° E. mag. for seven miles, we came to the lake, and, entering it, succeeded in reaching the southern shore after twelve miles of heavy walking, sinking over our boots every step—the horses having great difficulty in getting through. When we reached the southern shore, it was nearly sundown. Determined to push on, and reached the range, where we bivouacked on a patch of feed and a little water; Mount Elvire bearing N. 87° E. mag., about one mile distant; and Yeadie and Bulgar N. 8° E. mag. Rained lightly during the day. Being wet through from the splashings of the horses while crossing the lake, and from it raining throughout the night, and not having any covering, our situation was not the most pleasant. Jemmy informed me there was a fine permanent spring close to Mount Elvire; but we did not go to see it.

14*th*.—This morning, after ascending a range to have a view of the country, steered N. 288° E. mag., and then, travelling six miles, came to a branch of Lake Barlee running far to the southward, which we attempted to cross; but after travelling a mile and a half, the horses went down to their girths in the bog, and we had great difficulty in getting them to return, which, however, we ultimately succeeded in doing, and made another attempt, at a place where a series of islands appeared, to cross it, and, passing over without much difficulty, reached the opposite shore at sundown, where we bivouacked on a splendid grassy ride, with abundance of water in granite rocks, Mount Elvire bearing N. 108° E. mag., and Yeadie and Bulgar N. 45° E. mag.

15th.—Having finished our rations last night, we started at dawn, and steered towards Retreat Rock, where we were to meet the party. After travelling five miles, we came to that part of Lake Barlee which we attempted to cross, without success, on May 19th (on our outward track); but, leading our horses, we at last succeeded in crossing, and reached camp, all very tired, at twelve o'clock, finding all well. The party were encamped one mile north of our former bivouac, at some granite rocks with two fine water-holes.

16th.—Considerable delay having occurred in collecting the horses, we did not start till ten o'clock, when we travelled nearly along our out-ward track—passing Yeeramudder Hill, from the summit of which Mount Elvire bore N. 111° 30′ E. mag. about thirty-five miles distant—for about twenty-one miles, and bivouacked at some granite rocks with a little feed around them, which I found to be in south latitude 29° 8′ 47″ by meri-dian altitudes of Bootes (Arcturus) and Pegasi (Markab), and in longitude about 118° 59′ E.

17th.—Started at 8.45 a.m., and, steering about

west for twenty-five miles through dense thickets without feed, we camped without water on a small miserable patch, in south latitude 29° 7′ 13″ by meridian altitude of Bootes (Arcturus). Marked a small tree with " F. 1869." Being now in friendly country, I decided to give up keeping watch, which had been done regularly for the last two months.

18th (*Sunday*).—After starting the party, went, in company with Tommy Windich, to take bearings from a low hill, bearing N. 289°, distant about eight miles, after which we struck in the direction in which we expected to find the party ; but as, for some reason or other, they had not passed by, I anticipated they must have met with good feed and water, and camped, it being Sunday. However this may be, we kept bearing more and more to the southward, in hope of crossing the track, till after dark, when we reached the Warne Flats, and bivouacked. Not expecting to be absent more than a few days, we had neither rations nor rugs. Luckily, Tommy shot a turkey, which we roasted in the ashes, and made a very good meal. The night was bitterly cold, and, not having any rug, I slept with a fire on each side of me, and, considering the circumstances, slept fairly.

19th.—Made a first-rate breakfast off the remainder of the turkey, and then started in search of the party, making back towards where we

had left them, keeping well to the southward.
After spending nearly the whole of the day, and
knocking up the horses, we found the tracks of
the party nearly where we had left them yesterday morning, and, following along them for nine
miles, found where they had bivouacked last night;
and, it being now two hours after dark, we camped
also, having between us for supper an opossum,
which Tommy had luckily caught during the day.
The night was again very cold, and we had hardly
anything to eat, which made matters still worse.

20th.—Starting on the tracks at daybreak, followed them for about thirteen miles, and then we
found the party encamped on the east side of a
large bare granite rock called Meroin, Mount
Kenneth bearing N. 24° E. mag., about fifteen
miles distant. From a cliff, about one mile west
of the camp, took a splendid round of angles,
Mount Kenneth, Mount Singleton, and several
other known points being visible. By meridian
altitudes of sun, a Bootes (Arcturus), ε Bootes,
and a Coronæ Borealis, camp was in south
latitude 29° 10′ 49″, and longitude about 118°
14′ east.

21st.—At seven a.m., barometer 29·10; thermometer 35°. Started at 8.15 a.m. Steered
about west for fifteen miles, over country studded
here and there with granite rocks, with good feed
around them—in some places rock poison—and
then camped at a spring called Pullagooroo,

bearing N. 189° from a bare granite hill, three quarters of a mile distant, from which hill Mount Singleton bore N. 237° E. mag., by meridian altitudes of α Bootes (Arcturus) and ε Bootes. Pullagooroo is in south latitude 29° 7' 46". Finished our bacon this morning, and for the future will only have damper and tea.

22nd.—Steering a little to the north of west, through dense thickets without grass, we bivouacked at a very grassy spot called Bunnaroo, from which Mount Singleton bore N. 205° E. mag. By meridian altitudes of α Bootes (Arcturus), ε Bootes, and Coronæ Borealis, camp is in south latitude 28° 58', and in longitude about 117° 35' east.

23rd.—After starting the party with instructions to proceed straight to Mount Singleton, distant about thirty-two miles, I went, in company with Jemmy, to the summit of a high trap range in order to take a round of angles, and fix Nanjajetty, which was visible. While on our way to join the party, saw the tracks of two men and two horses, with two natives walking, and soon after found where they had bivouacked a few days before. Was much surprised at this discovery : suppose it to be squatters looking for country. Continuing, we found the tracks of our party, and overtook them, and encamped at a fine permanent spring— Mount Singleton bearing N. 146° E. mag. about three miles and a half distant. Reached the party at seven o'clock. There was a partial eclipse of the moon this evening.

24th.—There being splendid green feed around Mount Singleton, and as the horses were tired, I concluded to give them a day's rest. Went, in company with Mr. Monger and Jemmy, to the summit of Mount Singleton, which took us an hour to ascend; but, on reaching it, we were well repaid for the trouble by the very extensive view and the many points to which I could take bearings. Far as the eye could reach to the E. and S.E. were visible Lake Moore, Mount Churchman; to the north, conspicuous high trap ranges appeared; while to the west, within a radius of six miles, hills covered with flowers gave the country a pretty appearance. Further to the west a dry salt lake and a few trap hills appeared. Reached the camp at 2 p.m. On our way shot three rock kangaroos.

25th (Sunday).—Rested at camp near Mount Singleton, which I found to be in south latitude 29° 24′ 33″ by meridian altitude of sun, and longitude about 117° 20′ east.

26th.—Some delay having occurred in collecting the horses, did not start till 9 a.m., when we steered a little to the north of west towards Damparwar. For the first seven miles over rough trap hills lightly grassed, when we entered samphire and saltbush flats for four miles. Crossing a large marsh at a point where it was only 100 yards wide, and continuing through thickets, we camped at a spot with very little feed and no water, in south latitude 29° 21′ 48″. From this spot Mount Singleton bore N. 113° 20′ E. mag., distant about twenty miles. Here we met two natives, whom we had seen on our outward track at the Warne Corroboree. They were of course friendly, and slept at our camp; they had a great many dulgates and opossums, which they carried in a net bag, made out of the inner bark of the ordnance-tree, which makes a splendid strong cord. They informed us that a native had come from the eastward with intelligence relating to the encounter we had with the large tribe on May 31, adding that we had all been killed, and that all the natives in this vicinity had cried very much on hearing the news. This is another specimen of the narrations of natives, with whom a tale never loses anything by being carried.

27th.—Steering a little to the north of west for eighteen miles, we reached Damparwar Springs, a clear grassy spot of about 300 acres, on west side of a low granite hill. The spring was dry, but by digging a few feet obtained abundant supply. From the appearance of the country there has hardly been any rain in this neighbourhood for many months. Took a round of angles from a trap hill about two miles distant, Mount Singleton and many other points being visible. Met a party of friendly natives here. By meridian altitudes of a Bootes, a

Coronæ Borealis and α Lyræ (Vega), Dampar-war Spring is in south latitude 29° 16′ 32″, and longitude about 116° 47′ E.

28th.—Steering in a southerly direction, and following along the western margin of a salt lake, —most of the way over samphire flats, with thickets intervening, denser than usual,—we encamped on a small grassy spot, with plenty of water in granite rocks, called Murrunggnulgo, situated close to the west side of the lake, which I named Lake Monger. The native Jemmy, in company with some of his friends, stayed behind to-day in order to catch opossums, and did not join us this evening. By meridian altitudes of ε Bootes, α Coronæ Borealis, α Lyræ (Vega), and Aquilæ (Altair), Murrunggnulgo is in south latitude 29° 37′ 20″, Damparwar bearing about north mag.

29th.—Moving a little to the west of south for twenty miles, through dense thickets, by far the worst we have ever encountered, and destitute of feed, we reached Bera Bera, a grassy spot with a dry well, where water might be procured. Continuing N. 238° E. for about five miles, we reached and camped at some granite rocks, with a fine well of water called Wandanno, which I found to be in south latitude 29° 57′ 14″ by meridian altitudes of Lyræ (Vega) and Aquilæ (Altair). From Bera Bera, Mount Singleton bore N. 50° 30′ E. mag. about fifty miles distant.

Jemmy did not put in an appearance to-day, but
sent on a native to say he would join us in a
day or two.

30*th.*—Travelling about N. 212° E. mag. for
fourteen miles, over samphire flats, with thickets
intervening, we reached a fine grassy spot, with
water in granite rocks, called Gnookadunging.
Continuing about south for two and a half miles,
passed another small grassy spot called Ginbin-
ning; thence in about the general direction of N.
210° E. mag. For about eleven and a half miles,
over an immense sand-plain, running as far as
the eye could reach to the N.W. and S.E., we
camped in the centre of it at a spring called
Manginie, a sheep station belonging to Mr. James
Church. Towards the end of the day Bailey's
horse Tommy fairly gave in, and we had great
difficulty in getting him to camp, which Mr.
Hamersley and I did not reach until an hour after
dark. The night was cloudy, and I was unable
to get any observations, but luckily at daybreak
obtained meridian altitudes of Jupiter, which
placed Manginie Spring in S. latitude 30° 21′.

31*st.*—Steering about S.S.W. for thirteen miles,
we reached Cooroo Springs—a fine grassy spot
in winter—where we camped, the horses being
very tired. For the first seven miles over
scrubby sand-plains; thence to Cooroo, over
grassy country, with spearwood thickets intervening. Tommy shot a kangaroo this afternoon,

which was very acceptable, having had only damper and tea for several days past.

August 1st (Sunday).—Rested at Cooroo Springs. All very busy putting our ragged clothes in as good repair as possible. By meridian altitudes of sun, Lyræ (Vega), 32′ 15″. Read Divine Service. Jemmy has not yet overtaken us, so I conclude he has changed his mind, and does not intend following us. We are now about nine miles from Clarke's homestead, which bears about S.S.E.

2nd.—Travelling about S.S.E. for nine miles over grassy country, with York gums, &c., we reached the hospitable residence of Mr. Clarke, where we were very kindly received, and stayed a short time to hear the news. Resuming for eighteen miles along the road to Newcastle, we passed Mr. Donald MacPherson's, where I obtained some rations, and pushed on six miles farther, and bivouacked one mile south of Badgy-Badgy, with very short feed for our horses.

3rd.—Travelling along the road towards Newcastle for twenty-six miles, we camped one mile past Byen, and about sixteen miles from Newcastle.

4th.—Reached Newcastle at eleven o'clock, and had just time to report the safe return of the expedition before the mail left.

5th.—After handing over all the horses provided by the different settlers to their respective

owners, and bidding farewell to Mr. George
Monger (who intends proceeding to York), I
left Newcastle in company with Mr. M. Hamersley and Tommy Windich, leaving Morgan
and remainder of equipment to follow with the
cart which had been brought to Newcastle by
Ward and C. Adams. Reached Baylup at 4 p.m.

6th.—Made an early start; reached Guildford
at twelve o'clock, where we rested an hour. Then
resuming, reached Perth at 4 p.m., and reported
personally the results of the expedition, having
been absent 113 days, in which time I travelled
by computation over 2000 miles.

I now beg to make a few remarks with reference to the main object of the expedition,
which was the discovery of the remains of the
late Dr. Leichardt and party.

In the first place, Mr. Frederick Roe was informed by the native Weilbarrin, that two white
men and their native companions had been
killed by the aborigines, thirteen days' journey
to the northward, when he was at a spot called
Koolanobbing, which is in south latitude about
30° 53′, and longitude about 119° 14′ east. Mr.
Austin lost eleven horses at Poison Rock (nine
died, and two were left nearly dead), which is
in latitude 28° 43′ 23″ south, and longitude about
118° 38′ east, or about 130 miles from Koolanobbing, and in the direction pointed to by

the natives. I therefore imagine it to be very probable that the whole story originated from the horses lost by Mr. Austin at Poison Rock, as I am convinced the natives will say anything they imagine will please. Again, the account given us at Mount Churchman, on May 5th, appeared very straightforward and truthful. It was very similar to that related to Mr. Roe; but, on questioning the natives, they at last stated there were neither men nor guns left, only horses' remains, and pointed towards Poison Rock. Further, the native who gave all the information to Mr. Monger was one of our party. His tale, as related by Mr. Monger, also appeared very straightforward and truthful, that white men had been killed by the natives twenty years ago; that he had seen the spot, which was at a spring near a large lake, so large that it looked like the sea as seen from Rottnist, eleven days' journey from Ningham or Mount Singleton, in a fine country. The white men were rushed upon while making a damper, and clubbed and speared. He had often seen an axe which formed part of the plunder. All this appears feasible and truthful enough in print; but the question is, Of what value did I find it? Upon telling Jemmy what Mr. Monger stated he told him, he said he never told him that he had seen things himself, but that he had heard it from a native who had seen them, thus contradicting the whole

he had formerly stated to Mr. Monger. Moreover, the fine country he described we never saw,
what a native calls good country being where he
can get a drink of water and a wurrong; and
if there is an acre of grassy land they describe
it as a very extensive grassy country! This
I have generally found the case. As a specimen of the untruthfulness of these natives,
I may quote that my native Jemmy, who was
a first-rate fellow in every other respect, stated
to Mr. Monger and myself at York, that there
was a large river like that called the Avon
at York, to the eastward, knowing at the time
he would be found out to be telling a falsehood.
He even told Mr. George Monger, before leaving
Newcastle, to buy hooks, in order to catch the
fish that were in the river, and concluded by
stating that we would have great difficulty in
crossing it, as it ran a great distance north and
south. Almost every evening I questioned and
cross-questioned him respecting this river; still
he adhered to what he first stated! It may well
be imagined how disappointed we were on reaching the spot to find only a small brook running
into a salt marsh, with water in winter, but dry
in summer.

With reference to the country travelled over,
I am of opinion that it is worthless as a pastoral
or agricultural district; and as to minerals I am
not sufficiently conversant with the science to

offer an opinion, except that I should think it was worth while sending geologists to examine it thoroughly.

It now becomes my most pleasing duty to record my entire satisfaction with the manner in which all the members of the expedition exerted themselves in the performance of their respective duties. To Mr. George Monger and Mr. Malcolm Hamersley I am indebted for their co-operation and advice on all occasions. I am also deeply indebted to Mr. Hamersley for collecting and preserving all the botanical specimens that came within his reach, as well as the great trouble and care taken with the store department, placed under his immediate charge. To probation prisoner David Morgan my best thanks are due as the shoeing smith, as well as acting cook for the party the whole time. Of Tommy Windich (native) I cannot speak too highly, being very useful in collecting the horses, as well as a first-class huntsman, and really invaluable as a water finder. Accompanying me on many trying occasions, suffering often from want of water, he showed energy and determination deserving of the highest praise. Jemmy Mungaro was also a first-class bushman, and invaluable as a water finder. He was in many ways useful, and very obedient. His great failing was that he exaggerated—no tale ever losing anything in his charge. Nevertheless, I

have many things to thank him for, and therefore he deserves praise.

In conclusion, sir, allow me to thank you for
your kindness and advice, which has greatly
supported me in this arduous undertaking. I
much regret that an expedition which was so
efficiently equipped, and on which I was left so
free to act, has not resulted in more direct
benefit to the colony, to satisfy many who are
not capable of appreciating the importance of
such explorations.

I have, Sir, &c.,

JOHN FORREST,

Leader of Expedition.

The Hon. Capt. Roe, R.N., Surveyor-General.

So far as the mystery on which the fate of
Leichardt is involved was concerned, my expedition was barren of results; but the additional
knowledge gained of the character of the country
between the settled districts of Western Australia
and the 123rd meridian of east longitude, well
repaid me, and those of the party, for the exertions
we had undergone.

Shortly after my return I received an official
communication from Mr. Barlee, the Colonial
Secretary at Perth, announcing that his Excellency the Governor, with a view to mark his
sense of the value of my services as leader of
the expedition, had sanctioned the payment to
me of a gratuity of 50l. Mr. Monger and Mr.

Hamersley each received 25*l.*; Morgan, the probation prisoner, who had done good service in the expedition, especially in looking after the horses, was promised a remission of a portion of his sentence. Tommy Windich and Jemmy Mungaro, the natives, had each a single-barrel gun, with his name inscribed—presents which they highly valued.

So ended the first of my expeditions; and a very short time elapsed before I was called upon to undertake a longer, more hazardous, and more important journey.

CHAPTER III.

SECOND EXPEDITION.——FROM PERTH TO ADELAIDE, ROUND
THE GREAT BIGHT.

A new Exploration suggested.—Proposal to reach Adelaide by
way of the South Coast.—The experience derived from
Eyre's Expedition.—Survey of Port Eucla.—Official Instructions.—The Start.—Dempster's Station near Esperance
Bay.—The Schooner at Port Eucla.—Journal of the Expedition.

IMMEDIATELY on my return to Perth a new expedition was suggested by Dr. Von Mueller, whose
anxiety for the discovery of Leichardt was rather
increased than abated by the disappointment experienced. He proposed that I should start from
the upper waters of the Murchison River with a
light party and provisions for six months, and endeavour to reach Carpentaria. He thought, not
only would such an expedition almost certainly
find some traces of the lost explorer, but probably would make geographical discoveries of the
highest interest and importance. In a paper in
the *Colonial Monthly* he argued that—

" While those who searched after traces of the

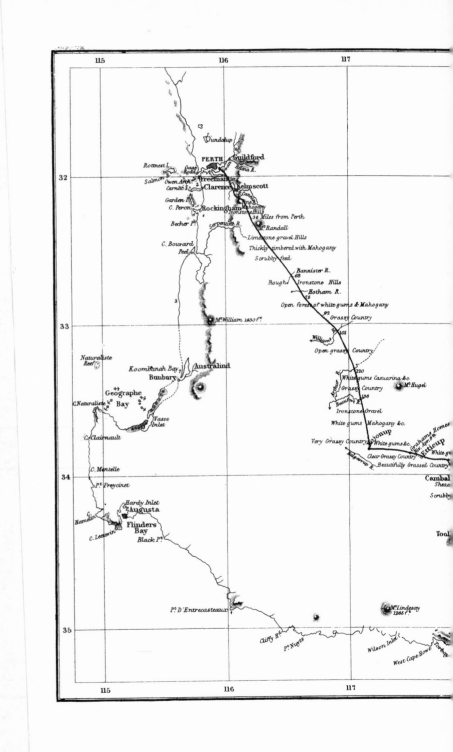

Very rich

Martinup Biv Apr 10th
Jam Trees & White Gums
Nigamp
Scrubby Country
Kybelup
Jam Trees &c
Granite
Sheaoak
York Gum &c
Sand Plains
Granite Rocks
Biv. Apr 11th

Stirling Range
Ellens Pk

Mt Manypeak
Bald I.

King George Sd

C. Knob

Pt Hood

Doubtful Island Bay

W. Mt Barren
Middle Mt Barren
Gairdner R.

Fitzgerald R.

Pallinup R.
Salt R.

Jerramungup
Biv. Apr 13th
Cowombelup
Wongamup
Scrubby
Granite Rocks
Red Cliffs
E. Mt Barren
Jam Trees

Biv. Apr 16th & 17th
Salt pools
Open Plains
Rough feed
Native Swamp
Darkannup
Jarrup

Open Plains
lightly grassed
Rough

Shoal Cape
Red Islet
West Group

Esperance Bay

Monbeup Biv. Apr 23rd & 24th
Granite Hills
Brackish Streams
Fresh Swamp
Swamp

Station I.
Dukes of Orleans

C. le Grand
Mondrain I.

Mt McGrath
Biv. May 10th

Saddleback Hill

Twin Peaks

Archipelago of the Re

lost party did not solve the primary objects of their mission, their labours have not been without importance to geographical science. The course of one traveller connected the southern interior of Queensland in a direct route with the vast pastoral depressions about Lake Torrens; the researches of another explorer, bent on ascertaining Leichardt's fate, unfolded to us a tract of table country, now already occupied by herds and flocks, not less in length than that of Sweden and Italy. . . . We should bear fully in mind how a line in Leichardt's intended direction would at once enable the squatters of North-East Australia to drive their surplus of flocks and herds easily across to the well-watered, hilly and grassy country within close proximity to the harbour of the north-west coast."

I should have been well satisfied to undertake an expedition in the proposed direction, starting from the head of the Murchison, and trying to connect my route with that of Mr. A. Gregory's down Sturt Creek; but the difficulty of obtaining funds and lack of support caused the project to be set aside or at least delayed. Mr. Weld, then Governor of Western Australia, who always heartily supported explorations, was in favour of an attempt to reach Adelaide by way of the south coast, and offered me the command of an expedition in that direction.

I readily accepted the offer, and at once busied

myself with the necessary preparations, but was far from being insensible to the difficulties of the undertaking. Of the route nothing was known except the disastrous experience of Mr. Eyre in 1840 and 1841. His remarkable narrative—interesting to all concerned in the history of explorations or in the records of energy, courage, and perseverance under the most discouraging circumstances—might have acted as a warning to future explorers against endeavouring to follow in his track. The fearful privations he endured, his narrow escape from the most terrible of all forms of death, were certainly not encouraging; but his experience might often be of service to others, pointing out dangers to be avoided, and suggesting methods of overcoming difficulties. At any rate, I was not deterred from the attempt to trace once more the coast of the Great Bight, and to reach the sister colony by that route. Eyre had not discovered any rivers, although it was possible that he might have crossed the sand-bars of rivers in the night. The difficulties he laboured under in his almost solitary journey, and the sufferings he endured, might have rendered him unable to make observations and discoveries more practicable to a better equipped and stronger party, while the deficiency of water on the route appeared to offer the greatest impediment. We were not, however, deterred from the attempt, and on the 30th of March, 1870, we started from Perth on a journey which

ALEXANDER FORREST.

all knew to be dangerous, but which we were sanguine enough to believe might produce considerable results.

That we were not disappointed the result will prove. Indeed, the difficulties were much fewer than we had been prepared to encounter; and in five months from the date of departure from Perth we arrived safely at Adelaide, completing a journey which Mr. Eyre had been more than twelve months in accomplishing.

My party was thus composed:—I was leader; the second in command was my brother, Alexander Forrest, a surveyor; H. McLarty, a police constable; and W. Osborne, a farrier and shoeing smith,—these with Tommy Windich, the native who had served me so faithfully on the previous expedition, and another native, Billy Noongale, an intelligent young fellow, accompanied us.

Before I enter upon the details of my journey it may be useful to state as briefly as possible the efforts made to obtain a better acquaintance with the vast territory popularly known as No Man's Land, which had been traversed by Eyre, and afterwards to summarize the little knowledge which had been obtained.

In 1860 Major Warburton—who afterwards, in 1873-74, succeeded in crossing the northern part of the great inland desert, after enduring great privations—contrived to reach eighty-five miles beyond the head of the Bight, and made several journeys from the coast in a north and north-westerly direction for a distance of about sixty miles. Traces of Eyre's expedition were then visible. The holes he had dug in search of water twenty years before were still there, and the records of his journey were of great value as guiding Warburton's movements. His experience of the nature of the country amply confirmed that of the previous explorer. He found the district to the north to be a dreary waste, destitute of food and water. Rain seldom fell, and, when it did, was immediately absorbed by the arid soil. Bustards and moles were the only living creatures. To the north-west there was a little grass, but the tract showing verdure was very small in extent, and beyond it was again the scorched, barren, inhospitable desert.

Two years afterwards other explorations were attempted, and especially should be noted Captain Delessier's. He was disposed to think more favourably of the nature of the country. The enterprise of squatters seeking for " fresh fields and pastures new,"—to whom square miles represent less than acres to graziers and sheep farmers in England—is not easily daunted. They made a few settlements ; but the scanty pasturage and the difficulty of obtaining water, by sinking wells, in some instances to the depth of over 200 feet, have been great drawbacks.

It might naturally be inquired why no attempts were made to reach the coast of the Great Bight by sea? Why so much suffering has been endured when a well-equipped vessel might have landed explorers at various points and been ready to afford them assistance? In his explorations to the north of Western Australia, Mr. F. Gregory had a convenient base of operations in the "Dolphin," a barque which remained on the coast. It might seem that similar aid could have been afforded to Warburton and others who attempted to trace the south-coast line. But for hundreds of miles along the shores of the Bight no vessel could reach the shore or lie safely at anchor. Long ranges of perpendicular cliffs, from 300 to 400 feet high, presented a barrier effectually forbidding approach by sea. About 1867, however, an excellent harbour was discovered about 260 miles to the west of Fowler's Bay. The South Australian Government at once undertook a survey of this harbour, and Captain Douglas, President of the Marine Board, the officer entrusted with this duty, reported in the most favourable terms. The roadstead, named Port Eucla, was found to afford excellent natural protection for shipping. There was, however, the less encouraging circumstance that it was situated a few miles to the west of the boundary of the colony, and consequently Western, and not South, Australia was entitled to the benefit of the discovery.

It was evident that Port Eucla, which Captain
Douglas carefully surveyed by taking soundings
and observing bearings, was the key to the exploration of this vast portion of the continent.
But, notwithstanding the propositions made to
the Government of Western Australia by the York
Agricultural Society for equipping an exploring
party, nothing was done until the beginning of
1870, when the Governor determined on equipping
an overland party intended to make its way, keeping
as far inland as possible, to Eucla, where assistance and supplies would await them. It was
this expedition which I was selected to command. The following copy of official instructions will show the object of the exploration and
the preparations made to insure a fair prospect of
a successful result:—

Colonial Secretary's Office, Perth,
March 29th, 1870.

Sir,—His Excellency the Governor, confiding in your
experience, ability, and discretion, has been pleased to entrust
to your charge and leadership an overland expedition, which
has been organized for the purpose of exploring the country
between the settled portions of this colony and the Port of
Eucla, situated near its east boundary.

Your party will consist of the following six persons, well
armed, and provisioned for two months, namely, yourself as
leader; Mr. Alexander Forrest, your brother, as second in
command; H. McLarty, a police-constable, third in command;
W. H. Osborne, farrier, &c.; and two reliable natives, one of
whom will be your former well-tried companion, Windich.
An agreement to serve under you on the expedition in the

above capacities will be signed by each European named previous to starting.

Ample stores and supply of provisions have been prepared for your use, and a suitable coasting vessel (the schooner "Adur") is engaged, under an experienced commander, to convey them where required, and to be at your disposal in aiding the operations of the expedition.

It is desirable the party should start from Perth as soon as all arrangements have been completed, and take the most convenient route to Esperance Bay, where men and horses can be recruited, further supplies from the coaster laid in, and a fresh start made for Eucla so soon as the first winter rains may lead to a prospect of the country being sufficiently watered.

About 120 miles to the eastward of the station of Messrs. Dempster, at the west end of Esperance Bay, lies Israelite Bay, under some islands, in front of which there is said to be anchorage. That being the nearest known anchorage westward of Eucla, it appears to offer a convenient spot whence fresh supplies might be drawn from your coaster with which to prosecute the remaining 300 miles; but this arrangement as to an intermediate place of call will be liable to modification, after consulting on the spot with the Messrs. Dempster, who are well acquainted with that part of the coast.

Between Israelite Bay and Eucla the route should be as far from the coast as circumstances and the nature of the country will admit.

At Eucla all the remaining provisions and stores that may be required should be landed, and the coaster despatched on her return to Fremantle with a report of your proceedings.

After recruiting at Eucla, five or six days might be employed with advantage in exploring the country to the northward, care being taken to place in security, by burying in casks or otherwise, such provisions, &c., as might not be necessary for the northern excursion.

On returning to Eucla from the north, the expedition is to make a final start overland for Adelaide, by such route as you may deem advisable. The Surveyor-General is of opinion that *viâ* Port Lincoln, and thence to Adelaide by steamer, would be the preferable route; but of this you will be the best judge, after receiving information from the various out-stations you will pass. Before leaving South Australia, you will dispose of your horses and such remaining stores and provisions as may not be further required, retaining all instruments and such pack-saddles and other articles of outfit as you may deem worth preserving for future service.

On arriving at Adelaide you will report yourself to his Excellency the Governor, and avail yourself of the first favourable opportunity of returning to Perth with your party, and with the remains of your outfit, either by any vessel about to proceed direct to the Swan, or by the earliest mail-steamer to King George's Sound. On application to his Excellency, Sir James Fergusson, you will be furnished with such means as may be necessary to defray your expenses from South to Western Australia, as well as during your stay in the former colony.

I am to impress on you the advisability of endeavouring, by every means in your power, to cultivate friendly relations with the aboriginal inhabitants of the country you are about to traverse.

Such are briefly the general instructions by which it is intended you should be governed in conducting the expedition entrusted to your care and guidance ; and I may add that the fullest confidence is placed in your energy, zeal, and discretion, for bringing it to a successful issue. The main objects of the undertaking are alone referred to; and, although a mode of accomplishing them is briefly alluded to, it is by no means intended to fetter your judgment in adopting such measures of minor details as may appear to you necessary for effectually carrying them out.

I have the honour to be, Sir, your obedient servant,
FRED. P. BARLEE.

The "Adur," chartered by the Government, was a vessel of thirty tons, owned by Mr. Gabriel

Adams. It gives me much pleasure to express my thanks to him and to Mr. Waugh, the master, and to the crew of the vessel, for the important services they performed, and the zeal they exhibited in rendering me assistance, not only on board the vessel, but also on shore.

We started from Perth on the afternoon of Wednesday, the 30th of March, 1870. His Excellency the Governor accompanied us for about three miles on the Albany Road. We had fifteen horses, and provisions sufficient for the journey to Esperance Bay, a distance of about 450 miles, where, it was arranged, further supplies would await us. By the 5th of April we had reached Kojonup, travelling in a north-easterly direction, and then rested four days, leaving for Jerramungup on the 9th, and reaching it on the 13th. Our first day's journey brought us to Mr. Graham's homestead, near which we bivouacked; thence our route lay in an easterly direction, at first through good grassy country with jam and white gum trees and shea oaks, by way of Etticup, Martinup (where we bivouacked on the night of the 10th), and Nigalup, beyond which were scrubby sand-plains extending south-wards towards the Stirling range. On the following night we camped near some granite rocks. The next day's journey extended to Koor-arkup, where we again rested. Our rate of travel was from twenty to twenty-five miles a day, and already we began to experience inconvenience from want of water. A little stream, the Pallinup, was salt, and there were salt pools on the route between our last camping-place and Koorarkup, where we were now resting.

Around Jerramungup was rich grassy country, but beyond it we passed over scrubby undulating plains for about sixteen miles, camping, on the night of the 14th, on a small branch of the Fitzgerald River, near some granite rocks called Dwertup. At this spot there was water, but very little feed for the horses. My observations showed that we were in latitude 33° 1' 15" south.

From this point the progress will be best narrated by extracts from my Diary. A reference to the map will show that as yet we had not reached the track of Eyre, who had followed the coast to King George's Sound; but by the 16th of April we had reached his line of route.

April 15th.—Travelled to the north of east, and at seven miles crossed the main branch of the Fitzgerald River; granite rocks in bed, and salt-water pools. After travelling over stony undulating country for twenty-one miles, camped on a small patch of feed, with water in some granite rocks, called Coombedup.

16th.—Continuing easterly over rough stony country, crossing several brooks with salt pools of water in them, we reached the Phillips River, and, after a good deal of searching, found some fresh water in a small brook near the river. The immense pools in the Phillips were as salt as sea water. Distance travelled about twenty-five miles.

17th (*Sunday*).—Did not travel. Went this morning, in company with McLarty, to the summit of a high hill in Eyre's Range, called Annie's Peak, which we reached after one and a half hour's hard climbing. It is the steepest hill I ever attempted to ascend. We had a splendid view of the sea—the first since leaving Perth—and I also obtained a fine round of angles and bearings. On our return, found Billy had shot five ducks, and Tommy soon returned with an emu. In the evening it very suddenly came on to thunder and lighten, and soon rained in torrents, and, as we were rather unprepared, we did not pass a very pleasant night.

18th.—Just as we had collected the horses it commenced to rain in torrents; got under way, however, by 9 o'clock, steering in about an easterly direction over sandy, scrubby country, and at ten miles crossed a brook with salt pools in it, and afterwards reached a large river of salt water, which we followed about two miles, and then camped at a spring called Jerdacut-tup. It rained in torrents the whole day, blowing hard from the southward, so that all were drenched when we halted.

19th.—After travelling about twenty-three miles, in an easterly direction, we reached a salt lake, called Parriup, and camped. Procured water on some granite rocks near camp.

20th.—Travelling nine miles, reached Mr. Campbell Taylor's station on the Oldfield River, and rested for the remainder of the day.

21st.—After starting the party, with instructions to reach and camp on north side of Stokes' Inlet, distant about twenty miles, I went with Mr. Taylor to the mouth of the Oldfield River, in order to take bearings to East Mount Barren, but was disappointed, the weather being very hazy. Accompanied by a native of Mr. Taylor's, followed on the tracks, but, night setting in, we made the best of our way to where I expected to find the party, but could see nothing of them, and were obliged to camp for the night without food, and, what was worse, without a fire, having neither matches nor powder with us. Luckily I had a rug, by which means I fared much better than my companion, who had only a small kangaroo skin. As it blew and rained in torrents most of the night, our position can be better imagined than described.

22nd.—Early this morning we were looking for the tracks of the party, but without success; finally we returned eight miles to the Margaret River, and, after a good deal of searching, found the tracks almost obliterated by the rain, and

followed along them. Upon nearing Stokes' Inlet we met Tommy Windich looking for us, he
having seen the tracks and last night's bivouac.
He informed me that they had camped about four
miles westward of the inlet, and we had therefore
passed them in the dark last night. Made all
haste to overtake the party; succeeded in doing
so, after a great deal of trouble, one hour and a
half after dark. Encamped on north side of
Barker's Inlet, at a small well of water called
Booeynup. We did justice to the supper, as we
had not had anything to eat for thirty-two hours.

23rd.—For the first nine miles over scrubby
sand-plains, kangaroos very numerous, when we
came into and skirted a chain of salt lakes and
marshes. Continuing over generally low country,
well grassed, for five miles, we reached and camped
at the old homestead of the Messrs. Dempster,
called Mainbenup.

24th (Sunday).—Left camp in company with
Billy Noongale, and proceeded to Esperance Bay,
distant twenty-four miles. On getting in view
of the Bay, was much disappointed to see no
schooner lying at anchor, and felt very anxious
for her safety. Was very kindly received by
Mrs. Andrew Dempster; the Messrs. Dempster
being away on Mondrain Island.

25th.—Went several times up on the hill, looking out for the " Adur," but was each time disappointed. On my return in the evening, found

the party had arrived from Mainbenup, and had camped.

26th.—Rained very heavily all last night. Shifted camp over one mile west of homestead to a sheltered spot, where there was feed and wood. No signs of the " Adur."

27th and 28th.—Rested at camp; the weather very stormy. The Messrs. Dempster returned from Mondrain Island this evening.

29th.—Shifted camp back to the homestead, and camped in a sheltered nook near the Head. On ascending the Look-out Hill this evening, was rejoiced to espy the "Adur" near Cape Le Grand, making in for the Bay, and at 8 o'clock went off in Messrs. Dempster's boat, and had the great pleasure of finding all hands well. They had experienced heavy weather, but everything was dry and safe, I cannot find words to express the joy and relief from anxiety this evening; all fears and doubts were at an end, and I was now in a position to attempt to carry out my instructions.

The Messrs. Dempster, whose hospitality was so welcome, are good specimens of the enterprising settlers who are continually advancing the frontiers of civilization, pushing forward into almost unknown regions, and establishing homesteads which hereafter may develope into important towns. In ten days we had journeyed

160 miles, and had enjoyed a foretaste of the nature of the country through which we should have to make our way. Four days' rest recruited our energies, and the arrival of the " Adur," with stores, gave all the party excellent spirits.

The last day of April was occupied with landing the stores required for immediate use, and the following day, being Sunday, we rested, and, observing the practice adopted in my previous expeditions, I read Divine Service to a somewhat larger congregation than I generally had around me.

The horses had suffered from sore backs, the result of saddles being stuffed with straw; and on the two following days we were all busy restuffing them with wool, and I set Osborn, the farrier, to work to widen and alter the iron-work, so as to make the saddles more comfortable and easy to the horses. From the 3rd to the 8th of May we remained at Mr. Dempster's, and I made a survey of his location, a tract of forty acres. On Saturday, the 7th, Mr. William Dempster left for Perth, and I had the opportunity of sending a report of our proceedings to that date to the Colonial Secretary, and also of forwarding private letters.

Sunday, the 8th, being our last day in Esperance Bay, was passed quietly, all attending Divine Service at Mr. Dempster's house; and on the following morning we prepared to start on the second stage of our journey. The "Adur" was to meet us again at Israelite Bay, about 120 miles to the eastward; and here I resume the extracts from my Diary:—

May 9th.—After collecting the horses, we saddled up and started *en route* for Israelite Bay, where I had instructed the master of the "Adur" to meet us. Bidding good-bye to our kind friends at Esperance Bay, travelled along the north shore for about eleven miles, when we left the coast and steered towards Mount Merivale, and camped at a spring on S.E. corner of a salt sake, Mount Merivale bearing N. 60° E. mag.; Frenchman's Peak N. 150° E. mag., and Remarkable Island N. 196° E. mag. The country for the last few miles is beautifully grassed, with numerous brackish streams running through. Commenced keeping watch this evening, two hours each, from 8 p.m. to 6 o'clock a.m. Marked a tree with the letter F. at our bivouac.

10th.—Travelled nearly due E. for twenty-four miles, through scrubby, sandy country without timber. Remarkable bare granite hills studded in every direction. Camped at a spring on S.E. side of granite hills, resembling a saddle. Passed Mount Hawes, leaving it a little to the north. From hill near camp, Mount Hawes bore N. 295° E. mag., Mount Merivale N. 278° E. mag.,

Frenchman's Peak N. 243° 30' E. mag., and the east side of Mondrain Island N. 207° 30' E. mag.

11*th*.—The horses having strayed back on the tracks last night, we were delayed till 10 o'clock, when only eight of them were brought in. Sent Tommy in search of the remainder, and, after waiting until 3 o'clock for his return, my brother, Osborn, and Billy, went with seven horses and loads; instructed to camp at the first place where there was feed and water, there being no feed at this camp. McLarty and myself waited until Tommy returned, which he did at sundown, having had to go back twenty-four miles to the bivouac of the 9th. There being scarcely any feed here, and it being too late to follow after the party, we tied up our horses for the night. Found it rather long hours watching, viz., about four hours each. By meridian altitude of sun, camp is in latitude 33° 90' 49" S.

12*th*.—Packed up and followed on the tracks of the party, and at ten miles found them camped on a branch of a creek which runs into Duke of Orleans Bay. Brackish streams plentiful: scrubby, sandy country. By meridian altitudes of sun and Arcturus, camp is in S. lat. 33° 51' 35".

13*th*.—Travelled in an easterly direction towards Cape Arid, passing at five miles a large creek, and at ten miles camped on a running brackish stream, which I named the Alexander.

Scrubby open country most of the way. Shot a few ducks from thousands that are in these rivers.

14th.—Continuing a little to the south of E. for ten miles, crossed a large brook, and at fourteen miles reached another creek. Followed it up a mile and camped on east side of a large salt lagoon, into which the brook empties. Splendid green feed around camp, but no water. Went with Billy to look for some, and, after going a mile and a half E., struck the Thomas River, where we met two natives, quietly disposed, who showed us the water, and, after filling our canteens, returned with us to camp.

15th (Sunday).—Shifted camp over to the Thomas River, one mile and a half, where there was plenty of water. Rained a little during the day. Grassy piece of country round camp—the first good feeding land seen since leaving Mount Merivale. About half a mile west of camp, Mount Ragged bore N. 43° 30′ E. mag., Mount Baring N. 53° 15′ E. mag., and S.W. point of Cape Arid N. 140° 30′ E. By meridian altitude of sun, camp was in south latitude 33° 50′ 7″, and longitude about 123° E. Billy shot five ducks this afternoon.

16th.—Got an early start and steered nearly E., accompanied by the two natives, over scrubby sand-plains for about twenty-one miles. We camped near the sea, a few miles to the westward of Cape Pasley. Filled our canteens about two miles back from where we camped, from which point Mount Ragged bore N. 11° E. mag., Cape Pasley N. 110° 30′ E. mag., and S.E. point of Cape Arid N. 214° E. mag.

17th.—Steering in an E.N.E. direction for about nineteen miles, we camped near Point Malcolm, Mount Ragged bearing N. 327° E. mag., and Point Dempster (Israelite Bay) N. 35° 15′ E. mag. Hope to reach Israelite Bay to-morrow, as it is only sixteen miles distant. There was no water at Point Malcolm, but luckily we had filled our canteens. The wind was strong from the westward, accompanied with light showers all day. Tommy shot a kangaroo this evening, and the two natives who were travelling with us from the Thomas River did ample justice to the supper, literally eating the whole night.

18th.—After starting the party, went in advance with Billy to prepare camp at Israelite Bay. When we reached it were delighted to find the "Adur" lying safely at anchor there; proceeding on board, found all well. Procured abundance of water by digging one foot deep in the sand-hills, and good feed a short distance from camp.

Our friends on the "Adur" were looking anxiously for us. We were two days behind the appointed time, and they feared some evil

had befallen us, not taking into consideration
the many delays incidental to such a journey
through strange and difficult country as we had
made. We had occupied ten days in reaching
Israelite Bay since leaving Mr. Dempster's
station, going an average of about twelve miles
a day, which would be a slow rate of progress
in a settled country, but which had sufficiently
tried our horses, they being now in a very reduced
condition from scarcity of feed. I resolved
to stay at the camp for eight or ten days to
recruit the horses, as there was good feed in
the vicinity; and we re-stuffed and re-fitted the
saddles and had the horses shod. I made a correct chart of the route from Esperance Bay,
and found that the coast-line, as laid down in
the Admiralty charts, was in many places in-
correct.

On the 24th of May we determined to celebrate the Queen's birthday. All hands from the
" Adur " came ashore, and I drew them up in
line under the Union Jack, which was duly
hoisted near the camp. We presented arms;
sang " God Save the Queen" vigorously, and
fired a salute of twenty-one guns, finishing with
three cheers. I venture to record that our vocal
efforts were as sincerely and heartily made in
the Australian wilderness as any which rang that
day in any part of her Majesty's wide dominions.
We were all highly delighted—not only feeling

that we had done our duty as loyal subjects, but other celebrations in more civilized places were forcibly recalled to memory.

I had fixed the 30th as the time for our fresh start, and we had enough to do in packing bags, and making general repairs and improvements in our outfit. Eucla Bay, the only other point at which we should be able to communicate with the coaster, was 350 miles to the east of Israelite Bay. The nature of the country was quite unknown, except so far as indicated by the not very encouraging record of Eyre's journey. We felt that we should inevitably have to encounter considerable difficulties, and perhaps even fail to reach Eucla. I deemed it right to give explicit directions to Mr. Waugh, the master of the schooner, so that, in the event of not meeting with us at the appointed place, he should have no difficulty as to the course to pursue, and to that end I gave him in writing the following instructions :—

Israelite Bay, 28th May, 1870.

Sir,—It being my intention to start for Eucla on Monday, the 30th instant, I have the honour to direct you will be good enough to make arrangements for leaving this place on the 7th of June, wind and weather permitting, and sail as direct as possible for Port Eucla, situated in south latitude 31° 43′, and east longitude 128° 52′ E.

You will remain at anchor in Port Eucla until the 1st September, long before which time I hope to reach and meet you there. No signs of myself or party appearing by that date, you will bury in casks under the Black Beacon, 400 lbs.

flour, 200 lbs. pork, 100 lbs. sugar, 10 lbs. tea, and four bags barley, together with the remainder of our clothing on board. You will be careful to hide the spot of concealment as much as possible, or by any other means that may suggest themselves. Also you will bury a bottle containing report of your proceedings.

All these matters had better be attended to a day or two before, and on the 2nd of September you will set sail and return with all despatch to this place (Israelite Bay), where, if I have been obliged to return, I will leave buried a bottle at this spot (arranged by us yesterday), which will contain instructions as to your future proceedings.

No signs of our return being found here, you will sail for Fremantle, calling at Esperance Bay on your way.

On arriving in Fremantle, you will immediately report your return to the Hon. the Colonial Secretary, and forward him a report of your proceedings, after which your charter-party will have been completed.

These arrangements are chiefly respecting your proceedings in the event of our not reaching Eucla; and I may add that, although I have every hope of reaching there in safety, still it is impossible to command success in any enterprise, and I have to impress upon you the necessity of these instructions being carried out, as nearly as possible, to the very letter. Wishing yourself and crew a prosperous voyage, and hoping soon to meet you in Port Eucla,   I have, &c.,

                              JOHN FORREST,
Mr. R. B. Waugh,   Leader of Expedition.
  Master of Schooner " Adur."

On Sunday, the 29th of May, all hands came ashore to dinner. It was certainly a festive party under rather extraordinary circumstances, but it was heartily enjoyed. So far as we were concerned the future was more than usually uncertain; but there was no feeling of despondency, and we

separated in the evening with mutual good wishes
and hopes for the success of the expedition. I
read Divine Service, and, situated as we were, a
small party remote from civilization, I think we all
felt more impressed than under ordinary circumstances would have been the case. We had
rested for eleven days. Good food had restored
the condition of the horses, and we rested in our
camp in good spirits, ready for the work we
were to begin on the following morning. My
observations showed that we were in latitude
33° 36′ 58″ S. and longitude about 123° 48′ E., the
variation of compass from a number of azimuths
being about 0° 46′ westerly.

The narrative is now continued in extracts
from my Diary :—

May 30*th.*—After bidding good-bye to the crew
of the " Adur," and to the two natives we have
had with us from the Thomas River, who were
now at the end of their country and were afraid
to come any further with us, we left Israelite Bay
en route for Eucla, and steered in a northerly
direction for about fifteen miles over salt marshes
and clay-pans, with dense thickets intervening,
destitute of grass. I was obliged to make for
the coast, and, following it for about eight miles,
we camped close to it, without water or feed, and
tied up our horses in latitude 33° 17′ 17″ by
meridian altitude of Arcturus and α Bootes.

31*st*.—Saddled up at dawn and continued along
the beach for four miles; came to a large sand-
patch, and found abundance of water by digging
one foot deep in the hollows. Camped on east
side of the sand-hills, with first-rate feed for the
horses. By meridian altitude of sun, camp is in
latitude 33° 13′ 46″ S.

June 1*st*.—After starting the party, went with
Tommy Windich to examine the country to the
N.W., and then, travelling nine miles over salt
marshes and samphire flats, with dense scrub intervening, we reached what is named on the
Admiralty Charts "The Front Bank," which, ascending, we found very steep and rough. At last,
gaining the summit, the country receded to the
north, level and thickly wooded, as far as the eye
could reach. We travelled about four miles to the
N.W., from where we ascended the range, and
then climbed a tree to have a view of the country,
which I found very level and thickly wooded with
mallee. I therefore determined to turn east, and,
if possible, reach the party to-night. Accordingly,
we reached the sea, and, following the tracks of
the party, came up with them at about 10 p.m.,
encamped on N.E. side of an immense sand-patch,
about twenty-five miles from our last night's
bivouac. There was abundance of water on the
surface in the hollows of the sand-hills.

2*nd*.—There being no feed near camp, saddled
up and continued towards Point Culver for four

miles and camped, with only some coarse grass growing on the white sand-hills for our very hungry horses. Found plenty of water by digging. This is a poor place for the horses : intend making a flying trip to the N.E. to-morrow. By meridian altitude of sun and Arcturus, camp is in latitude 32° 55′ 30″ south, and longitude 124° 25′ east.

3rd.—Started with my brother and Billy to examine the country to the N.E., and travelled in about a N.E. direction for twenty-five miles over very level country, but in many places most beautifully grassed. We camped on a splendid flat, without water.

4th.—Started at dawn and travelled in a southerly direction for nine miles, when we found a rock water-hole containing one gallon, and had breakfast. Continuing for four miles, we reached the cliffs, which fell perpendicularly into the sea, and, although grand in the extreme, were terrible to gaze from. After looking very cautiously over the precipice, we all ran back quite terror-stricken by the dreadful view. Turning our course westward along the cliffs, we reached camp at 5 o'clock, and found all well. We saw several natives' tracks during the day.

5th (*Sunday*).—Rested at camp. Read Divine Service. Intend making preparations to-morrow for starting on Tuesday morning, and attempt to reach the water shown on Mr. Eyre's track, in longitude 126° 24′ E., 150 miles distant, by carrying thirty gallons of water with us and walking in turns, so as to have the horses to carry the water. Intend allowing each man one quart and each horse two quarts per day. Feel very anxious as to the result, as it will take five or six days; but it is the only resource left. After explaining my views to my companions, and pointing out the great probability of our meeting with small rock water-holes, was much relieved by the sanguine way in which they acquiesced in the plans, and the apparent confidence they placed in me.

6th.—Filled the water-cans, and got everything ready for a start to-morrow morning.

7th.—Started at 9 a.m., carrying over thirty gallons of water with us. One of the drums leaked so much that we left it at camp. Travelled along our outward tracks of the 4th, and camped at our former bivouac, with splendid feed, but no water for our horses.

8th.—Started early, and steered about N.E. through dense mallee thickets, destitute of grass or water, for eighteen miles. We came upon a small patch of open grassy land, and camped without water for our horses. This is the second night our horses have been without water, but the grass has been fresh, and they do not yet appear to have suffered much. Marked a tree at camp, " F., 1870." My brother, I am sorry to say, left his revolver at our last night's bivouac, and did not notice it until this evening, when it was too far to send back to look for it. By meridian altitude of Arcturus, camp is in latitude 32° 34' 20" south, and longitude 124° 59' east.

9th.—Made an early start, steering N.E., and at one mile found a rock water-hole containing fifteen gallons, which we gave the tired, thirsty horses, and, continuing, chiefly through dense mallee thickets, with a few grassy flats intervening, for twenty-two miles, found another rock water-hole holding about ten gallons, which we also gave the horses, and, after travelling one mile from it, camped on a large grassy flat, without water for the horses. Our horses are still very thirsty, and have yet seventy miles to go before reaching the water in longitude 126° 24' E. Am very thankful for finding the little water to-day, for if we had none, our situation would be somewhat perilous, and some of the horses would probably show signs of distress to-morrow. Latitude of camp, 32° 20' 35" S. by Arcturus, and longitude 125° 16' E.

10th.—Steering E.N.E. over generally open country, grassy flats, &c., thinly wooded, for twenty-one miles, found a small rock water-hole containing three gallons, which we put into our canteens. After travelling three miles further, camped on the edge of a grassy flat, and gave our horses half a gallon each from our canteens. Our horses appear fearfully distressed this evening. For the last ninety-six hours they have only had two gallons each. Latitude of camp 32° 11′ 5″ S., longitude 125° 37′ E.

11*th*.—Found, on collecting the horses, that four were missing. Those found were in a sad state for want of water, and there was not a moment to lose. I therefore at once told Tommy to look for those missing, and, after saddling up, sent the party on with my brother, with instructions to steer easterly for nearly fifty miles, when they would reach the water in longitude 126° 24′ E. I remained behind to await Tommy's return, and, after an hour's awful anxiety, was rejoiced to see him returning with the ramblers. We lost no time in following after the party, and at two miles came to a water-hole they had emptied and given to the horses (fifteen gallons), and at five miles overtook them. After travelling ten miles, found another water-hole with fifteen gallons, which we also gave our horses, they being still very thirsty. At fourteen miles found a water-hole holding three gallons, which we transferred to our canteens; and at fifteen miles camped on a small but very grassy flat, close to which we found a water-hole of ten gallons, which I intend giving the horses to-morrow morning. Although the horses are still very thirsty, they are much relieved, and are willing to feed. We all felt tired from long, weary, and continued walking. By meridian altitude of Arcturus, camp is in latitude 32° 13′ S., and longitude 125° 51′ E.

12*th* (*Sunday*).—After giving the horses the little water found by Tommy last evening, we struck a little to the south of east over generally grassy country, slightly undulating for three miles, when, being in advance, walking, I found a large water-hole with about 100 gallons of water in it. It being Sunday, and men and horses very tired, I halted for the day, as there was most luxuriant feed round camp. Our horses soon finished the water, and looked much better after it. Although now without water, we are in comparative safety, as the horses have had nearly sufficient. We are now only thirty-two miles from the water shown on Mr. Eyre's chart, in longitude 126° 24′ E. Latitude of camp 32° 13′ 35″ S., and longitude 125° 54′ E.

13*th*.—Made an early start, and steering a little to the south of east, keeping straight for the water in longitude 126° 24′ E. At eighteen miles got a view of the sea, and beheld the sand-hills about fifteen miles ahead. Here we saw some natives' fires close to us. Approaching them, we came upon an old woman, and my brother and Tommy soon brought a man to bay. There were about twenty round us; they appeared very frightened. After detaining them half an hour, and treating them as kindly as possible, we bade them farewell and continued our journey. The natives were entirely naked. After we left the natives, we came to where the cliffs leave the sea, in longitude

126° 12′ E. From here Point Dover was clearly visible, and I cannot express my feelings when gazing on the scene. To the westward, those grand precipitous cliffs, from 200 to 300 feet high, and Point Dover, near which Mr. Eyre's overseer was murdered, could easily be discerned; and while thinking over his hardships and miseries, we turned our faces eastward, and there saw, within a few miles, the water we so much needed. We then descended the cliffs and reached the sea shore, which we followed for about twelve miles, reaching the first sand-patch at about 10 o'clock p.m. There was good feed all around, but we could not, from the darkness, find any water. Gave our horses all we had with us, about fifteen gallons.

14th.—This morning searched the sand-patches for water, without success; I therefore packed up and proceeded towards another large patch, four miles distant, going in advance with Billy. After we left, Tommy found a place used by the natives, where water could be procured by digging. He, however, followed after Billy and myself. On reaching the sand-patch we saw the place where water could be procured by digging; we also found sufficient to satisfy our horses on some sandstone flats. We were soon joined by the party, who were overjoyed to be in perfect safety once more, and we were all thankful to that Providence which had guarded us over 150 miles without finding permanent water. We soon pitched camp, and took

the horses to the feed, which was excellent. Returning, we were surprised to see a vessel making
in for the land, and soon made her out to be the
"Adur." Although the wind was favourable for
Eucla, she made in for the land until within about
three miles, when she turned eastward, and, although
we made fires, was soon out of sight. I afterwards
ascertained that they were not sure of their longitude, having no chronometer on board, and therefore wished to see some landmark.

15*th.*—Dug two wells to-day, and found good
water at seven feet from the surface. Lined them
with stakes and bushes to keep them from filling
in. In the afternoon we all amused ourselves
shooting wattle-birds, and managed to kill fifteen.

16*th.*—Dug another well and bushed it up,
the supply from the two dug yesterday being
insufficient, and obtained an ample quantity of
splendid fresh water. By a number of observations, camp is in latitude 32° 14′ 50″ S., and longitude 126° 24′ E., the variation of compass being
about 1° 6′ easterly. The horses are improving
very quickly, there being splendid feed round the
sand-patches.

17*th.*—Went with Tommy Windich for a walk
eastward along the beach, and returned a little
inland. Passed over some patches of beautiful
grassed country. Saw a pine pole standing on one
of the hummocks near the beach, probably erected
by Mr. Eyre, as I am not aware of any one else

having been here. We could not find any of his camps, however; doubtless the sand has long since covered them.

18th.—Making preparations for a flying trip inland on Monday.

19th (*Sunday*).—Read Divine Service. Every appearance of rain.

20th.—Started this morning, in company with McLarty and Tommy Windich, to explore the country to the northward. The first twelve miles north was through very dense thickets and sandy hills, when we reached the cliffs, which we ascended with difficulty, and steering about N.N.E. for the first three miles, through dense mallee thickets, we emerged into a generally grassy country, and travelled over beautifully-grassed downs. We camped at a rock water-hole of fifteen gallons, about twenty-five miles from main camp.

21st.—Steering about north for one mile, we found a rock water-hole holding about thirty gallons; and continuing for thirteen miles over grassy plains, thinly wooded, the country became very clear and open, and at twenty-five miles there was nothing but plains, gently undulating, of grass and salt-bush in view. Far as the eye could reach to the N.W., N., and N.E., this clear and grassy country extended; and being now fifty miles from camp, with the prospect of finding water diminishing as we travelled northward, I determined to return. Accordingly struck S.W., and after travelling twelve miles found a small water-hole of three gallons, and camped for the night. Set watch as follows : myself 7 to 11, McLarty 11 to 3.30 a.m., and Tommy from 3.30 to 6 a.m. We found them rather long hours.

22*nd*.—Saddled up at dawn, and steering southerly over clear, open, grassy plains for twenty-eight miles, we reached the cliffs, and rested an hour ; after which we continued our journey and reached camp a little after dark, finding all well.

23*rd*. — Made preparations for a start for Eucla to-morrow, and put everything in travelling order. During my absence, Osborn had got the horses' feet in order, and the pack-saddles had been overhauled, and repairs generally made. In looking round the camp, Tommy Windich found shoulder-blade of a horse, and two small pieces of leather. They no doubt belonged to Mr. Eyre's equipment, and, on reference to his journal, I find he was here obliged to kill a horse for food. In his journal he writes thus : " Early on the morning of the 16th April, 1841, I sent the overseer to kill the unfortunate horse, which was still alive but unable to rise from the ground, having never moved from the place where he had first been found lying yesterday morning. The miserable animal was in the most wretched state possible, thin and emaciated by long and continued suffering, and labouring under some complaint that in a very few hours, at the farthest, must have ter-

minated its life." I cut off part of the shoulder-
blade, and have since given it, together with
the pieces of leather, to his Excellency Governor
Weld.

24th.—Started at 8.30 a.m. *en route* for Eucla.
Steering in a N.N.E. direction for fifteen miles,
reached the cliffs, and after following along them
two miles, found a large rock water-hole, but in an
almost inaccessible spot. While I was examining
the cliffs near, to find a place where we could get
the horses up, Tommy heard a coo-ey, and after
answering it a good many times, we were surprised to see two natives walking up towards us,
unarmed. I approached and met them; they did
not appear at all frightened, and at once began to
eat the damper I gave them. We could not understand anything they said. I beckoned them
to come along with us, which they at once did,
and followed so closely after me as to tramp on
my spurs. They pointed to water further ahead.
After walking about a mile, four more natives
were seen running after us, who, on joining,
made a great noise, singing, and appearing very
pleased. Shortly afterwards two more followed,
making seven in all; all entirely naked, and
every one circumcised. We found the water
alluded to on the top of the cliffs, but, it being
too late to get the horses up, we turned off to the
southward half a mile, and camped on a small
grassy flat, without water for the horses. The

seven natives slept at our fire. We gave them as much damper as they could eat. They had not the least particle of clothing, and made pillows of each other's bodies, and resembled pigs more than human beings.

25th.—The horses began to stray towards morning, and at 3 a.m. I roused Billy and brought them back. After saddling up, went to the cliffs, and with two hours' hard work in making a path and leading up the horses (two of which fell backwards), we managed to gain the summit. The seven natives accompanied us, and giving one of them the bag containing my rug to carry over to the water, I was surprised to see him trotting off with it. Calling Tommy, we soon overtook him and made him carry it back to the party. After giving our horses as much as they required from the fine water-holes, I motioned five of the natives to leave us and two to accompany us, which they soon understood, and appeared satisfied. Travelling in an E.N.E. direction for twenty-one miles, over rich grassy table-land plains, thinly wooded, we camped on a very grassy spot, without water for our horses. By meridian altitude of Arcturus, camp is in latitude 31° 52′ 30″ south, and longitude 126° 53′ E.

26th (Sunday).—Finding the two natives entirely useless, as we could not understand them, and had to give them part of the little water we carried with us, motioned them to return, which they appeared very pleased to do. Steering in an easterly direction for two miles, over downs of most luxuriant grass, we found a large rock water-hole holding over 100 gallons. It was Sunday, and all being tired, we camped for the day. In every direction, open gently undulating country, most beautifully grassed, extended. By meridian altitude of sun, camp is in latitude 31° 53′ S. Read Divine Service. Tommy and Billy went for a stroll, and returned bringing with them two small kangaroos, (the first we have shot since leaving Israelite Bay,) which proved a great treat. The natives also found a fine water-hole about a mile from camp. Gave the horses all the water at this place. Every appearance of rain.

27th.—Made rather a late start, owing to some of the horses straying. Steered in an E.N.E. direction, and at ten miles found a small water-hole, and at twenty-one miles another, both of which we gave our horses, and at twenty-four miles camped on a grassy spot, without water for our horses. For the first fifteen miles grassy, gently undulating, splendid feeding country extended in every direction, after which there was a slight falling off, scrubby at intervals. By meridian altitude of Arcturus, camp was in latitude 31° 46′ 43″ S., and longitude 127° 17′ E.

28th.—Had some difficulty in collecting the horses, and made a late start, steering in about an E.N.E. direction for the first five miles, over very grassy flats, &c., when it became more dense and scrubby until twenty miles, after which it improved a little. At twenty-four miles we camped on a grassy rise, without water, in south latitude 31° 41′, and longitude 127° 40′ E. Our horses appeared distressed for want of water, the weather being very warm.

29th.—Had to go back five miles to get the horses this morning. After saddling up, travelled in about an easterly direction for twenty-four miles, and camped on a grassy rise, close to a small rock water-hole. During the day, found in small rock-holes sufficient to give each horse about three gallons. The country was generally very grassy, although in some places rather thickly wooded. McLarty was very foot-sore from heavy and long walking. By meridian altitude of Arcturus, camp is in latitude 31° 45′ S., and longitude 128° 2′ E.

30th.—Hearing the horses make off, I roused Billy and brought them back; they had gone two miles. Packed up, and steering in an east direction over generally very grassy country with occasional mallee thickets, for about twenty-two miles, we came to a splendidly-grassed rise, and found a fine rock water-hole on it, containing about 100 gallons, which our horses soon finished being fearfully in want, the day being very warm. We are now only thirty miles from Eucla. For the last two days McLarty has been so lame that I have not allowed him to walk—his boots hurting his feet.

July 1*st*.—Made an early start, every one being in high spirits, as I told them they should see the sea and Eucla to-day. Travelling about east over most beautifully-grassed country, at five miles found a large water-hole, holding 100 gallons; but our horses, not being thirsty, did not drink much. This is the first rock water-hole we have passed without finishing since we left Point Culver. After ten miles reached the cliffs, or Hampton Range, and had a splendid view of the Roe Plains, Wilson's Bluff looming in the distance, bearing N. 77° 30′ E. mag.

Descending the cliffs with difficulty, we followed along the foot of them, which was beautifully grassed, and, after travelling twelve miles, beheld the Eucla sand-hills. On my pointing them out, every heart was full of joy, and, being away some distance, I heard the long and continued hurrahs from the party! Eucla was all the conversation! I never before remember witnessing such joy as was evinced on this occasion by all the party. After travelling five miles further we camped close to the cliffs, at a small water-hole, Wilson's Bluff bearing N. 85° E. mag., and the Delissier sand-hills N. 90° E. mag. We might have reached Eucla this evening, but I preferred doing so to-morrow, when we could have the day before us to choose camp. We are now again in safety, Eucla being only seven miles distant, after having travelled 166 miles without finding permanent water,—in fact, over 300 miles with only one place where we procured permanent water, viz., in longitude 126° 24′ E. I trust we all recognized with sincerity and thankfulness the guiding and protecting Father who had brought us through in safety. By observation, the camp was in latitude 31° 42′ S.

2nd.—Made an early start and steered straight for the anchorage, distant about five miles, having first ascended the range to have a view of the country, which was very extensive. Far as the eye could reach to the westward the Roe Plains and Hampton Range were visible; while to the eastward lay Wilson's Bluff and the Delissier sandhills; and three miles west of them we were delighted to behold the good schooner "Adur," riding safely at anchor in Eucla harbour, which formed by no means the least pleasing feature of the scene to our little band of weary travellers. Made at once for the vessel, and, on reaching her, found all well and glad to see us. She was anchored between the Red and Black Beacons. The latter had been blown down, but shall be re-erected. There being no water at the anchorage, moved on to the Delissier sandhills, where we found water by digging two and a half feet from the surface. Camped on west side of the sand-hills. Landed barley, &c.,

from the boat. There was good feed for the
horses under the Hampton Range, about a mile
and a half distant.

The next day was Sunday. The crew of the
" Adur " came ashore and dined with us, and, as
usual, I read Divine Service. On the following
morning I went aboard the schooner and examined
the log-book and charts. We painted the Red
and Black Beacons, and Mr. Adams having trimmed
up a spar, we erected a flagstaff thirty-four feet
high. I occupied myself the next day with preparing a report to be sent to the Colonial Secretary. My brother went off to the boat and brought
ashore the things we required. We were busy on
the following days packing up and shipping things
not required for the trip to Adelaide, and I gave
the master of the " Adur " instructions to sail
with all despatch for Fremantle.

The following report, which I sent back by the
" Adur," describes the progress then made with
somewhat more detail than in my Journal :—

Port Eucla, 7th July, 1870.

SIR,—It is with much pleasure I have the honour to report,
for the information of his Excellency the Governor, the safe
arrival here of the expedition entrusted to my guidance, as also
the meeting of the schooner " Adur."

Leaving Esperance Bay on the 9th of May, we travelled in
au easterly direction, over plains generally poorly grassed, to
Israelite Bay (situated in latitude 33° 36′ 51″ S., and longitude
123° 48′ E.), which we reached on the 18th May, and met the

" Adur," according to instructions issued to the master. Here we recruited our horses and had them re-shod, put the pack-saddles in good order, packed provisions, &c., and gave the master of the " Adur" very strict and detailed instructions to proceed to Eucla Harbour, and await my arrival until the 2nd of September, when, if I did not reach there, he was to bury provisions under the Black Beacon and sail for Fremantle, *vià* Israelite and Esperance Bays. Everything being in readiness, on the 30th of May we left Israelite Bay *en route* for Eucla, carrying with us three months' provisions. Keeping near the coast for sixty miles, having taken a flying trip inland on my way, we reached the sand-patches a little to the west of Point Culver, in latitude 32° 55' 34" S., and longitude 124° 25' E., on the 2nd of June.

On the 3rd went on a flying trip to the N.E., returning on the 4th along the cliffs and Point Culver. I found the country entirely destitute of permanent water, but, after leaving the coast a few miles, to be, in places, beautifully grassed. On the coast near the cliffs it was very rocky, and there was neither feed nor water. Finding there was no chance of permanent water being found, that the only water in the country was in small rocky holes—and those very scarce indeed—and the feed being very bad at Point Culver, I determined, after very mature consideration, to attempt at all hazards to reach the water shown on Mr. Eyre's track in longitude 126° 24' E., or 140 miles distant.

In accordance with these arrangements, on the 7th day of June started on our journey, carrying over thirty gallons of water on three of our riding horses, and taking it in turns walking. Travelled about N.E. for four days, which brought us to latitude 32° 11' S., and longitude 125° 37' E., finding, during that time, in rocky holes, sufficient water to give each horse two gallons. On the fifth day we were more fortunate, and were able to give them each two gallons more, and on the sixth day (the 12th June, Sunday) found a large rock hole containing sufficient to give them five gallons each, which placed us in safety, as the water in longitude 126° 24' E. was only thirty-two miles distant. Continuing, we reached the water on Tuesday, June 14th, and by observation found it to be in latitude 32° 14′ 50″ S., and longitude 126° 24′ E., the variation of the compass being about 1° 6′ easterly.

The country passed over between Point Culver and longitude 126° 24′ E., was in many places beautifully grassed, level, without the slightest undulation, about 300 feet above the sea, and not very thickly wood. It improves to the northward, being clearer and more grassy, and the horizon to the north, in every place where I could get an extensive view, was as uniform and well-defined as that of the sea. On the route from Point Culver to longitude 126° 24′ E., we were from twenty to twenty-five miles from the sea.

Recruiting ourselves and horses till the 30th, I took a flying trip to the northward. For the first twelve miles from the sea was through a dense and almost impenetrable scrub, when we reached the cliffs, and after ascending them we came into the same description of level country that we travelled over from Point Culver, save that this was more open and grassy, and became still clearer as we proceeded north, until, at our farthest point north, in latitude 31° 33′ S., and longitude 126° 33′ E., scarcely a tree was visible, and vast plains of grass and saltbush extended as far as the eye could reach in every direction. We found a little water for our horses in rock holes. Returning, we reached camp on June 22nd. On the 23rd we were engaged making preparations for a start for Eucla. In looking round camp, Tommy Windich found the shoulder-blade of a horse and two small pieces of leather belonging to a packsaddle. The shoulder-blade is no doubt the remains of the horse Mr. Eyre was obliged to kill for food at this spot.

On June 24th started for Eucla, carrying, as before, over thirty gallons of water, and walking in turns. On the 25th found on the top of the cliffs a large rock hole, containing sufficient water to give the horses as much as they required, and on the 26th were equally fortunate. From the 26th to the 30th we met with scarcely any water, and our horses appeared very distressed, more so as the weather was very warm. On the evening of the 30th, however, we were again fortunate enough to find a water-hole containing sufficient to give them six gallons each, and were again in safety, Eucla water being only thirty miles distant. On the morning of the 1st day of July we reached the cliffs, or Hampton Range (these cliffs recede from the sea in longitude 126° 12' E., and run along at the average distance of twelve or fifteen miles from the sea until they join it again at Wilson's Bluff, in longitude 129° E. They are very steep and rough, and water may generally be found in rock holes in the gorges. I, however, wished to keep further inland, and therefore did not follow them), and shortly afterwards we beheld the Wilson's Bluff and the Eucla sandhills. Camped for the night near the Hampton Range, about five miles from Eucla Harbour, and on the 2nd July, on nearing the anchorage, discovered the schooner "Adur" lying safely at anchor, which proved by no means the least pleasing feature to our little band of weary travellers. Camped on west side of Delisser sand-hills, and found water by digging.

The country passed over between longitude 126° 24' E., as a grazing country, far surpasses anything I have ever seen. There is nothing in the settled portions of Western Australia equal to it, either in extent or quality ; but the absence of permanent water is the great drawback, and I do not think water would be procured by sinking, except at great depths, as the country is at least three hundred feet above the sea, and there is nothing to indicate water being within an easy depth from the surface. The country is very level, with scarcely any undulation, and becomes clearer as you proceed northward.

Since leaving Cape Arid I have not seen a gully or watercourse of any description—a distance of 400 miles.

The route from longitude 126° 24' E. to Eucla was generally about thirty miles from the sea.

The natives met with appeared friendly and harmless ; they are entirely destitute of clothing, and I think not very numerous.

Very little game exists along the route ; a few kangaroos were seen, but no emus—an almost certain sign, I believe, of the scarcity of water.

The health of the party has been excellent; and I cannot speak too highly of the manner in which each member of the expedition has conducted himself, under circumstances often of privation and difficulty.

All our horses are also in splendid condition; and when I reflect how great were the sufferings of the only other Europeans who traversed this route, I cannot but thank Almighty God who has guarded and guided us in safety through such a waterless region, without the loss of even a single horse.

I am afraid I shall not be able to get far inland northward, unless we are favoured with rain. We have not had any rain since the end of April, and on that account our difficulties have been far greater than if it had been an ordinary wet season.

I intend despatching the " Adur " for Fremantle to-morrow. The charter-party has been carried out entirely to my satisfaction. With the assistance of the crew of the " Adur " I have re-painted the Red and Black Beacons. The latter had been blown down; we, however, re-erected it firmly again. I have also erected a flagstaff, thirty feet high, near camp on west side of Delisser sand-hills, with a copper-plate nailed on it, with its position, my name, and that of the colony engraved on it.

We are now within 140 miles from the nearest Adelaide station. I will write to you as soon as I reach there. It will probably be a month from this date.

Trusting that the foregoing brief account of my proceedings, as leader of the expedition entrusted to my guidance, may meet with the approval of his Excellency the Governor,

I have, &c.,
JOHN FORREST,
Leader of Expedition to Eucla and Adelaide.

The Hon. the Colonial Secretary,
Perth, W. A.

We had now accomplished rather more than half the distance between Perth and Adelaide, but there was still a gap of 140 miles to be bridged over. We bade good-bye to our friends on board the " Adur," and were now thrown entirely

on our own resources. I resume the extracts
from my Journal :—

July 8th.—Started in company with my brother
and Billy, having three riding horses and a pack
horse, to penetrate the country to the northward. Travelled in a northerly direction for
about twenty-seven miles, over plains generally
well grassed, and then bivouacked. From the
camp only plains were in sight, not a tree visible.
Did not meet with a drop of water on our way,
and, having brought none, we had to do without
it. This season is too dry to attempt to cross
these vast grassy plains, and I shall return to
camp to-morrow—the attempt to get inland without rain only exhausting ourselves and horses to
no purpose.

9th.—After collecting the horses, which had
strayed back on the tracks, we steered in a
S.S.W. direction, and reached camp a little
after sundown. Did not find any water, except
about half a gallon, during the two days, and,
the weather being warm, the horses were in a
very exhausted state when they reached camp.
Found the " Adur" had left yesterday afternoon.

10th (Sunday).—Rested at Eucla. Read Divine
Service.

11th.—Osborn busy with the shoeing. Went
with Billy to Wilson's Bluff, and saw the boun-
dary-post between South and Western Australia,

placed by Lieutenant Douglas. Returned at sundown.

12*th*.—Erected the flagstaff with the Union Jack flying, and nailed a copper plate to the staff, with the following engraved on it:—

"WESTERN AUSTRALIA. ERECTED BY
J. FORREST, JULY 12TH, 1870."

From the flagstaff, Wilson's Bluff bore N. 70° 15′ E. mag., and the Black Beacon N. 246° 20′ E. mag., and it is situated in latitude 31° 41′ 50″ S.

13*th*.—There was a total eclipse of the moon in the morning. All busy preparing for a start for the Head of the Bight to-morrow. Buried a cask eight feet west of flagstaff, containing 100lbs. flour, 130lbs. barley, 16 new sets of horse-shoes, shoeing nails, &c. Nailed a plate on flagstaff, with "DIG 8 FEET WEST" on it. Took a ride to the Black and Red Beacons, to examine country round Eucla.

14*th*.—Bidding farewell to Eucla and the Union Jack, which we left on the flagstaff, we started for the Head of the Bight, carrying over thirty gallons of water with us, and walking in turns. Ascended the cliffs without difficulty, and passed the boundary of the two colonies; then left the sea, and, steering in an E.N.E. and N.E. direction until a little after dark, camped on a grassy piece of country, without water for our horses.

Distance travelled about twenty-six miles. By observation camp is in latitude 31° 30′ 42″ S., and longitude 129° 20′ E.

15*th*.—Started at daylight, and travelled E.N.E. for seven miles, when we bore E. over generally level country, well grassed, but entirely destitute of water. We camped at sundown on a grassy rise, without water for our horses. Distance travelled, thirty-four miles. The horses have not had any water for two days, and show signs of distress. Intend starting before daylight, as there is a good moon.

16*th*.—At 1 a.m. went with Billy to bring back the horses, which had again made off. After returning, saddled up, and at 4.50 a.m. got under way, steering a little to the south of east in order to make the cliffs, as there might be water in rock holes near them. At eighteen miles came to the sea, but could find no water. At thirty miles saw a pile of stones, and at thirty-three miles saw a staked survey line. Camped on a grassy piece of country, two miles from the sea. This is the third day without a drop of water for the horses, which are in a frightful state. Gave them each four quarts from our water-drums, and I hope, by leaving a little after midnight, to reach the Head of the Bight to-morrow evening, as it is now only forty miles distant. By observation, camp is in latitude 31° 32′ 27″ S., and longitude 130° 30′ E.

17*th*.—Was obliged to get up twice to bring

back the horses, and at four o'clock made a start.
The horses were in a very exhausted state; some
having difficulty to keep up. About noon I
could descry the land turning to the southward,
and saw, with great pleasure, we were fast
approaching the Head of the Great Australian
Bight. Reached the sand-patches at the extreme
Head of the Bight just as the sun was setting,
and found abundance of water by digging two
feet deep in the sand. Gave the horses as much
as I considered it safe for them to have at one
time. I have never seen horses in such a state
before, and hope never to do so again. The horses,
which four days ago were strong and in good
condition, now appeared only skeletons, eyes sunk,
nostrils dilated, and thoroughly exhausted. Since
leaving Eucla to getting water at this spot, a
period of nearly ninety hours, they had only
been allowed one gallon of water each, which was
given them from our water-drums. It is wonderful how well they performed this journey;
had they not started in good condition, they
never could have done it. We all felt very tired.
During the last sixty hours I have only had about
five hours' sleep, and have been continually in
a great state of anxiety—besides which, all have
had to walk a great deal.

18th.—This is a great day in my journal and
journey. After collecting the horses we followed
along the beach half a mile, when I struck N. for

ARRIVAL AT THE GREAT AUSTRALIAN BIGHT.—FRESH WATER FOUND.

Peelunabie well, and at half a mile struck a
cart track from Fowler's Bay to Peelunabie.
After following it one mile and a quarter, came
to the well and old sheep-yards, and camped.
Found better water in the sand-hills than in the
well.   There is a board nailed on a pole directing
to the best water, with the following engraved
on it : " G. Mackie, April 5th, 1865, Water 🖙
120 yards." Upon sighting the road this morning, which I had told them we should do, a loud
and continued hurrahing came from all the party,
who were overjoyed to behold signs of civilization again ; while Billy, who was in advance with
me, and whom I had told to look out as he would
see a road directly, which he immediately did,
began giving me great praise for bringing them
safely through such a long journey. I certainly
felt very pleased and relieved from anxiety,
and, on reviewing the long line of march we
had performed through an uncivilized country,
was very sensible of that protecting Providence
which had guided us safely through the undertaking.

19th.—Steered in an easterly direction along an
old track towards Wearing's well, as I intend
going inland, instead of along the coast to Fowler's
Bay.   Travelled for sixteen miles through a barren
and thickly-wooded country, sand-hills, &c.   We
camped on a small grassy flat, without water.
Being now in the settled districts I gave over

keeping watch, which we had regularly done since the 9th of May.

20th.—Continuing for fifteen miles, we reached a deserted well called Wearing's; it was about 200 feet deep, and after joining all the tether-ropes, girths, bridle reins, halters, &c., we managed to get up a bucket full, but after all our trouble it was quite salt. We therefore continued our journey S.E. for Fowler's Bay, and at four miles saw some fresh sheep tracks, and shortly afterwards saw the shepherd, named Jack, who was very talkative. He told us he had been to Swan River, and thought it was quite as good as this place. He also said there was a well of good water about eight miles further on. This was a pleasant surprise, the nearest well on my chart being sixteen miles distant: this was a new well sunk since the survey. We therefore pushed on, although our horses were very tired, and reached the well, where there was a substantial stone hut; met the shepherd, whose name was Robinson. He said he knew who we were, having heard about three months ago that we might be expected this way. He was as kind and obliging as it was possible to be, in his circumstances. Had a difficulty in drawing water for the horses, the well being nearly 200 feet deep, and there was not a bite for the poor creatures to eat, except a few miles off. As it was now an hour after dark, I turned them out, and left them to do the best they could. The old shepherd kept talking most of the night, and said we looked more like people just come from Fowler's Bay than having come overland from Western Australia.

21*st*.—The horses strayed off in many directions during the night, and they were not all collected till after noon, when we continued our journey for four miles, and finding a small piece of feed, we camped without water for the horses. Many of the horses were in a very critical state, and one was completely knocked up.

22*nd*.—Again were delayed by the rambling of the horses until nearly noon, when we travelled along the road towards Fowler's Bay. After ten miles, watered the horses at a well called Waltabby, and two miles further on camped, with scarcely any feed for the horses. One of the horses completely gave in to-day, and we had great difficulty in getting him to camp. By meridian altitude of Arcturus, camp is in latitude 31° 34' 28" S.

23*rd*.—Although the feed was short, our horses did not stray, and after saddling up we continued along road for two and a half miles, and reached Colona, the head station of Degraves and Co., of Victoria, where we were most hospitably received by Mr. Maiden, the manager. At his desire camped, and turned out the horses on a piece of feed kept for his horses, and intend remaining over Sunday. We accepted his kind invitation to make ourselves his guests while we remained. He informed me that the South Australian Government had instructed the mounted trooper at Fowler's Bay to proceed to the Head of the Bight and give us every information and assistance in his power. I am glad we have saved him the journey.

24th.—Rested at Colona. In the afternoon was rather surprised at the arrival of Police-trooper Richards and party, who were on their way to try and find out our whereabouts. He handed me a circular for perusal, stating that anything I required would be paid for by the South Australian Government.

25th.—Left Colona, accompanied by Police-trooper Richards and party. Mr. Maiden also accompanied us a few miles, when he returned, bearing with him my sincere thanks for his kindness to myself and party. After travelling eleven miles, we reached the hospitable residence of Messrs. Heathcote and Mathers, where we stayed to dinner, and, although pressed to stay, pushed on seven miles and camped at a well called Pintumbra.

26th.—Rested at Pintumbra, as there was good feed for our tired and hungry horses. Police-trooper Richards and party also remained with us.

27th.—Travelled towards Fowler's Bay, and at ten miles reached Yallata, the residence of Mr. Armstrong, where we had dinner, and afterwards reached Fowler's Bay and put up at the police-station.

28*th* *to* 31*st.*—Remained at Fowler's Bay, re-cruiting ourselves and horses, and wrote the following letters to the Honourable the Colonial Secretary, Western Australia, and to his Excellency Sir James Fergusson, Governor of South Australia :—

Fowler's Bay, 29th July, 1870.

SIR,—I have the honour to report, for the information of his Excellency the Governor, the safe arrival here of the exploring expedition under my command, and beg to give you a brief outline of our proceedings since the departure of the schooner "Adur" from Port Eucla.

On the 8th of July, started on a flying trip north from Eucla, with fourteen days' provisions, but was unable to penetrate more than thirty miles (which was over clear open plains of grass, &c., scarcely a tree visible), on account of the scarcity of water, not meeting with a drop of water on the whole journey. Returned to Eucla on the 9th, and, as summer had apparently set in, and there appeared no likelihood of rain, I decided to at once start for Fowler's Bay and Adelaide.

On the 14th, therefore, we started, carrying with us about thirty gallons of water. After great privation to our horses, and not meeting with a drop of water for 135 miles, by travelling day and night we reached the Head of the Bight on the evening of the 17th July, and found abundance of water by digging in the sand-hills.

Our horses had been ninety hours without a drop of water, and many of us were very weary from long marching without sleep. Many of the horses could scarcely walk, and a few were delirious ; they, however, all managed to carry their loads. They have not, however, yet recovered, but with a few days' rest I hope to see them well again. There being very little feed at the Head of the Bight, we continued our journey, and on the 23rd July reached Colona (head station of Degraves and Co.), where we met Police-trooper Richards, who was on his way to the Head of the Bight to meet us, in accordance with instructions from his Excellency Sir James Fergusson.

Leaving Colona on the 25th, we reached Fowler's Bay on the 27th July, all well.

We are now about 600 miles from Adelaide. Our route will be through the Gawler Ranges, skirting the south end of Lake Gairdner, and thence to Port Augusta and Adelaide, which we shall probably reach in five or six weeks from date.

By this mail I have written to his Excellency Sir James Fergusson, apprising him of our safe arrival, as well as giving him a brief account of our journey. According to present arrangements we shall, at latest, be in Perth by the October mail.

Trusting that these proceedings may meet with the approval of his Excellency the Governor, I have, &c.,

JOHN FORREST,
Leader of Expedition to Eucla and Adelaide.
The Hon. the Colonial Secretary, Perth,
        Western Australia.

_____

Fowler's Bay, 29th July, 1870.

SIR,—In accordance with my instructions from the Government of Western Australia, I have the honour to report, for the information of his Excellency Sir James Fergusson, that the exploring expedition, organized by that Government and placed under my command, has reached this place in safety.

With his Excellency's permission, I will give a brief account of our journey since leaving Perth.

Leaving Perth on the 30th March, we reached Esperance Bay, the station of the Messrs. Dempster, on the 25th April, and remained to recruit our horses until the 9th May, when we continued in an easterly direction for about 130 miles, and reached Israelite Bay, in latitude 33° 37′ S. and longitude 123° 48′ E., where we met a coasting vessel with our supplies, &c.

Left Israelite Bay on May 30th, and reached the water shown on Mr. Eyre's track in longitude 126° 24′ E. on the 14th June, depending wholly on rock water-holes during the journey. Here we recruited and made a trip inland for fifty miles, finding the country to be very clear and well grassed, but entirely destitute of permanent water.

Leaving longitude 126° 24′ E. on 24th June, we reached Eucla on the 2nd July, depending again solely on rock water-holes, our horses often being in great want of water. At Eucla we again met the coaster with supplies, &c.

After despatching the coaster on her return to Swan River, attempted to get inland north of Eucla; but, owing to the scarcity of water and the dryness of the season, was unable to get more than thirty miles inland. I therefore concluded to continue the journey towards Adelaide, and accordingly left Eucla on July 14th, reaching the Head of the Great Australian Bight on the evening of the 17th, after a very hard and fatiguing journey, without a drop of water for our horses for ninety hours, in which time we travelled 138 miles.

Men and horses were in a very weary state when we reached the water, which we found by digging in the sand-hills at the extreme Head of the Bight. Continuing, we reached Fowler's Bay on the 27th July.

From longitude 124° 25′ E. to Port Eucla, in longitude 128° 53′ E., our route was from twenty to thirty miles from the sea, and in the whole of that distance we only procured permanent water in one spot, viz. that shown on Mr. Eyre's track in longitude 126° 24′ E.

On our route we passed over many millions of acres of grassy country, but I am sorry to say I believe entirely destitute of permanent water. The natives met with were friendly, but to us altogether unintelligible. The health of my party has been excellent, and we have reached this place without losing a single horse.

Before reaching Fowler's Bay, we were met by Police-trooper Richards, who was on his way to meet us, in accordance with instructions from his Excellency. I am truly thankful for this, as he has been of great service to us, and has been very attentive to our requirements. I hope to reach Adelaide in five weeks from date. My route will be through the Gawler Ranges to Port Augusta, and thence to Adelaide.

Trusting that this short account of our journey may not be wholly uninteresting to his Excellency, I have, &c.,

JOHN FORREST,

Leader of Expedition from Western Australia.

The Private Secretary, Government House,

    Adelaide, South Australia.

August 1st.—Left Fowler's Bay, accompanied by Police-trooper Richards, *en route* for Port Augusta. Travelled fourteen miles in about an E.N.E. direction and camped. Rained lightly this evening.

2nd.—Reached Pinong station. Distance travelled, thirty miles. Passed several huts and wells. The whole journey was over most beautifully-grassed country.

3rd.—Left Pinong, and, after travelling thirty miles, reached a spot called Athena; then camped, leaving Charra station about seven miles to the southward. Passed a few huts and wells during the day.

4th.—At seventeen miles reached Denial Bay, when we turned off towards Hosken and Broadbent's stations, and at thirteen miles further camped on a very grassy rise, with two small rock water-holes, called Merking. By meridian altitude of α Lyræ (Vega), found it to be in latitude 32° 12′ 36″ S.

5th.—After travelling eight miles, came to a

deserted station of Hosken and Broadbent's, and found abundance of water in a rock water-hole called Chillandee. As the horses were very tired, and there was splendid feed for them, we camped here for the remainder of the day.

6th.—Left Chillandee, and after travelling twenty-six miles, passed Madebuckela, the homestead of Mr. Hosken, where we camped at a deserted hut, with splendid feed and water for the horses.

7th.—Travelled towards Gawler Ranges for thirteen miles, and camped at a spot called Conkabeena, from which the ranges were clearly visible.

8th.—Continuing in an easterly direction for twelve miles, we reached Wollular, a granite hill with plenty of water on the rocks; after which proceeded due east for twelve miles, through dense thickets and sandy hills, when we came on a small patch of grassy land and camped, Mount Centre bearing N. 95° E. mag.

9th.—Continuing towards Mount Centre for eighteen miles, over a succession of salt lakes and very sandy hills and scrub, we reached a road making a little farther north, which was followed, and after travelling five miles came to Narlibby, and camped on most beautiful feed.

10th.—After taking wrong roads and going a good deal out of our way, we reached Paney station and camped at the police-station.

11th and 12th.—Rested at Paney, as the horses

were very tired, and there was splendid feed for them. Police-trooper Richards intends returning to-morrow to Fowler's Bay. He has given us every assistance in his power, and deserves our very sincere thanks for his kindness and attention.

13*th to* 17*th.*—Travelling towards Port Augusta, accompanied for half the distance by Police trooper O'Shanahan, from Paney station.

18*th.*—Reached Port Augusta. Telegraphed to his Excellency Sir James Fergusson, informing him of our arrival. Camped five miles from Port Augusta, at a small township named Stirling.

19*th.*—Received telegram from his Excellency Sir James Fergusson, congratulating us on our success. Camped a few miles from Mount Remarkable.

20*th.*—Passed through Melrose, and on the 23rd reached Clare, where I had the pleasure of meeting Mr. John Roe, son of the Hon. Captain Roe, our respected Surveyor-General.

On August 24th reached Riverton, and on the 25th Gawler. On the 26th we arrived at Salisbury, twelve miles from Adelaide. Through all these towns we have been most cordially received, and I shall never forget the attention and kindly welcome received on the journey through South Australia.

On the 27th August we left Salisbury, and for

PUBLIC WELCOME AT ADELAIDE.

an account of our journey from there to Adelaide I cannot do better than insert an extract from the *South Australian Register* of August 27th, 1870 :—

"On Saturday morning the band of explorers from Western Australia, under the leadership of Mr. Forrest, made their entrance into Adelaide. They left Salisbury at half-past nine o'clock, and when within a few miles of the city were met by Inspector Searcy and one or two other members of the police force. Later on the route they were met by an escort of horsemen, who had gone out to act as a volunteer escort. At Government House Gate a crowd of persons assembled, who gave them a hearty cheer as they rode up. The whole party at once rode up to Government House, where they were received by his Excellency, who was introduced to all the members of the expedition, and spent a quarter of an hour in conversation with Mr. Forrest, and in examining with interest the horses and equipments, which all showed signs of the long and severe journey performed. Wine having been handed round, the party withdrew, and were again greeted at Government Gate by hearty cheers from the crowd, which now numbered several hundreds. They then proceeded by way of Rundle Street to the quarters assigned them at the police barracks. The men are to remain at the barracks, and the officers are to be entertained at the City of Adelaide Club."

From August 28th to September 12th we remained in Adelaide, having been most kindly received by all with whom we came in contact. We saw as much of the country as possible. I disposed of my horses and equipment by public auction ; then left in the steamer " Alexandra " with the whole of my party on the 12th, reaching King George's Sound on the 17th at 1 a.m. Left King George's Sound on the 19th, and arrived in Perth on the 27th, where we were most cordially welcomed by his Excellency the Governor and the citizens of Perth, having been absent 182 days.

In the foregoing I have attempted to give a faithful and correct account of our proceedings, and, in conclusion, beg to make a few remarks respecting the character and the capabilities of the country travelled over.

In about longitude 124° E. the granite formation ends, at least on and near the coast; but from longitude 124ᶜ to the Head of the Bight, a distance of over 400 miles, there is no change in the formation, being limestone and high table land the whole distance.

The portion most suited for settlement is, I believe, between longitude 126° 12′ E. and longitude 129° E., near Eucla harbour, or, in other words, the country to the north of the Hampton Range—the country north of the range being most beautifully grassed, and I believe abundance of water could be procured anywhere under the range by sinking twenty or thirty feet. There is also under the same range a narrow strip of fine grassy country for the whole length of the range, viz. about 160 miles. I have every confidence that, should the country be settled, it would prove a remunerative speculation, and, if water can be procured on the table land, would be the finest pastoral district of Western Australia.

Before I conclude, I have the pleasing duty to record my entire appreciation of every member of the party. I need not particularize, as one and all had the interest and welfare of the expedition at heart, and on no occasion uttered a single murmur.

Finally, sir, my best and most sincere thanks are due to his Excellency Governor Weld for the very efficient manner in which the expedition was equipped. It is chiefly owing to the great zeal and desire of his Excellency that I should have everything necessary that the success of the enterprise is attributable.

I have, &c.,

JOHN FORREST,

Leader of Expedition.

The Honourable F. P. Barlee, Esq.,
　Colonial Secretary, Western Australia.

CHAPTER IV.

RECEPTION AT ADELAIDE AND RETURN TO PERTH.

Departure from Gawler and Arrival at Adelaide.—Appearance
of the Party.—Public Entrance.—Complimentary Banquet.
—Grant by the Government of Western Australia.

ON Saturday, the 27th of August, we reached Adelaide. On the previous day we had left Gawler
for Salisbury, where we rested until the following
morning, when we started at half-past nine o'clock
for Adelaide. A few miles from there we were met
by the chief inspector of police and some troopers
sent to escort us, and soon afterwards a volunteer
escort of horsemen gave us a friendly welcome. We
were heartily cheered as we entered the town and
then rode to Government House, where we were
received in the most cordial manner by the Governor, Sir James Fergusson. After a brief time
spent in examining the horses (which were all the
worse for the long and arduous journey) also the
equipments, and in partaking of refreshments, we
left the Government House, the people cheering
lustily, and passed through King William and

Rundle Streets on the way to the City of Adelaide Club. My brother and self stayed there while in town, and the others at the police barracks, where man and horse enjoyed the much-needed rest and refreshment.

It may interest the reader to quote from the *South Australian Advertiser* the description of our appearance when we first entered Adelaide:—" It was a genuine Australian bush turn-out, the trappings, water-drums, and other necessaries being admirably adapted for the purpose. The horses looked somewhat the worse for wear; but, considering the immense distance that they have travelled, their condition was not to be complained of, and a few weeks in the Government paddocks will put them in capital condition. The officers and men, both white and black, look the picture of health, and their satisfaction at having completed their long and arduous task is beaming from their countenances."

Whatever our countenances may have expressed, I know we felt an intense satisfaction at having been enabled to discharge the duty we had undertaken.

On the evening of the 3rd of September Sir James Fergusson entertained us at dinner, and many old colonists who, in their time, had been engaged in exploring expeditions, were among the guests. Mr. Barlee, the Colonial Secretary of Western Australia, who arrived in Adelaide a day or two after we had reached it, was present with me at the luncheon on the occasion of the inauguration of the Northern Railway Extension at Kooringa. In replying to the toast of "The Visitors," he took the opportunity of thanking the South Australian people and the Government for the courtesy and kindness extended to me and the members of my party, who, he said, had carried out the instructions so successfully and in a manner which made him proud of the colony to which he belonged. He hoped that the line of communication that had been opened might soon lead to much better and closer intercommunication between the colonies.

With characteristic consideration and kindness Governor Weld, immediately on receiving my report from Eucla, addressed a private letter to my father, congratulating him on my success.

Anxious to lose no time in reporting myself to my Government, I only remained in South Australia about a fortnight, and then left for Perth in the " Branch " mail steamer, and arrived there on Tuesday, the 27th of September. The City Council determined to give us a public reception and present an address. A four-in-hand drag was despatched to bring us into the city, and a procession, consisting of several private carriages, a number of the citizens on horseback, and the volunteer band, escorted us. The city flag was flying at the Town Hall, and there was a liberal display of similar tokens from private dwellings. The Governor and his aide-de-camp came out five miles to meet us, and accompanied us to the beginning of the city, where he handed us over to the Council, meeting us again at the Government offices. A crowd had collected in front of the Government offices, where we were to alight, and amid cheering and general hand-shaking we entered the enclosure.

Here his Excellency the Governor received us with warm congratulations, and the City Council presented the address, which was read by the chairman, Mr. Glyde. He said,—

" Mr. Forrest,—In the name of the citizens I have the very great pleasure to bid you a cordial welcome on your safe return to Perth. We sincerely congratulate yourself and party on the success which has attended your adventurous expedition overland to Adelaide. It must have been gratifying to you to have been selected to lead this expedition, and to follow such explorers as Captain Roe, Gregory, Austin, and others, of whom West Australia may well be proud. Your expedition, however, has an additional interest from the fact that its leader and members were born in the colony. I trust, sir, that at no distant date you may have the satisfaction to see the advantages realized which the route opened by your expedition is calculated to effect.

I had had no reason to expect such a marked official reception, and could only express the pleasure I experienced in knowing that the colonists so fully appreciated my efforts to carry out successfully the task confided to me.

The Governor also offered his congratulations, and three cheers having been given the party, and three more for the Governor, we left for our quarters highly gratified with the reception. His Excellency gave a large dinner-party to celebrate our return, and on Monday, the 24th of October, a public demonstration of welcome was afforded by a banquet to which we were invited by the citizens. The following is a report from the Perth journal :—

COMPLIMENTAY BANQUET TO MR. JOHN FORREST.

ON Monday evening last a Complimentary Banquet was given to Mr. Forrest, the explorer, at the " Horse and Groom " tavern. About seventy sat down to dinner, among whom were his Excellency the Governor, the Private Secretary, the Colonial Secretary, the Surveyor-General, Captain Roe, and many of the leading inhabitants of Perth and Fremantle. The chair was taken by Captain Roe. On his right was his Excellency the Governor, and on his left the guest of the evening—Mr. Forrest. The vice-chair was filled by Mr. Landor. After the cloth had been removed, the chairman, Captain Roe, rose and proposed " the Queen," a lady whom the people could not consider without being proud of the sovereign by whom they were governed.

The Chairman said he rose to propose another toast, which, he trusted, was not always given as a matter of course, but with heartfelt satisfaction. It was the health of the " Heir Apparent to the Throne." (Cheers). The Prince of Wales will, it is hoped, one day fill the throne of his illustrious mother —may that day be far distant!—but, when that day does arrive, may he display the exemplary virtues of his illustrious mother and the sterling qualities that distinguished his great father!

The Chairman, in proposing the next toast, " His Excellency

the Governor," said he had some difficulty in doing so, particularly as the subject of it was on his right hand that evening;
yet he considered the gratitude of the colonists was due to her
Majesty's Government for selecting a gentleman who was so
well qualified to benefit the colony. He believed his Excellency
was the man to drag the colony out of the hole (cheers);
and he believed his Excellency was the man to attain for us
that prosperity we so much desired (hear, hear); but we must
do our utmost to support him in the effort to secure it. It was
impossible for any man to perform one hundredth part of what
was wanted of him; yet he believed his Excellency would do
all in his power to benefit the colony in every way. Let every
one give his Excellency that strenuous support necessary to
attain prosperity, and we would attain success. He trusted
that when the term of his Excellency's sojourn amongst us
had arrived, he would remember with pleasure the days he had
spent in Western Australia. The toast was drunk with cheers
and enthusiasm.

His Excellency the Governor, who was received most cordially, rose to thank them for the very kind manner in which
they had received the toast which had been proposed by the
worthy chairman. The chairman was right in saying that they
might rely upon his doing his best for the benefit of the country,
but they must not be disappointed ; he could not do everything,
but they might depend upon it he would do what he considered
right for the people and the colony, without the fear or favour
of any. But "many men of many minds," as the old school
copy says. People thought widely different, but he would do
his best for the welfare of the colony. (Cheers). He did not,
however, rise to speak of himself; the toast that evening was
in honour of Mr. Forrest, and at the present moment, viewing
the state of Europe, looking at the fact that at this very time
two of the largest nations in the world are carrying on a deadly
strife; that on either side deeds of daring have been done,
which we all admire, and by which we are all fascinated — and
why ? Because the human mind admired daring and enterprise. But war devastated the world — war meant misery, des-
titution, widows, orphans, and destruction, yet we behold all

these with a species of fascination. But not only in time of war, but at a period of peace, are the highest feelings of human nature and the noblest instincts of mankind brought out. It was in a spirit of daring, of self-sacrifice, of love of fame and science, that induced the gentleman, whose health will be duly proposed to you this evening, to undertake the task he has so successfully completed. The same motives, no doubt, led the warrior into the battle-field, as the explorer into a new and unknown country. He, like the warrior, combated dangers regardless to self. Peace, then, has triumphs as well as war. Mr. Forrest and his party well deserve the triumphs they have secured in their successful journey from this colony to Adelaide. The benefits conferred on the colony can best be appreciated by those who have the greatest capacity of looking into futurity, and as long as Australia has a history, the names of Mr. Forrest and his companions will be borne down with honour. To himself it will be a source of pleasure to know that the first year of his administration will be rendered memorable by the exertion, zeal, and enterprise of Mr. Forrest. His Excellency resumed his seat amidst loud and continued applause.

Captain Roe said a very pleasing duty now devolved upon him ; it was to recognize services well done and faithfully performed. It was always satisfactory to have our services recognized, and the leader of the expedition over a distance of more than 2000 miles, from Perth to Adelaide, so successfully, was deserving of esteem. That expedition had brought the colony into note, and the good results from it would soon be apparent. He personally felt more than he could say on the subject. He felt more in his heart than he could express in words. He trusted that the success of Forrest and his party would be a solace to him in his latest day, and that in their latter days they would look back with pride to the energy and pluck they displayed in their younger. He called upon them to drink " The health and success of Mr. Forrest and his companions during life." (Loud and continued cheering.)

Mr. Barlee: One more cheer for the absentees—Mr. Forrest's companions. (Immense cheering.)

A Voice: One cheer more for the black fellows. (Applause.)

Mr. Forrest, who was received with enthusiasm, said he felt quite unequal to the task of responding to the toast which had been so ably and feelingly proposed by Captain Roe, and so kindly received by his fellow-colonists. He was extremely gratified to find that his services had been so highly appreciated, and were so pleasing to his friends and fellow-colonists. He was much flattered at the kind way in which himself and his party had been received by his Excellency Governor Fergusson and the people of South Australia; but he must say he he was much better pleased at the reception he received from his Excellency Governor Weld and the citizens of Perth on his return. He was sorry he did not see round the table his companions of the expedition—some had gone out of town—but he must say that during the whole of their long and severe march, oftentimes without water, not one refused to do his duty or flinched in the least for a single moment. On the part of himself and his companions, he sincerely thanked them for the very kind manner in which they had drunk their health. (Great applause.)

Mr. Landor rose and said he had a toast to propose—it was the "Members of the Legislative Council"—and in doing so he would like to make a few observations upon the old. That evening they had had the pleasure of hearing one of the oldest of the Council, one who had seen more trial and suffering than any other, and to whom the grateful task fell that evening of introducing to you one who was new in travel; and, while admiring that act, he could not but call to mind the hardships that that gentleman had endured in former days. In times gone by parties were not so well provisioned as they were now, and he remembered the time when Captain Roe, short of provisions, discovered a nest of turkey's eggs, and, to his consternation, on placing them in the pan found chickens therein. But things have altered. Captain Roe belonged to an old Council, and it is of the new he proposed speaking. From the new Council great things are expected, and of the men who have been selected a good deal might be hoped. We all wanted progress. We talked of progress; but progress, like the philosopher's stone, could not be easily attained. He hoped and

believed the gentlemen who had been elected would do their
best to try to push the colony along. He trusted the gentlemen
going into Council would not, like the French, get the colony
into a hole; but, if they did, he trusted they would do their
best to get it out of the hole. What the colony looked for was,
that every man who went into the Council would do his duty.
He had much pleasure in proposing the new members of
Council with three times three.

Mr. Carr begged to express his thanks for the very flattering
manner in which the toast of the new Council had been proposed and seconded. As a proof of the confidence reposed in
them by their constituents, he could assure them that they
would faithfully discharge their duties to them in Parliament,
and work for the good of the colony generally. (Cheers.)
Again thanking them for the honour done the members of
the new Council, Mr. Carr resumed his seat amidst great
applause.

Mr. Leake (who, on rising, was supposed to follow Mr. Carr)
said his rising was not important. As the next toast fell to his
lot, he would ask them to charge their glasses. The toast that
was placed in his hands was to propose the health of his friend,
Mr. Barlee, the Colonial Secretary. He trusted they would
join him in giving Mr. Barlee a hearty welcome after his travels
in "foreign parts." Mr. Barlee started on his journey with the
approval of the entire colony, and that the acts of the Government had always the approval of the colonists was more than
could be said at all times. (Laughter.) Mr. Barlee's visit to
the other colonies must have been beneficial, and he trusted
Mr. Barlee would that evening give them his experience of the
other colonies. We have not had an opportunity of hearing of
Mr. Barlee, or what he has done since he was in Adelaide. In
Adelaide Sir J. Morphett, the Speaker of the House of Assembly, had said that Mr. Barlee was a hard-working man, and
that was a good deal to say for a man in this part of the world.
(Loud laughter.) Mr. Barlee, no doubt, would that evening
give them a history of his travels, and tell them what he had
done in Adelaide, Melbourne, and Sydney. Mr. Barlee was a
proven friend of the colonists and of West Australia. He would

ask them to join him in drinking the health of Mr. Barlee with three hearty cheers. (Drunk with enthusiasm.)

Mr. Barlee, who on rising was received with unbounded applause, said it would be impossible for him to conceal the fact that he was much pleased at the hearty manner in which his health had been proposed and received that evening. He did not require to leave the colony to know the good feeling of his fellow-colonists for him, nor to acquire testimony as to his quality as a public officer. There was one matter, however, he very much regretted, and that was that he was not present at the ovation given by the people of South Australia to Mr. Forrest and his party. Mr. Forrest had passed through Adelaide one day before his arrival. Mr. Forrest and his party had attracted attention not only in South Australia, but also, as he found, in all the other Australian colonies. Having done so much, we were expected to do more in the way of opening up the large tract of country that had been discovered. It was our duty to assure the other colonies that the country would carry stock, and stock would be forthcoming. If Mr. Forrest in former days established his fame as an explorer, his late expedition only proves that he must commence *de novo*. Of the modesty and bearing of Mr. Forrest and his party in South Australia he could not speak too highly. There was, however, one exception, and that was his friend Windich (native). He was the man who had done everything; he was the man who had brought Mr. Forrest to Adelaide, and not Mr. Forrest him. He (Mr. Barlee) was in his estimation below par to come by a steamer, and he walked across (laughter); and it was an act of condescension that Windich even looked upon him. (Great laughter.) He was quite aware Mr. Leake, in asking him to give an account of his travels in foreign parts, never seriously intended it. If he did, he would only keep them until to-morrow morning. He would say that his was a trip of business, and not pleasure, and hard work he had. Morning and night was he at work, and he trusted he would be spared to see the results of some of his efforts to benefit West Australia. (Loud cheers.) He considered, what with our lead and copper-mines, our Jarrah coal-mines, and the prospect of an auriferous country being found, a new era was dawning on the colony. (Cheers.) For the first time in the last sixteen years he had the pleasure of drinking that evening the health of the members of the Legislative Assembly. He was not yet a member of that Council, but it was probable he would be a member, and have important duties to discharge therein. He was proud to learn the quiet and orderly manner in which the elections had been conducted, and the good feeling and harmony that existed on all sides, and to learn that the defeated candidates were the first to congratulate the successful ones on their nomination. He sincerely trusted that the same quiet good feeling and harmony would remain and guide the Council in their deliberations hereafter.

Other complimentary toasts having been duly honoured, the company broke up.

While the citizens of Perth were thus exhibiting encouraging approval of our exertions, official recognition, in a practical form, was not wanting. On the 6th of October, Captain Roe forwarded to me the following communication :—

Surveyor-General's Office, Perth,
6th October, 1870.

Sir,—Having submitted to the Governor your report of the safe return to head-quarters of the overland expedition to Eucla and Adelaide, entrusted to your leadership, I have much pleasure in forwarding to you a copy of a minute in which his Excellency has been pleased to convey his full appreciation of your proceedings, and of the judgment and perseverance displayed in your successful conduct of the enterprise.

In these sentiments I cordially participate, and, in accordance with the wish expressed in the minute, I beg you will convey to the other members of the expedition the thanks of his Excellency for their co-operation and general conduct.

As a further recognition of the services of the party, his

Excellency has been pleased to direct that the sum of **Two Hundred Pounds** be distributed amongst them, in the following proportions, payable at the Treasury, namely—

To the Leader of the expedition	.	£75
„ Second in command	. .	50
„ H. McLarty and R. Osborne, £25 each	. . . .	50
„ Aborigines, Windich and Billy, £12 10s.	. . . .	25
	Total	£200

I am, Sir, your obedient servant,

J. S. ROE, Surveyor-General.

John Forrest, Esq.,
Leader of Expedition, &c., &c.

The following is the minute referred to in the above :—

HONOURABLE SURVEYOR-GENERAL,—I beg that you will convey to Mr. John Forrest, leader of the Eucla expedition, the expression of my appreciation of the zeal, judgment, and perseverance which he has displayed in the successful conduct of the enterprise committed to his charge. Great credit is also due to the second in command, and to every member of the party. All have done their duty well, and to them also I desire to render my thanks.

It is with much pleasure that, with the advice of my Executive Council, I authorize a gratuity of 200l., to be divided in the proportions you have submitted to me.

(Signed)   FRED. A. WELD.

1st October, 1870.

It will be remembered that the York Agricultural Society had previously proposed an overland expedition, but had not succeeded in obtaining official sanction, it being then believed that Eucla could be best approached from the sea. After my return the Society held a meeting, at which his Excellency the Governor was present, when my report of the expedition was received with every mark of approval of my labours.

CHAPTER V.

THE success which had attended my previous
expeditions, and the great encouragement received
from the Government and public of each colony,
made me wish to undertake another journey for
the purpose of ascertaining whether a route from
Western Australia to the advanced settlements of
the Southern colony was practicable. I also hoped
to contribute, if possible, towards the solution of the
problem, What is the nature of the interior ? My
first journey, when I succeeded in penetrating
for about 600 miles into the unknown desert of
Central Australia, had convinced me that, although
there might, and doubtless would, be considerable
difficulties to be encountered, there were no in-

superable obstacles except a probable failure in the supply of water. That certainly was the most formidable of all the difficulties that would no doubt have to be encountered; but on the previous journey the scarcity of water had been endured, not without privation and suffering, but without any very serious result. At any rate, the expedition I desired to undertake appeared to be of an extremely interesting character. It might contribute to the knowledge of an immense tract of country of which hardly anything was known; it might also be the means of opening up new districts, and attaining results of immense importance to the colonies. Perhaps, too, I was animated by a spirit of adventure—not altogether inexcusable—and, having been successful in my previous journeys, was not unnaturally desirous of carrying on the work of exploration.

In 1871 an expedition went out to the eastward of Perth under command of my brother, Mr. A. Forrest, in search of fresh pastoral country. It was a very good season, but the expedition was too late in starting. It succeeded in reaching latitude 31° S., longitude 123° 37′ E., and afterwards struck S.S.E. towards the coast; then, with considerable difficulty, it reached Mount Ragged and the Thomas River, and, continuing westerly, got as far as Esperance Bay, the homestead of the Messrs. Dempster. This expedition discovered a considerable tract of good country, some of which has been taken up and stocked. It was equipped on very economical principles, and did not cost more than 300*l.*

The leader had been previously with me as second in command on the journey to Adelaide in 1870, and afterwards accompanied me in 1874 from the west coast through the centre of the western part of Australia to the telegraph line between Adelaide and Port Darwin.

He received great credit from the Government for the energy and perseverance displayed on this expedition—a character borne out by future services as second in command with me.

In July, 1872, I addressed the following letter to the Honourable Malcolm Fraser, the Surveyor-General :—

Western Australia, Perth,
July 12th, 1872.

Sir,—I have the honour to lay before you, for the consideration of his Excellency the Governor, a project I have in view for the further exploration of Western Australia.

My wish is to undertake an expedition, to start early next year from Champion Bay, follow the Murchison to its source, and then continue in an east and north-east direction to the telegraph line now nearly completed between Adelaide and Port Darwin ; after this we would either proceed north to Port Darwin or south to Adelaide.

The party would consist of four white and two black men, with twenty horses, well armed and provisioned for at least six months.

The total cost of the expedition would be about 600*l.*, of which sum I hope to be able to raise, by subscriptions, about 200*l.*

The horses will be furnished by the settlers, many having already been promised me.

The geographical results of such an expedition would necessarily be very great ; it would be the finishing stroke of Australian discovery ; would be sure to open new pastoral country ; and, if we are to place any weight in the opinions of geographers (among whom I may mention the Rev. Tenison Woods), the existence of a large river running inland from the watershed of the Murchison is nearly certain.

Referring to the map of Australia you will observe that the proposed route is a very gigantic, hazardous, and long one ; but, after careful consideration, I have every confidence that, should I be allowed to undertake it, there are reasonable hopes of my being able to succeed.

Minor details are purposely omitted ; but, should his Excellency favourably entertain this proposition, I will be too glad, as far as I am able, to give further information on the subject.

Trusting you will be able to concur in the foregoing suggestions.   I have, &c.,

JOHN FORREST.

To this letter the Governor appended the following memorandum :—

Mr. J. Forrest, in a most public spirited manner, proposes to embark in an undertaking, the dangers of which, though not by any means inconsiderable, would be outweighed by the advantages which might accrue to this colony, and which would certainly result in a great extension of our geographical knowledge.   Should he succeed in this journey, his name will fitly go down to posterity as that of the man who solved the last remaining problem in the Australian continent ; and, whatever may come after him, he will have been the last (and certainly, when the means at his disposal and the difficulties of the undertaking are considered, by no means the least) of the great Australian explorers.

The honour to be gained by him, and most of the advan-

tages, will ultimately fall to this colony, which is his birth-
place ; and for my own part I shall be very proud that such
a design should be carried out during my term of office.   I
wish that the means of the colony were sufficient to warrant
the Government in proposing to defray the entire cost of the
expedition, and I think it would be a disgrace to the colony
if it did not at least afford some aid from public funds.

These papers will be laid before the Legislature, and the
Government will support a vote in aid, should the Legislature
concur.

FRED. A. WELD.

July 20th, 1872.

This memorandum showed that his Excellency
thoroughly sympathized with my reason for desir-
ing to undertake the expedition. The proposition, supported by official approval, was acceded
to by the Legislative Council, which voted the
400*l.* stated to be required in addition to the
200*l.* which I hoped to be able to raise by subscription.

Just at this time, however, South Australia was
making great efforts to solve the problem I had
undertaken to attempt, preparations being made
for the departure of three expeditions. Stuart's
great feat of crossing the continent from south to
north had been followed by other successful efforts
in the same direction. Another result was the
establishing a line of telegraph from Adelaide to
Port Darwin. This might therefore be considered
the eastern boundary of the unknown districts,
and moreover was the point of departure for
the South Australian expeditions in a westerly

direction.   It was also the limit I desired to
reach, and, reaching it, I should achieve the
object I had so much at heart.   Of the South
Australian expeditions, only one was successful in
getting to the western colony, and that one, led by
Colonel Warburton, involved much suffering and
was comparatively barren of practical results.
Besides, as we afterwards knew, the route selected
by him was so far to the north as not to interfere
with my project.

The following letter to me expresses the official
estimate of the result of Colonel Warburton's
expedition :—

Surveyor-General's Office, Perth,
March 27th, 1874.

The gist of the information I have from Colonel Warburton
may be summed up in a few words.   From the MacDermot
Ranges in South Australia to the head of the Oakoon River
(about 150 miles from the coast), keeping between the paral-
lels of 20° and 22° south latitude, he traversed a sterile country,
in which he states horses could not possibly exist— they would
starve, as they could not live on the stunted scrub and herbage
which the camels managed to keep alive on.

The general character of the country seen was that of a high,
waterless, slightly undulating, sandy table-land, with in some
parts sand deserts in ridges most harassing to traverse. There
was nothing visible in the way of water courses in which water
could be ratained ; but they were successful in finding, at long
distances, sufficient to maintain themselves and their camels as
they fled, as it were for their lives, westward over the Sahara,
which appears to be in a great part a desolate wilderness, de-
void of life or of anything life sustaining. Though this
is a grim picture put before you, yet I would not have you

daunted. Your task is a different one, and one which all the colony is looking forward to see successfully completed by you·

I have, &c.,

(Signed) MALCOLM FRASER, Surveyor-General.

Governor Weld, however, decided that it might be better to postpone my expedition, as it would not be advisable to appear to enter into competition with the other colony; besides which it might be of considerable advantage to wait and avail ourselves of the results of any discoveries that might be made by the South Australian explorers. Another reason for delay was that I was required to conduct a survey of considerable importance, which it was desirable should be completed before undertaking the new expedition.

It may assist my readers to understand the references in the latter part of my Journal if I state that in April, 1873, Mr. Gosse, one of the South Australian explorers, quitted the telegraph line about forty miles south of Mount Stuart; that the farthest point in a westerly direction reached by him was in longitude 126° 59′ E.; and that Mr. Giles, a Victorian explorer, had reached longitude 125°, but had been unable to penetrate farther.

Some records of these expeditions, and a copy of the chart made by Mr. Gosse, were in my possession, when at length, in March, 1874, I set to work on the preliminary arrangements for the expedition. Before leaving Perth I received from

the Surveyor-General the following outline of instructions for my general guidance :—

Western Australia, Surveyor-General's Office,
Perth, 17th March, 1874.

SIR,—The arrangements connected with the party organized
for the purpose of proceeding on an exploratory expedition
to the north-eastern division of this territory having now been
completed, I am directed to instruct and advise you generally
in the objects and the intention of the Government in regard
to it.

The chief object of the expedition is to obtain information
concerning the immense tract of country from which flow the
Murchison, Gascoigne, Ashburton, DeGrey, Fitzroy, and other
rivers falling into the sea on the western and northern shores
of this territory, as there are many good and reasonable
grounds for a belief that those rivers outflow from districts
neither barren nor badly watered.

Mr. A. C. Gregory, coming from the northwards by Sturt's
Creek, discovered the Denison Plains, and it may be that from
the head of the Murchison River going northwards there are
to be found, near the heads of the rivers above alluded to,
many such grassy oases ; and, looking at the success which
has already attended the stocking of the country to the
eastward of Champion Bay, and between the heads of the
Greenough River and Murchison, it will be most fortunate for
our sheep farmers if you discover any considerable addition to
the present known pasture grounds of the colony ; and by this
means no doubt the mineral resources of the interior will be
brought eventually to light. Every opinion of value that has
been given on the subject tells one that the head of the
Murchison lies in a district which may prove another land of
Ophir.

In tracing up this river from Mount Gould to its source,
and in tracing other rivers to and from their head waters,
detours must be made, but generally your course will be
north-east until you are within the tropics ; it will then be

discretionary with you to decide on your route, of which there
is certainly a choice of three, besides the retracing of your
steps for the purpose, perhaps, of making a further inspection
of the good country you may have found.

Firstly,—There is to choose whether you will go westward,
and fall back on the settlements at Nicol Bay or the
De Grey River, on the north-west coast.

Secondly,—To consider whether you might advantageously
push up Sturt's Creek, keeping to the westward of
Gregory's track.

Thirdly,—To decide whether or not you will go eastward
to the South Australian telegraph line.

Possibly this latter course may be the most desirable and
most feasible to accomplish, as the telegraph stations, taking
either Watson's Creek or Daly Waters, are not more than
300 miles from the known water supply on Sturt's Creek ;
and, supposing you do this successfully, the remaining distance
down the telegraph line to Port Darwin is a mere bagatelle,
provided an arrangement can be made with the South
Australian Government to have a supply of provisions at
Daly Waters.

In the event of your going to Port Darwin, the plan probably will be to sell your equipment and horses, returning
with your party by sea ; but in this and in other matters of
detail there is no desire to fetter you, or to prevent the
proper use of your judgment, as I am fully aware that your
sole object is in common with that of the Government—the
carrying to a satisfactory result the work to be done.

I hope that before you individually leave we shall have the
pleasure of welcoming Colonel Warburton, and I have no
doubt will be able to obtain some valuable information from
him.

Having now dwelt generally on the objects of the expedition, I will go more into details.

Your party will consist of yourself as leader, Mr. Alexander
Forrest as surveyor and second in command, James Sweeney
(farrier), police-constable James Kennedy, and two natives,
Tommy Windich and Tommy Pierre, making six in number

and twenty horses. The party will be well armed ; but by
every means in your power you will endeavour to cultivate
and keep on friendly relations with all the aborigines you may
fall in with, and avoid, if possible, any collision with them.

The provisions and other supplies already arranged for
are calculated to serve the party for eight months. The expedition will start from Champion Bay, to which you will
at once despatch by sea the stores to be obtained here ; and
the men and horses should proceed overland without delay.
You will be probably able to charter carts or drays to take
most of your impedimenta from Geraldton to Mr. Burges's
farthest out-station on the Murchison ; this will save you 200
miles of packing, and husband the strength of your horses
for that distance.

Having the assistance of Mr. Alexander Forrest as surveyor
to the party, you will do as much reconnaissance work in
connexion with the colonial survey as it may be possible ;
and also, by taking celestial observations at all convenient
times, and by sketching the natural features of the country
you pass over, add much to our geographical knowledge. All
geological and natural history specimens you can collect and
preserve will be most valuable in perfecting information concerning the physical formation of the interior.

You will be good enough to get the agreement, forwarded
with this, signed by the whole of the party.

I am, &c.,

MALCOLM FRASER,

Surveyor-General.

On the 18th of March, 1874, the expedition
quitted Perth. Colonel Harvest, the Acting-
Governor, wished us a hearty God-speed, which
was warmly echoed by our friends and the public
generally. The Surveyor-General and a party
accompanied us for some distance along the road.
Ten days afterwards we reached Champion Bay,

where we intended to remain for three days, having settled to commence our journey on the 1st of April. We had enough to do in preparing stores, shoeing horses, and starting a team with our heaviest baggage to a spot about fifty miles inland. On the 31st March we were entertained at dinner by Mr. Crowther (Member of the Legislative Council for the district) at the Geraldton Hotel. It was from that point we considered the expedition really commenced, and my Journal will show that we numbered our camps from that place. Our final start was not effected without some trouble. The horses, happily ignorant of the troubles which awaited them, were fresh and lively, kicking, plunging, and running away, so that it was noon before we were fairly on the move. Our first day's journey brought us to a place named Knockbrack, the hospitable residence of Mr. Thomas Burges, where we remained two days, the 3rd being Good Friday. On the 4th we were again on our way—a party of friends, Messrs. E. and F. Wittenoom, Mr. Lacy, and others, accompanying us as far as Allen Nolba. We camped that night at a well known as Wandanoe, where, however, there was scarcely any feed for the horses, who appeared very dissatisfied with their entertainment, for they wandered away, and several hours were spent on the following morning in getting them together.

Our route lay by way of Kolonaday, North

Spring, Tinderlong, and Bilyera to Yuin, Mr. Burges's principal station, which we reached on the 9th, and remained until Monday the 13th. Then we started on a route east-north-east, and camped that night at a rock water-hole called Beetinggnow, where we found good feed and water. My brother and Kennedy went on in advance to Poondarrie, to dig water-holes, and we rejoined them there on the 14th. This place is situated in latitude 27° 48′ 39″ S., and longitude 116° 16′ 11″ E.

On the following day we were very busy packing up the rations, for I had arranged to send back the cart, gone on in advance. We had eight months' provisions, besides general baggage, and I certainly experienced some difficulty in arranging how to carry such a tremendously heavy load, even with the aid of eighteen pack-horses, and a dozen natives who accompanied us. I intended to start on the 16th, but one of the horses was missing, and, although Pierre and I tracked him for five miles, we were compelled to give up the search for that night, as darkness came on, and return to camp. On the following day, however, we followed up the tracks, and caught the horse after a chase of twenty miles. He had started on the return journey, and was only a mile from Yuin when we overtook him.

By half-past nine on the morning of the 18th we had made a fair start. The day was intensely hot, and as we had only three riding-horses, half of the party were compelled to walk. We travelled in a north-easterly direction for eleven miles, and reached a spring called Wallala, which we dug out, and so obtained sufficient water for our horses. I may mention here that Colonel Warburton and other explorers who endeavoured to cross the great inland desert from the east had the advantage of being provided with camels—a very great advantage indeed in a country where the water supply is so scanty and uncertain as in Central Australia. As we ascertained by painful experience, a horse requires water at least once in twelve hours, and suffers greatly if that period of abstinence is exceeded. A camel, however, will go for ten or twelve days without drink, without being much distressed. This fact should be remembered, because the necessity of obtaining water for the horses entailed upon us many wearying deviations from the main route and frequent disappointments, besides great privation and inconvenience to man and beast.

The 19th was Sunday, and, according to practice, we rested. Every Sunday throughout the journey I read Divine Service, and, except making the daily observations, only work absolutely necessary was done. Whenever possible, we rested on Sunday, taking, if we could, a pigeon, a parrot, or such other game as might come in our way as special fare. Sunday's dinner was an institution for which, even in those inhospitable wilds, we had a great respect. This day, the 19th, ascertained, by meridian altitude of the sun, that we were in latitude 27° 40′ 6″ S. We had several pigeons and parrots, which, unfortunately for them, but most fortunately for us, had come within range of our guns. While thus resting, Police constable Haydon arrived from Champion Bay, bringing letters and a thermometer (broken on the journey), also a barometer. When he left we bade good-bye to the last white man we were destined to see for nearly six months.

After the usual difficulty with the horses, which had again wandered, we started on Monday, the 20th, at half-past ten, and steering about 30° E. of north for seven miles, came to a spring called Bullardo, and seven miles farther we camped at Warrorang, where there was scarcely any water or feed. We were now in latitude 27° 33′ 21″ S., Cheangwa Hill being N. 340° E. mag.

I now take up the narrative in the words of my Journal, which will show the reason for ultimately adopting the third of the routes which the letter of instructions left to my discretion.

April 21*st*.—Continued on N. 340° E. to Cheangwa Hill four miles; thence northerly, passing Koonbun, and on to a place called Pingie, on the Sandford River. From camp to Pingie,

Barloweery Peaks bore N. 322° E. mag., Cheang-wa Hill N. 207° E., latitude 27° 19′ 33″. Found water by digging. Rather warm; barometer rising. Clear flats along water-courses; otherwise dense thickets.

22nd.—Continued northerly; at twelve miles crossed the dividing range between the Sandford and other creeks flowing into the Murchison. Camped at a granite hill called Bia, with a fine spring on its north side. Got a view of Mount Murchison, which bore N. 7° E. mag. from camp. Fine grassy granite country for the first eight miles to-day. Splendid feed at this camp. Travelled about fifteen miles. Latitude by meridian altitude of Regulus 27° 7′ S. Walking in turns every day.

23rd.—Steering a little west of north over level country for six miles, with a few water-courses with white gums in them, we came into granite country with bare hills in every direction. Kept on till we came to a brook with pools of fresh water, where we camped about one mile from the Murchison River. Latitude 26° 52′ 38″, Mount Murchison bearing N. 50° E. Went with Pierre to a peak of granite N. 50° E., about one mile and a half from camp, from which I took a round of angles and bearings. Travelled about eighteen miles to-day.

24th.—At one mile reached the Murchison River, and followed along up it. Fine grassy flats,

good loamy soil, with white gums in bed and
on flats. Travelled about fourteen miles, and
camped. Rather brackish water in the pools.
Latitude of camp 26° 42′ 43″ by Regulus. Shot
seven ducks and eight cockatoos. Saw several
kangaroos and emus. Rain much required.
Mount Murchison bears from camp N. 122° E.,
and Mount Narryer N. 14° E. mag.

25th.—Continued up river for about nine miles,
and camped at a fine spring in the bed of river,
of fresh water, which I named Elizabeth Spring;
it is surrounded by salt water, and is quite fresh.
Mount Narryer bore from camp N. 4° E. mag.,
and Mount Murchison N. 168° 30′ E. mag.
Windich shot an emu, and some ducks were also
shot. Fine grassy country along river; white
gums in flats; large salt pools. Very hot weather;
thermometer 90° in pack-saddle.

26th (Sunday).—Did not travel to-day. Plotted
up track and took observations for time and longitude. Barometer 29·18; thermometer 83° at 6 p.m.
Latitude of camp 26° 35′ 8″ S. by Regulus.

27th.—Travelled up river for about sixteen
miles; camped at a fine fresh pool in latitude
26° 24′ 52″ S., Mount Narryer bearing N. 238°
E., and Mount Dugel N. 334° E. mag. Fine
grassy country along river. Shot six ducks; great
numbers were in the river, also white cockatoos. Very warm mid-day; cloudy in evening.
Marked a tree F on the right bank of river.

28*th.*—Followed up the river. Fine pools for the first six miles, with numbers of ducks in them. After travelling about twenty miles we lost the river from keeping too far to the east, and following branches instead of the main branch,— in fact, the river spreads out over beautifully-grassed plains for many miles. Fearing we should be without water, I pushed ahead, and after following a flat for about six miles, got to the main river, where there were large pools of brackish water. As it was getting late, returned in all haste, but could not find the party, they having struck westward. I got on the tracks after dark, and, after following them two miles, had to give it up and camp for the night, tying up my horse alongside. Neither food nor water, and no rug.

29*th.*—I anxiously awaited daylight, and then followed on the tracks and overtook the party, encamped on the main branch of the river, with abundance of brackish water in the pools. Shot several cockatoos. From camp Mount Narryer bore N. 211° 30′ E. mag., and Mount Dugel 225° 15′ E. mag. Camp is in latitude 26° 6′ 12″. Marked a tree with the letter F on right bank of river.

30*th.*—Two of the horses could not be found till half-past twelve. After this we continued up the river over well-grassed country for about ten. miles. Camped at a small pool of fresh water, in latitude 26° 2′ 52″, which we luckily found by tracking up natives. Large pools of salt water in river. Three walking and three riding every day. Set watch to-night, two hours each.

May 1st.—Followed up river, keeping a little to the south of it for about fifteen miles. We camped on a splendid grassy flat, with a fine large pool of fresh water in it. Shot several ducks. This is the best camp we have had—plenty of grass and water—and I was very rejoiced to find the month commence so auspiciously. Barometer 29·10; thermometer 78° at 5.30 p.m.; latitude 26° 0′ 52″ S. Sighted Mount Gould, which bore N. 58° E. mag. Marked a white gum-tree $\frac{F}{20}$, being 20th camp from Geraldton.

2nd.—Steered straight for Mount Gould, N. 58° E., for sixteen miles, when I found I had made an error, and that we had unknowingly crossed the river this morning. After examining the chart, I steered S.E. towards Mount Hale, and, striking the river, we followed along it a short distance and camped at some brackish water, Mount Hale bearing N. 178° E., and Mount Gould N. 28° E. Barometer 28·96; thermometer 77° at 5.30 p.m. As Pierre was walking along, he suddenly turned round and saw four or five natives following. Being rather surprised, he frightened them by roughly saying, "What the devil you want here?" when they quickly made off. Windich and I then tried to speak to them, but could not find them. Latitude 25° 57′ 32″ S.; longitude about 117° 20′ E.

3rd (Sunday).—Went to summit of Mount Hale in company with Pierre, and after an hour's hard work reached it. It was very rough and difficult to ascend. The rocks were very magnetic; the view was extensive; indeed, the whole country was an extended plain. To the east, plains for at least thirty miles, when broken ranges were visible. Mount Gould to the N.N.E. showed very remarkably. Mount Narryer range was visible. To the south, only one hill or range could be seen, while to the S.E. broken ranges of granite were seen about thirty miles distant. Mount Hale is very lofty and rugged, and is composed of micaceous iron ore, with brown hematite; being magnetic, the compass was rendered useless. Returned about one o'clock. Windich and the others had been out searching for fresh water, and the former had seen three natives and had a talk with them. They did not appear frightened, but he could not make anything out of them. They found some good water. Barometer, at 6.30 p.m., 28·88; thermometer 76°. Took observations for time and longitude. We are much in want of rain, and thought we should have had some, but the barometer is rising this evening. To-morrow we enter on country entirely unknown.

4th.—Started at nine o'clock, and, travelling N.E. for three miles, came to junction of river

from Mount Gould, when we got some fresh water,
also met two natives, who were friendly, and they
accompanied us.   We took the south or main
branch of river, and, steering a little south of
east for about nine miles, over splendidly-grassed
country, we camped on a small pool of fresh water
on one of the courses of the river, Mount Gould
bearing N. 334° 30′ E. mag., and Mount Hale
N. 228° 30′ E. mag.   Barometer 28·90; thermometer 76° at 6 p.m. ; latitude 25° 54′ 37″ by
Regulus.   Marked a tree $_{22}^{F}$, being 22nd camp
from Geraldton.

5th.—We travelled up easterly along the river,
which spreads out and has several channels, sometimes running for miles separately, then joining
again.   There were many fine fresh pools for the
first four miles, after which they were all salt, and
the river divided into so many channels that it
was difficult to know the main river.   After
travelling about sixteen miles over fine grassy
plains and flats, we were joined by seven natives,
who had returned with the two who had left us
this morning.   They told us that there was no
fresh water on the branch we were following, and
we therefore followed them N. 30° E. for seven
miles (leaving the river to the southward),
when they brought us to a small pool in a
brook, where we camped, Mount Gould bearing
N. 285° 30 E. mag., Mount Hale N. 250° E.
mag.   Latitude 25° 52′ from mean of two ob-

servations. Barometer 28·78; thermometer 77°
at 6 p.m.

6th.—Three of the natives accompanied us to-
day. We travelled east for six miles, when I
ascended a rise and could see a river to the north
and south; the one to the north the natives say
has fresh water. As the natives say there is plenty
of water ahead, N. 70° E., we continued onwards
to a hill, which I named Mount Maitland. After
about twenty miles we reached it, but found the
spring to be bad, and after digging no water came.
For our relief I tied up the horses for some time
before letting them go. Ascending the hill close
to the camp, I saw a very extensive range, and
took a fine round of angles. The compass is useless on these hills, as they are composed of micaceous iron ore, with brown hematite, which is very
magnetic. To the east a line of high, remarkable
ranges extend, running eastwards, which I have
named the Robinson Range, after his Excellency
Governor Robinson. One of the highest points
I named Mount Fraser, after the Honourable
Commissioner of Crown Lands, from whom I
received much assistance and consideration, and
who has aided the expedition in every possible
way; the other highest point, Mount Padbury,
after Mr. W. Padbury, a contributor to the Expedition Fund. The river could be traced for thirty
miles by the line of white gums, while to the south
long lines of white gums could also be seen. I

am not sure which is the main branch, but I intend following the one to the north, as it looks the largest and the natives say it has fresh water. Barometer 28·45; thermometer 69° at 6 p.m.; latitude 25° 46′ S. The last thirty-five miles over fine grassy plains, well adapted for sheep-runs; and water could, I think, be easily procured by digging, as well as from the river.

7*th.*—The three natives ran away this morning, or at least left us without asking leave. We had to keep watch all last night over the horses to keep them from rambling. Got an early start, and steering N. 70° E. for about twelve miles, we reached the river, and camped at a fresh pool of splendid water. This is a fine large branch; it is fresh, and I believe, if not the main, is one of the largest branches. The country is now more undulating and splendidly grassed, and would carry sheep well. The whole bed of the river, or valley, is admirably adapted for pastoral purposes, and will no doubt ere long be stocked. Latitude 25° 42′ 12″ S., and longitude about 118° 9′ E. Barometer 28·57; thermometer 75° at 5.30 p.m. Marked a white gum on right bank of river $\frac{F}{25}$, being the 25th camp from Champion Bay.

8*th.*—Continued up the river for about fifteen miles, the stream gradually getting smaller, many small creeks coming into it; wide bed and flat. Fine grassy country on each side, and some per-

manent pools in river. Camped at a small pool
of fresh water, and rode up to a low ridge to the
N.E., from which I got a fine view to the eastward. I do not think the river we are following
goes much farther; low ranges and a few hills
alone visible. Barometer 28·48; thermometer
70° at 6 o'clock p.m.; latitude 25° 47′ 53″ by
meridian altitude of Jupiter.

9th.—Continued along river, which is gradually
getting smaller, for about thirteen miles over
most beautiful grassy country, the best we have
seen. White gums along bed. I believe the river
does not go more than twenty miles from here, it
being now very small. Found a nice pool of water
and camped. Barometer 28·48; thermometer
68° at half-past five o'clock.

10th (Sunday).—Went with Windich south
about eight miles to a low range, which I rightly
anticipated would be a watershed. Could see a
long line of white gums; believe there may be a
river to the south, or it may be the salt branch of
the Murchison. Returned to camp at two o'clock;
plotted up track. Barometer 28·52; thermometer 69° at 6 p.m. Mount Fraser bears
N. 328° E. mag. from camp, which is in latitude
25° 51′ 46″, longitude about 118° 30′ E. The
country is very dry indeed; in fact, we could not
be more unfortunate in the season thus far. I
only trust we may be blessed with abundance of
rain shortly, otherwise we shall not be able to
move onwards.

11*th*.—Continued up river, which is getting very small, over beautifully-grassed country, and at seven miles came to a fine flat and splendid pool of permanent water. Although a delightful spot, I did not halt, as we had come such a short distance. Here we met six native women, who were very frightened at first, but soon found sufficient confidence to talk and to tell us there was plenty of water ahead. As they always say this, I do not put any faith in it. We continued on about east for eight miles to a high flat-topped hill, when we got a view of the country ahead and turned about N.E. towards some flats, and at about eight miles camped on a grassy plain, with some small clay-pans of water. Splendid feeding country all along this valley—I may say for the last 100 miles. Heard a number of natives cooeying above our camp, but did not see them. Barometer 28·37; thermometer 68° at six o'clock p.m.; latitude 25° 51′ S. by meridian altitude of Jupiter.

12*th*.—Started E.N.E. for four miles, then north three miles to the range, where we searched over an hour for water without success. We then travelled S.E. for five miles and south one mile and a half to a water-hole in a brook, by digging out which we got abundance of water. About a quarter of a mile farther down the brook found a large pool of water and shot six ducks. As soon as we unloaded, it commenced to rain, and

kept on steadily till midnight. I am indeed pleased
to get this rain at last, as the country is very
dry. Splendid open feeding country all to-day,
and the camp is a beautifully-grassed spot.
Marked a white gum-tree $\frac{F}{29}$, close to the pool or
spring on the right bank of this brook.

13th.—Continued on, steering about south-east,
as the flat we have been following the last week is
now nearly at an end. Afterwards determined to
bear southward, in order to see where the south
branch of the river goes to. For the first six
miles over most magnificent grassed country.
Ascended a low range to get a view of the country.
The prospect ahead, however, not cheering. Took
round of bearings. A very conspicuous range
bore about south, which I named Glengarry Range,
in honour of Mr. Maitland Brown, a great supporter
of the expedition; while to the south-east only one
solitary hill could be seen, distant about twenty
miles. We, however, continued for about ten
miles over most miserable country, thickets and
spinifex, when we reached some granitic rocks and
a low rise of granite, on which we found sufficient
water to camp. Barometer 28·12; thermometer
60° at 5.30 p.m.; latitude 25° 57′ 11″ S. by
Regulus.

14th.—Steered S.E. for about fourteen miles
to a stony low range, thence E.N.E. and east and
south for six miles, turning and twisting, looking
for water. Windich found some in a gully and we

camped. Spinifex for the first fourteen miles, and miserable country. The prospect ahead not very promising. Barometer 28·06; thermometer 83° at 5 p.m. Every appearance of rain. Latitude 26° 8′ 31″ S., longitude about 119° 18′ E.

15th.—Raining lightly this morning. I did not proceed, but gave the horses rest.

16th.—Continued east for five miles, when we found three of the horses were missing; returned with Windich, and found them near camp, having never started at all. Seeing white gums to the south-east, we followed for five miles down a fine brook (which I named Negri Creek, after Commander Nègri, founder of the Geographical Society of Italy), with fine grassy country on each side. Afterwards it joined another brook, and went south-east for about three miles, where it lost itself in open flats. Struck south for two miles to some large white gums, but found no water. After long looking about I found water in a gully and camped. Distance travelled about twenty miles. Spinifex and grassy openings the first five miles to-day. Barometer 28·20; thermometer 67° at 6 o'clock p.m.; latitude 26° 16′ 8″ by Jupiter. Windich shot a turkey.

17th (Sunday).—The horses rambled far away, and it was noon before they were all collected. Shifted three and a half miles north, where there was better feed and water. Went on to a low hill on the north of our last night's camp, and got a fine view of the country to the south and south-east. Two remarkable flat-topped hills bore S.E., which I named Mount Bartle and Mount Russell, after the distinguished President and Foreign Secretary of the Royal Geographical Society. Saw a long line of white gums (colalyas) running E. and W. about ten miles distant, looking very much like a river. To the east and north the view was intercepted by long stony rises, apparently covered with spinifex. Large white gum clumps studded the plains in every direction. Evidences of heavy rainfall at certain times to be seen everywhere. Barometer 28·28; thermometer 72° at 5 p.m. ; latitude 26° 13′ 4″ S.

18th.—Steered S.S.E. for four miles, then S.E. generally, towards the flat-topped hills seen yesterday, and which bore 144° E. mag. from Spinifex Hill. At six miles crossed a low range covered with spinifex, after which we passed over country generally well grassed, some of it most beautifully, and white gums very large in clumps were studded all over the plains. At about twenty-two miles reached the flat-topped hills, and camped, finding some water in a clay-pan. The line of white gums I find are only large clumps studded over extensive plains of splendidly-grassed country. No large water-course was crossed, but several small creeks form here and there, and afterwards run out into the plains, finally finding their way into the Murchison. It was sundown when we camped. Walked over twenty miles myself to-day. Barometer 28·38 ; thermometer 60° at six o'clock ; latitude 26° 27′ 38″ S., longitude about 119° 42′ E.

19*th*.—Continued in a north-easterly direction for about eight miles over fine grassy plains, and camped at some water in a small gully with fine feed. I camped early in order to give the backs of the horses a good washing, and to refit some of the pack-saddles. Passed several clay-pans with water. We have not seen any permanent water for the last eighty miles. I much wish to find some, as it is very risky going on without the means of falling back. The country seems very deficient of permanent water, although I believe plenty could be procured by sinking. Barometer 28·46 ; thermometer 63° at 5 p.m. ; latitude 26° 23′ 39″ S. Left a pack-saddle frame and two pack-bags hanging on a tree.

20*th*.—Steering N.E. for five miles over fine grassy plains, came to a low stony range, ascending which we saw, a little to the south, a line of (colalya) white gums, to which we proceeded. Then following up a large brook for about five miles N.E., we camped at a small water-hole in the brook. In the afternoon I went with Pierre about one mile N.E. of camp to the summit of a rough range and watershed, which I believe is the easterly watershed of the Murchison River. All the creeks to the west of this range (which I named Kimberley

Range, after the Right Honourable Lord Kimberley, the Secretary of State for the Colonies) trend
towards the Murchison, and finally empty into the
main river. From this range we could see a long
way to the eastward. The country is very level,
with low ranges, but no conspicuous hills. Not
a promising country for water, but still looks
good feeding country. This range is composed
of brown hematite, decomposing to yellow (tertiary), and is very magnetic, the compass being
useless. Bituminous pitch found oozing out of the
rocks—probably the result of the decomposition
of the excrement of bats. It contains fragments
of the wing cases of insects, and gives reactions
similar to the bituminous mineral or substance
found in Victoria. Barometer 28·285; thermometer 63° at 5 p.m. On summit of watershed,
barometer 28·15; thermometer 69°; latitude 26°
17' 12", longitude about 119° 54' E.

21st.—Continued on N.E., and, travelling over
the watershed of the Murchison, we followed along
a gully running N.E.; then, passing some water-
holes, travelled on and ascended a small range,
from which we beheld a very extensive clear plain
just before us. Thinking it was a fine grassy plain
we quickly descended, when, to our disgust, we
found it was spinifex that had been burnt. We
continued till three o'clock, with nothing but
spinifex plains in sight. I despatched Windich
towards a range in the distance, and followed after

as quickly as possible.   When we reached the
range we heard the welcoming gunshot, and, continuing on, we met Tommy, who had found abundance of water and feed on some granite rocks.
We soon unloaded, and were all rejoiced to be in
safety, the prospect this afternoon having been anything but cheering.   Distance travelled about thirty
miles.   Barometer 28·22 ; thermometer 56° at 6
p.m.   Cold easterly wind all day.   About eighteen
miles of spinifex plains.   Latitude 26° 0′ 53″
by Arcturus and ε Boötis.

22nd.—Did not travel to-day, the horses being
tired, and the country ahead did not seem very
inviting.   Windich found a native spring about
a mile to the N.E.   This is a very nice spot, surrounded as it is by spinifex.   Variation 2° 40′ W.
by observation.

23rd.—Continued on N.E. for about twelve
miles over spinifex plains and sandy ridges.   Went
on ahead with Windich, and came to a gorge and
some granite rocks with abundance of water, and
were soon joined by the party. Barometer 28·30 ;
thermometer 60° at 6 p.m. ;   latitude 25° 53′ 52″
by Altair.

24th (Sunday).—We rested at camp.   I was
all day calculating lunar observations.   Barometer
28·22 ; thermometer 64° at 5.30 p.m.

25th.—Travelled onwards about N. 40° E. for
eight miles, passing a low granite range at six
miles.   Came to a fine brook trending a little

south of east, which we followed downwards seven
miles, running nearly east. This brook was full
of water, some of the pools being eight or ten feet
deep, ten yards wide, and sixty yards long. It
flowed out into a large flat, and finally runs into
a salt lake. I named this brook Sweeney Creek,
after my companion and farrier, James Sweeney.
Leaving the flat, we struck N.N.E. for four miles,
and came to a salt marsh about half a mile wide,
which we crossed. Following along, came into some
high ranges, which I named the Frere Ranges,
after Sir Bartle Frere, the distinguished President
of the Royal Geographical Society. Found a
small rock water-hole in a gully and camped.
Water appears exceedingly scarce in these ranges.
It is very remarkable that there should have been
such heavy rain twelve miles back, and none
at all here. Rough feed for horses. Distance
travelled about twenty-seven miles. These
ranges run east and west, and are the highest we
have seen. The marsh appears to follow along
the south side of the range. Barometer 28·38;
thermometer 70° at 5.30 p.m.; latitude 25° 43′
44″ by Arcturus.

26th.—Ascended the Frere Ranges and got a
fine view to the north and east. Fine high hills
and ranges to the north; a salt marsh and low
ranges to the east and S.E. Continued on N.E.
for four miles, then N.N.W. for three miles, passing
plenty of water in clay-holes and clay-pans in bed

of marsh, we camped at a fine pool in a large
brook that runs into the marsh, which I called Kennedy Creek, after my companion James Kennedy.
The prospect ahead is very cheering, and I hope
to find plenty of water and feed for the next 100
miles. Latitude 25° 38′ 44″ S. ; barometer 28·42 ;
thermometer 41° at 10 p.m. Marked a white gum-
tree $\frac{F}{40}$ close to camp in bed of river. The banks
of the brook at this spot are composed of purple-
brown slate (Silurian).

27th.—Followed up the Kennedy Creek, bearing
N.N.E. and N. for about seven miles, passing a
number of shallow pools, when we came to some
splendid springs, which I named the Windich
Springs, after my old and well-tried companion
Tommy Windich, who has now been on three exploring expeditions with me. They are the best
springs I have ever seen—flags in the bed of the
river, and pools twelve feet deep and twenty chains
long—a splendid place for water. We therefore
camped, and found another spot equally good a
quarter of a mile west of camp in another branch.
There is a most magnificent supply of water and
feed—almost unlimited and permanent. A fine
range of hills bore north-west from the springs,
which I named Carnarvon Range, after the Right
Honourable the present Secretary of State for the
Colonies. The hills looked very remarkable, being
covered with spinifex almost to their very summit.
We shot five ducks and got three opossums this

afternoon, besides doing some shoeing. There is an immense clump of white gums at head of spring. Barometer 28·34; thermometer 46° at 11 p.m. Marked a large white gum-tree $\frac{F}{41}$ on west side close to right bank of river, being our 41st camp from Geraldton. Latitude 25° 22′ 26″ S., longitude about 120° 42′ E.

28th.—Steering N. 30° E. for eleven miles, we came to a rough hill, which I ascended, camped on north side of it, and found water in a gully. The view was very extensive but not promising —spinifex being in every direction. A bold hill bore N. 31° E. mag., about seven miles distant to the N.N.W., which I named Mount Salvado, after Bishop Salvado, of Victoria Plains, a contributor to the Expedition Fund The Carnarvon Ranges looked very remarkable. To the E. and N.E. spinifex and low ranges for fifteen miles, when the view was intercepted by spinifex rises—altogether very unpromising. Barometer 28·26; thermometer 70° at 5 p.m; latitude 25° 24 11″ S.

29th.—Steered E.N.E. for seven miles, when we came to some fine water in a gully, which we did not camp at, owing to my being ahead with Windich, and my brother not seeing a note I left telling him to remain there while I went on to get a view ahead. Passing this at ten miles, we reached a low spinifex hill capped with rock, from which a remarkable hill was visible, which I named Mount

Davis, after my friend Mr. J. S. Davis, who was
a contributor to the Expedition Fund. Mount
Salvado was also visible. Spinifex in every direction, and the country very miserable and unpromising. I went ahead with Windich. Steering
about N. 15° E. for about eight miles over spinifex
sand-hills, we found a spring in a small flat, which
I named Pierre Spring, after my companion
Tommy Pierre. It was surrounded by the most
miserable spinifex country, and is quite a diamond
in the desert. We cleared it out and got sufficient water for our horses. To the N., S., and E.
nothing but spinifex sand-hills in sight. Barometer
28·44; thermometer 70° at 5 p.m. ; latitude 25°
14′ 34″ S. by Altair.

30*th*.—Steering E.N.E. over spinifex red sand-
hills for nine miles, we came to a valley and followed down a gully running N.N.E. for two miles,
when it lost itself on the flat, which was wooded
and grassy. About a mile farther on we found a
clay-pan with water, and camped, with excellent
feed. The country is very dry, and I should think
there has not been any rain for several months.
The appearance of the country ahead is better
than it looked yesterday. I went onwards with
Windich to-day, and found the water. Barometer
28·46; thermometer 66° at 5.30 p.m.; latitude
25° 10′ 32″.

31*st* (*Sunday*).—Rested at camp. Took observations for time. Left two pack-saddle bags
hanging on a tree.

June 1st.—Barometer 28·38; thermometer 45° at 8 a.m. In collecting the horses we came on an old native camp, and found the skull of a native, much charred, evidently the remains of one who had been eaten. Continued on about N.E. along a grassy flat, and at five miles passed some clay-pans of water, after which we encountered spinifex, which continued for fifteen miles, when we got to a rocky range, covered with more spinifex. Myself and Windich were in advance, and after reaching the range we followed down a flat about N. for six miles, when it joined another large water-course, both trending N.N.W. and N.W. We followed down this river for about seven miles, in hopes of finding water, without success. Night was fast approaching, and I struck north for four miles to a range, on reaching which the prospect was very poor; it proved to be a succession of spinifex sand-hills, and no better country was in view to the N.E. and E. It was just sundown when we reached the range; we then turned east for two miles, and south, following along all the gul-lies we came across, but could find no water. It was full moon, so that we could see clearly. We turned more to the westward and struck our out-ward tracks, and, following back along them, we met the party encamped at the junction of the two branches mentioned before. We kept watch over the horses to keep them from straying. Mine and Windich's horses were nearly knocked up, and Windich himself was very ill all night.   Latitude 24° 55′ 19″ S.

2nd.—Early this morning went with Pierre to look for water, while my brother and Windich went on the same errand.   We followed up the brook about south for seven miles, when we left it and followed another branch about S.S.E., ascending which, Pierre drew my attention to swarms of birds, parroquets, &c., about half a mile ahead. We hastened on, and to our delight found one of the best springs in the colony.   It ran down the gully for twenty chains, and is as clear and fresh as possible, while the supply is unlimited.   Overjoyed at our good fortune, we hastened back, and, finding that my brother and Windich had not returned, packed up and shifted over to the springs, leaving a note telling them the good news.   After reaching the springs we were soon joined by them. They had only found sufficient water to give their own horses a drink; they also rejoiced to find so fine a spot.   Named the springs the Weld Springs, after his Excellency Governor Weld, who has always taken such great interest in exploration, and without whose influence and assistance this expedition would not have been organized.   There is splendid feed all around. I intend giving the horses a week's rest here, as they are much in want of it, and are getting very poor and tired.   Barometer 28·24; thermometer 71° at 5 p.m.   Shot a kangaroo.

3rd.—Rested at Weld Springs. Light rain this morning. The horses doing well, and will improve very fast. Towards evening the weather cleared, which I was sorry for, as good rains are what we are much in need of. Did some shoeing. Barometer 28·13; thermometer 61° at 5 p.m.

4th.—Barometer 28·16; thermometer 53° at 8 a.m. Rested at Weld Springs. Shod some of the horses. Repairing saddles. Rating chronometer. Windich shot an emu. Horses doing first-rate, and fast improving.

5th.—Barometer 28·28; thermometer 53° at 6 p.m. Rested at Weld Springs. Shoeing and saddle-stuffing. Ten emus came to water; shot twice with rifle at them, but missed. Rated chronometer.

6th.—Rested at Weld Springs. Took three sets of lunars. Pierre shot a kangaroo. Marked a tree $\frac{F}{46}$ on the east side of the spring at our bivouac, which is in latitude 25° 0' 46" S., longitude about 121° 21' E. Mended saddles. Horses much improved, and some of them getting very fresh.

7th (Sunday).—Pierre shot an emu, and the others shot several pigeons. This is a splendid spot; emus and kangaroos numerous, pigeons and birds innumerable, literally covering the entire surface all round the place in the evenings. We have been living on game ever since we have been here. Intend taking a flying trip to-morrow; party to follow on our tracks on Tuesday. Read

Divine Service.   Barometer 28·38 ; thermometer
55° at 7 p.m.

8th.—Started with Tommy Pierre to explore
the country E.N.E. for water, leaving instructions
for my brother to follow after us to-morrow with
the party.   We travelled generally E.N.E. for
twenty miles over spinifex and undulating sand-
hills, without seeing any water.   We turned east for
ten miles to a range, which we found to be covered
with spinifex.   Everywhere nothing else was to
be seen ; no feed, destitute of water ; while a
few small gullies ran out of the low range, but all
were dry.   Another range about twenty-four miles
distant was the extent of our view, to which we
bore. At twenty miles, over red sandy hills covered
with spinifex and of the most miserable nature,
we came to a narrow samphire flat, following which
south for two miles, we camped without water and
scarcely any feed.   Our horses were knocked up,
having come over heavy ground more than fifty
miles.   The whole of the country passed over
to-day is covered with spinifex, and is a barren
worthless desert.

9th.—At daybreak continued east about four
miles to the range seen yesterday, which we found
to be a low stony rise, covered with spinifex. The
view was extensive and very gloomy.   Far to the
north and east, spinifex country, level, and no
appearance of hills or water-courses.   To the
south were seen a few low ranges, covered also

with spinifex; in fact, nothing but spinifex in sight, and no chance of water. Therefore I was obliged to turn back, as our horses were done up. Travelling south for five miles, we then turned W.N.W. until we caught our outward tracks, and, following them, we met the party at 3 o'clock, coming on, about twenty miles from the Weld Springs. Our horses were completely done up. We had not had water for thirty-one hours. We all turned back, retreating towards the springs, and continued on till 10 o'clock, when we camped in the spinifex and tied up the horses.

10*th.*—We travelled on to the springs, which were only about three miles from where we slept last night, and camped. I intend staying here for some time, until I find water ahead or we get some rain. We are very fortunate in having such a good depôt, as the feed is very good. We found that about a dozen natives had been to the springs while we were away. They had collected some of the emu feathers, which were lying all about. Natives appear to be very numerous, and I have no doubt that there are springs in the spinifex or valleys close to it. Barometer 28·08; thermometer 62° at 5.30 p.m.

11*th.*—Rested at the Weld Springs. Shot an emu; about a dozen came to water. My brother and Windich intend going a flying trip E.S.E. in search of water to-morrow. Barometer 28·15; thermometer 60° at 5 p.m.

12*th*.—My brother and Windich started in search of water; myself and Pierre accompanied them about twelve miles with water to give their horses a drink. About ten o'clock we left them and returned to camp.

13*th*.—About one o'clock Pierre saw a flock of emus coming to water, and went off to get a shot. Kennedy followed with the rifle. I climbed up on a small tree to watch them. I was surprised to hear natives' voices, and, looking towards the hill, I saw from forty to sixty natives running towards the camp, all plumed up and armed with spears and shields. I was cool, and told Sweeney to bring out the revolvers; descended from the tree and got my gun and coo-eyed to Pierre and Kennedy, who came running. By this time they were within sixty yards, and halted. One advanced to meet me and stood twenty yards off; I made friendly signs; he did not appear very hostile. All at once one from behind (probably a chief) came rushing forward, and made many feints to throw spears. He went through many manœuvres, and gave a signal, when the whole number made a rush towards us, yelling and shouting, with their spears shipped. When within thirty yards I gave the word to fire: we all fired as one man, only one report being heard. I think the natives got a few shots, but they all ran up the hill and there stood, talking and haranguing and appearing very angry. We re-loaded our guns,

ATTACKED BY THE NATIVES AT WELD SPRINGS.

and got everything ready for a second attack, which I was sure they would make. We were not long left in suspense. They all descended from the hill and came on slowly towards us. When they were about 150 yards off I fired my rifle, and we saw one of them fall, but he got up again and was assisted away. On examining the spot we found the ball had cut in two the two spears he was carrying; he also dropped his wommera, which was covered with blood. We could follow the blood-drops for a long way over the stones. I am afraid he got a severe wound. My brother and Windich being away we were short-handed. The natives seem determined to take our lives, and therefore I shall not hesitate to fire on them should they attack us again. I thus decide and write in all humility, considering it a necessity, as the only way of saving our lives. I write this at 4 p.m., just after the occurrence, so that, should anything happen to us, my brother will know how and when it occurred.—5 p.m. The natives appear to have made off. We intend sleeping in the thicket close to camp, and keeping a strict watch, so as to be ready for them should they return to the attack this evening. At 7.30 my brother and Windich returned, and were surprised to hear of our adventure. They had been over fifty miles from camp E.S.E., and had passed over some good feeding country, but had not found a drop of water. They and their horses had been over thirty hours without water.

14*th* (*Sunday*).—The natives did not return to the attack last night. In looking round camp we found the traces of blood, where one of the natives had been lying down. This must have been the foremost man, who was in the act of throwing his spear, and who urged the others on. Two therefore, at least, are wounded, and will have cause to remember the time they made their murderous attack upon us. We worked all day putting up a stone hut, ten by nine feet, and seven feet high, thatched with boughs. We finished it; it will make us safe at night. Being a very fair hut, it will be a great source of defence. Barometer 28·09; thermometer 68° at 5 p.m. Hope to have rain, as without it we cannot proceed.

15*th*.—Finished the hut, pugging it at the ends, and making the roof better. Now it is in good order, and we are quite safe from attack at night, should they attempt it again, which I think is doubtful, as they got too warm a reception last time. I intend going with Windich to-morrow easterly in search of water. Barometer 29·09 at 5 p.m.; thermometer 62°.

16*th*.— Left the Weld Springs with Windich and a pack-horse carrying fourteen gallons of water. Steered S.E. for twelve miles over spinifex, after which we got into a grassy ravine, which we followed along three miles, passing some fine clay-holes which would hold plenty of water if it rained. We then turned E.N.E. for twelve miles over spinifex, miserable country, when we struck the tracks of my brother and Windich on their return, June 13th. We followed along them S.E. for four miles, and then S.E. to a bluff range about eighteen miles, which we reached at sundown. Spinifex generally, a few grassy patches intervening, on which were numbers of kangaroos. We camped close to the bluff, and gave the horses one gallon of water each out of the cans. Just when the pannicans were boiled, heard noises which we thought were natives shouting. We instantly put out the fire and had our supper in the dark, keeping a sharp look-out for two hours, when we were convinced it must have been a native dog, as there were hundreds all round us, barking and howling. The weather is heavy and cloudy, and I hope to get some rain shortly. We slept without any fire, but it was not very cold.

17*th.*—As the horses did not ramble far, we got off early and followed along and through the ranges E.S.E. about, the distance being eighteen miles. Passed some splendid clay-pans quite dry. The flats around the ranges are very grassy, and look promising eastwards, but we cannot find any water. Kangaroos and birds are numerous. Being about seventy miles from camp, we cannot go any farther, or our horses will not carry us back. We therefore turned, keeping to the south of our outward track, and at about eleven miles found some water in some clay-holes, and camped at

about 3 o'clock in the afternoon. There is sufficient water to last the party about a week, but not
more. The weather is dark and threatening, and
I believe there will be rain to-night, which will be a
great boon, and will enable us to travel along
easily. It is in circumstances such as I am at
present placed that we are sure to implore help
and assistance from the hand of the Creator; but
when we have received all we desire, how often we
forget to give Him praise!

18th.—Rained lightly last night, and we had a
nice shower this morning. Yet did not get very
wet, as we had our waterproofs. Fearing that
the rain would obliterate the tracks and the party
be unable to follow them, I decided to return
towards Weld Springs. Therefore followed
along our outward track, but found, to our
sorrow, that there had been no rain west of our
last night's camp. We pushed along and got
within eighteen miles of Weld Springs and camped
without water, having left the cans behind, thinking we should find plenty cf rain-water.

19th.—We had to go about two miles for our
horses this morning; after which, we made all
haste towards Weld Springs, as I knew the party
would be coming on along our tracks to-day.
When we were within six miles of the spring we
met the party, but, being obliged to take our
horses to water, I decided that all should return
and make a fresh start to-morrow. The natives

had not returned to the attack during our absence, so I conclude they do not intend to interfere with us further. On our way to-day we passed some fine rock holes, but all were quite dry. Rain is very much required in this country.

20th.—Started at 9.30 a.m., and steering S.E. towards the water found on the 17th for twenty-four miles; thence E.S.E. for eight miles, and camped without water on a small patch of feed. The last ten miles was over clear spinifex country of the most wretched description. The country all the way, in fact, is most miserable and intolerable. Barometer 28·50; thermometer 56° at 8 p.m.; latitude 25° 13′ 36″ S. by meridian altitude of Arcturus. Left the rum-keg and a pair of farriers pincers in the stone hut at Weld Springs.

21st (Sunday).—Got an early start, and continued on E.S.E. At about three miles reached a spring on a small patch of feed in the spinifex and camped, but found, after digging it out, that scarcely any water came in. I have no doubt that it will fill up a good deal in the night; but, our horses being thirsty, I re-saddled and pushed on to the water about sixteen miles ahead, which we reached at 4 p.m. There is not more than a week's supply here, therefore I intend going ahead with Pierre to-morrow in search of more. The country ahead seems promising, but there is a great deal of spinifex almost everywhere. From Weld Spring to our present camp is all spinifex,

o

with the exception of a few flats along short
gullies. Latitude 25° 22′ 50″ S., longitude about
121° 57′ E. Barometer 28·50 ; thermometer 62°
at 5 p.m.

22nd.—Left camp in company with Tommy
Pierre, with a pack-horse carrying fifteen gallons
of water. Steered S.E. for four miles, then east
for about eight miles over fine grassy country,
then S.E. towards a high range about twenty-five
miles distant. After going about three miles,
struck a flat trending S.S.E., which we followed
down about four miles, passing two small clay-
holes with water in them ; then we struck S.E.
for four miles, and came to a large brook
trending S.E., which we followed along until it
lost itself on the plain about six miles. Fine
grassy country all the way, and game abundant.
There were a few gallons of water here and there
in the brook, but none large enough to camp at.
I then turned east, and at about seven miles
reached the hill seen this morning, which I named
Mount Moore, after Mr. W. D. Moore, of Fremantle, a subscriber to the Expedition Fund.
Ascending the hill we had an extensive view
to the S.W., S., and S.E. Fine grassy country
all round and very little spinifex. To the south
about nine miles we saw a lake, and farther off a
remarkable red-faced range, which I named Timperley Range, after my friend Mr. W. H. Timperley,
Inspector of Police, from whom I received a great

deal of assistance before leaving Champion Bay.
A remarkable peak, with a reddish top, bore
S.S.E., which I named Mount Hosken, after
Mr. M. Hosken, of Geraldton, a contributor to
the expedition. I made south towards the lake,
and at one mile and a half came on to a gully in
the grassy plain, in which we found abundance of
water, sufficient to last for months. We therefore
camped for the night, with beautiful feed for the
horses. I was very thankful to find so much
water and such fine grassy country, for, if we had
not found any this trip, we should have been
obliged to retreat towards Weld Springs, the
water where I left the party being only sufficient
to last a few days. The country passed over to-
day was very grassy, with only a little spinifex, and
it looks promising ahead. Distance from camp
about thirty-five miles.

23rd.—Steering south for about eight miles, we
reached the lake, which I named Lake Augusta.
The water is salt, and about five miles in circum-
ference. Grassy country in the flat; red sand-hills
along the shore. It appeared deep, and swarmed
with ducks and swans. Pierre shot two ducks,
after which we pushed on N.E. for about twelve
miles to a low rocky bluff, which we ascended and
got a view of the country ahead—rough broken
ranges to the east and south. We continued on
east for six miles, when, on approaching a rocky
face of a range, we saw some natives on top of it,

watching us. Approaching nearer, we heard them haranguing and shouting, and soon afterward came within . thirty yards of one who was stooping down, looking intently and amazedly at us. I made friendly signs, but he ran off shouting, and apparently much afraid. He and several others ran up and joined the natives on the cliff summit, and then all made off. We turned, and steering E.N.E. for six miles, and then east for about fourteen miles, the last few miles being miserable spinifex country, we camped, with poor feed, amongst some spinifex ranges. A good deal of grassy country the first part of the day. Kangaroos very numerous, and emus also. Evidences of the natives being in great numbers.

24th.—Ascended a red-topped peak close to our bivouac and got a view ahead. A salt lake was visible a few miles to the east, towards which we proceeded. Passing along samphire flats and over red sand-hills, we got within a mile of the lake. The country close to it not looking promising, I determined to turn our faces westward towards the party. Steering a little south of west for three miles, we struck a large brook trending N.E. into the lake, and, following it up a mile, found a fine pool of fresh water, with splendid feed. This is very fortunate, as it is a good place to bring the party to. Elated with our success, we continued on westerly, passing some fine rock water-holes, half full of water, and at twenty miles from the pool we found a springy hole, with plenty of water in it, within a few hundred yards of our outward track. We had missed it going out; it is in the centre of a very fine grassy plain. Kangaroos and emus numerous, also natives. Giving the horses water, we pushed on for twelve miles and camped on some fine grassy flats. Every appearance of rain.

25th.—Having finished all our rations last night, I shot two kangaroos while out for the horses, and brought the hind quarters with us. Continuing westerly for about ten miles, we reached the water, our bivouac on the 22nd. I awaited the arrival of the party, which should reach here this morning. At two o'clock heard gunshots, and saw my brother and Windich walking towards us. Found that they had missed our tracks and were camped about a mile higher up the gully, at some small clay-holes. We got our horses and accompanied them back. Rained this evening more than we have had before. Very cloudy. Barometer 28·18, but inclined to rise. Everything had gone on well during my absence.

26th.—Did not travel to-day, as there was good feed and water at this camp. My brother, Windich, and Pierre rode over to Lake Augusta to get some shooting, and returned in the afternoon with a swan and two ducks. On their way out they saw a native and gave him chase. He climbed up a small tree, and, although Windich

expended all his knowledge of the languages of
Australia to get him to talk, he would not open
his lips, but remained silent; they therefore left
him to get down from the tree at his leisure.
Re-stuffed some of the pack-saddles. Marked a
tree $^F_{50}$, being our 50th camp from Geraldton.
Barometer 28·40; thermometer 50° at 6 p.m. ;
weather cleared off and fine night. Latitude
25° 37′ 38″ S. ; longitude about 122° 22′ E.

27th.—Erected a cairn of stones on S.E. point
of Mount Moore, after which continued on and
reached the spring found by me on the 24th; distance fifteen miles. The last six miles poor
spinifex country. Fine and grassy round spring.
Barometer 28·54; thermometer 56° at 7 p.m.;
latitude 25° 37′ 53″ by Arcturus. Marked a
tree $^F_{51}$, being the 51st camp from Geraldton.

28th (Sunday).—Rested at spring. Found the
variations to be 1° 52′ W. by azimuths.

29th.—Reached the pool found by me on
the 24th; distance seventeen miles. Latitude
25° 41′ 22″ S. ; longitude about 122° 53′ E.
Splendid feed round camp. Marked a tree $^F_{52}$,
being the 52nd from Geraldton. About two miles
west of camp I ascended a remarkable hill and
took a round of bearings, naming it Mount Bates,
after the Secretary of the Royal Geographical
Society.

30th.—Left camp $^F_{52}$ in company with Tommy
Windich, taking one pack-horse, to find water

ahead eastward. Steered E.N.E. over salt marshes and spinifex sand-hills, and at about eleven miles found water in some clay-pans, and left a note telling my brother to camp here to-morrow night. Continued on and found several more fine water-pans and fine grassy patches. Ascended a range to get a view ahead. In every direction spinifex, more especially to the north; to the east some low ranges were visible, about twenty miles distant, towards which we proceeded. On our way we surprised an emu on its nest and found several eggs; we buried four with a note stuck over them, for the party to get when they came along, and took three with us. Soon after this the horse Windich was riding (Mission) gave in, and we had great difficulty in getting him along. I was much surprised at this, for I considered him the best horse we had. We reached the range and found water in some of the gorges, but no feed; spinifex everywhere. We continued on till dark, passing some natives' fire, which we did not approach,—then camped with scarcely any feed. I hope to have better luck to-morrow. We have found plenty of water, but no feed; this is better than having no water and plenty of feed. We had one wurrung, four chockalocks, and three emu eggs, besides bread and bacon, for tea to-night, so we fared sumptuously.

July 1st.—Got off early and continued easterly

to a low stony range three miles off, over spinifex sandy country. Found a rock water-hole and gave our horses a drink. Continuing about east to other ranges, which we followed along and through, and from range to range, spinifex inter-vening everywhere, and no feed, a few little drops of water in the gullies, but not sufficient for the party to camp at. When we had travelled about fifteen miles, we turned north for three miles, and again east, through and over some ranges. No feed and scarcely any water. Saw a range about twenty-five miles farther east—spinifex all the way to it. Mission being again knocked up, although carrying only a few pounds, we camped about three o'clock at a small hole of water in a gully—only large enough to serve the party one night—the first to-day that would even do that. The last forty miles was over the most wretched country I have ever seen; not a bit of grass, and no water, except after rain; spinifex everywhere. We are very fortunate to have a little rain-water, or we could not get ahead.

2nd.—Steered towards the range seen yester-day a little south of east, and, after going twelve miles, my horse completely gave in, Mission doing the same also. I had hard work to get them along, and at last they would not walk. I gave them a rest and then drove them before me, fol-lowing Windich till we reached the range. Found a little water in a gully, but no feed. Spinifex all

ON THE MARCH.—THE SPIN'FEX DESERT.

the way to-day; most wretched country. We ascended the range, and the country ahead looks first-rate; high ranges to the N.E., and apparently not so much spinifex. We continued N.E., and after going four miles camped on a patch of feed, the first seen for the last sixty miles. I was very tired, having walked nearly twenty miles, and having to drive two knocked-up horses. I have good hopes of getting both feed and water to-morrow, for, if we do not, we shall be in a very awkward position.

3rd.—Soon after starting, found a little water in a gully and gave our horses a drink. Ascended a spur of the range and had a good view ahead, and was very pleased with the prospect. Steering N.E. towards a large range about fifteen miles off, we found a great deal of spinifex, although the country generally was thickly wooded. I rode Mission, who went along pretty well for about twelve miles, when Williams gave in again, and Mission soon did the same. For the next six miles to the range we had awful work, but managed, with leading and driving, to reach the range; spinifex all the way, and also on the top of it. I was very nearly knocked up myself, but ascended the range and had a very extensive view. Far to the north and east the horizon was as level and uniform as that of the sea; apparently spinifex everywhere; no hills or ranges could be seen for a distance of quite thirty miles. The prospect was very cheerless and disheartening. Windich went on the only horse not knocked up, in order to find water for the horses. I followed after his tracks, leading the two poor done-up horses. With difficulty I could get them to walk. Over and through the rough range I managed to pull them along, and found sufficient water to give them a good drink, and camped on a small patch of rough grass in one of the gorges. Spinifex everywhere; it is a most fearful country. We cannot proceed farther in this direction, and must return and meet the party, which I hope to do to-morrow night. We can only crawl along, having to walk and lead the horses, or at least drag them. The party have been following us, only getting a little water from gullies, and there is very little to fall back on for over fifty miles. I will leave what I intend doing until I meet them. I am nearly knocked up again to-night; my boots have hurt my feet, but I am not yet disheartened.

4th.—We travelled back towards the party, keeping a little to the west of our outward track; and after going five miles found some water in clay-holes, sufficient to last the party about one night. Two of our horses being knocked up, I made up my mind to let the party meet us here, although I scarcely know what to do when they do arrive. To go forward looks very unpromising, and to retreat we have quite seventy miles with scarcely any water and no feed at all. The prospect is very cheerless, and what I shall do depends on the state of the horses, when they reach here. It is very discouraging to have to retreat, as Mr. Gosse's farthest point west is only 200 miles from us. We finished all our rations this morning, and we have been hunting for game ever since twelve o'clock, and managed to get a wurrung and an opossum, the only living creatures seen, and which Windich was fortunate to capture.

5th (*Sunday*).—Early this morning Windich and I went in search of more water. Having nothing to eat, it did not take us long to have a little drink of water for our breakfast. Went a few miles to the N.W. and looked all round, but only found a small rock water-hole. Windich got an opossum out of a tree. We returned about twelve o'clock and then ate the opossum. At about one o'clock we saddled up and made back towards the party, which I thought should have arrived by this time. When about two miles we met them coming on; they had been obliged to leave two horses on the way, knocked up, one named Fame, about twenty-four miles away, and Little Padbury about eight miles back; all the others were in pretty good trim, although very hungry and tired. We returned to the little water, which they soon finished. I was glad to meet the party again, although we were in a bad position. Intend returning to-morrow to the range left by the party this morning, where there is enough water for half a day, and search that range more thoroughly. The horses will have a good night's feed and I have every confidence that, if the worst comes, we shall be able to retreat to a place of safety. Found my brother in good spirits. We soon felt quite happy and viewed the future hopefully. I was sorry to lose the horses, but we cannot expect to get on through such a country without some giving in. The country is so dry; the season altogether dry, otherwise we could go ahead easily. A good shower of rain is what is required. It has been very warm the last three days, and I hope much for a change. Read Divine Service. Latitude 25° 31′ 45″ S., longitude about 124° 17′ E. Barometer 28·62 at 4 p.m.

6th.—Retreated back to the water left by the party in the range fourteen miles S.W. At one mile we gave the horses as much water as they required from some rock holes. After reaching the water and having dinner, Pierre and myself, and my brother and Windich, started off on foot to examine the range for water, but could find only a few gallons. I think there will be sufficient water to last us here to-morrow, and we will give the country a good searching. If we fail, there must be a retreat westwards at least seventy miles. Barometer 28·53 ; thermometer 64° at 5 p.m.

7th.—Early this morning Pierre and I and my brother and Windich started off in search of water,

as there was scarcely any left at camp. Unless
we are fortunate enough to find some, retreat is in-
evitable. Pierre and myself searched the range
we were camped in, while Windich and my brother
went further south towards another range. We
searched all round and over the rough ranges
without success, and reached camp at one o'clock.
To our relief and joy learnt that my brother and
Windich had found water about five miles S.S.E.,
sufficient to last two or three weeks. This was
good news; so after dinner we packed up and
went over to the water. The feed was not very
good, but I am truly thankful to have found it, as
a retreat of seventy miles over most wretched
country was anything but cheering. Barometer
28·52; thermometer 70° at 5 p.m.; latitude 25°
43′ 8″ by Arcturus.

8th.—Rested at camp. Devoted the day to
taking sets of lunar observations. There is very
little feed about this water, and to-morrow my
brother and Pierre go on a flying trip ahead. It
is very warm to-day, and has been for the last
week. Barometer 28·59; thermometer 79° at 5
p.m.

9th.—Very cloudy this morning, although the
barometer is rising. My brother and Pierre
started on the flying trip; intend following on their
tracks on Saturday. Could not take another set
of lunars on account of the cloudy weather. Was
very busy all day repairing pack-saddles and put-

ting everything in good order. Did away with
one pack-saddle, and repaired the others with the
wool. Shall leave here with twelve pack-horses,
and three running loose and two riding, besides
the two that are on flying trip. Barometer 28·59 ;
thermometer 69° at 5 p.m.

10th.—Finished repairs and got everything
ready for a good start to-morrow morning, when
we will follow my brother's and Pierre's tracks.
Cloudy day, but barometer does not fall. Marked
a tree $\frac{F}{59}$, being our 59th bivouac from Geraldton. Hung up on the same tree four pack-bags
and one pack-saddle frame. Barometer 28·56 ;
thermometer 74° at 5 p.m. Tommy Windich
shot a red kangaroo this afternoon, and also
found a fine rock water-hole about one mile N.E.
of camp.

11th.—Followed on the tracks of my brother
and Pierre, south seven miles to a rough broken
range — spinifex and rough grass all the way.
Thence we turned S.E. for three miles ; then N.E.
and E. over most wretched spinifex plains for nine
miles, when we got on to a narrow grassy flat, and,
following it along about four miles, came to some
water in a clay-pan, sufficient for the night, and
camped. With the exception of this narrow flat
the country passed over to-day is most miserable
and worthless, and very dusty. Another hot day.
Barometer 28·70 ; thermometer 67° at 5 p.m ; latitude 25° 52' 30" S.

12*th* (*Sunday*).—Our horses finished all the water. We got off early, and, steering east, followed my brother's and Pierre's tracks for eight miles, when we reached a low rise, and a fine rock water-hole holding over a hundred gallons of water. While we were watering our horses we heard gunshots, and soon beheld my brother and Pierre returning. They had good news for us, having found some springs about twenty-five miles to the eastward. They had seen many natives; but for an account of their proceedings I insert a copy of his journal. Barometer 28·60 ; thermometer 60°. We camped for the day. Latitude 25° 53′ 23″ S. Read Divine Service.

A. FORREST'S JOURNAL.

July 10*th*.—Steered east from the rock hole for the first fifteen miles, over clear open sand-plains and red sand-hills covered with spinifex ; then S.S.E. for ten miles over similar country to a rough range ; after going nearly all round it only found about one gallon of water. As my horse was very tired, I almost gave up all hopes of finding any, as it would take us all our time to get back ; however, I went S.E. for seven miles further, and found about fifty gallons in a rock hole, but not a blade of grass near it. As it was nearly dark, and no feed near, I bore south for a low range about five miles distant, and found a little feed but no water, and camped. My horse completely gave in ; I had great difficulty in getting him to the range.

11*th*.—Again bore west on our return to meet the party. After going seven miles we saw a beautiful piece of feeding country—the first we had seen for the last 130 miles—and after looking for water, and our fondest hopes beginning to fail, we at last followed what seemed to be the largest gully to its head, when we were gratified in beholding abundance of water, with several springs, and good feed in the flats below. My horse was completely knocked up, and I was glad to be able to give him a rest. After being an hour here, Pierre, who is always on the look-out, saw two natives, fully armed and in war costume, making for us. I was soon on my legs and made towards them, but as soon as they saw us they began to move off, and were soon out of sight in the thicket. At two o'clock continued on W.N.W. for twelve miles, camped in a thicket, and, after taking off our saddles and making a fire, were very much surprised to find a party of eight or nine natives going to camp close to us, and a number more coming down the hill. As it was just dark we thought it best to move on a few miles, which we did after dark. I believe, myself, they intend attacking us after dark.   A. FORREST.

13*th*.—Steering straight for the water found by my brother, about E.S.E. for twenty-five miles, over most miserable spinifex country, without a break. Just before we got to the water Windich shot an emu. We saw two natives, who made off. Many fires in every direction. Latitude 26° 5′ 10″ S., longitude about 124° 46′ E. Fine water at this place. I have no doubt water is always here. I named it the Alexander Spring, after my brother, who discovered it. Abundance of water also in rock holes.

14*th*.—Rested at Alexander Spring. Eating emu was our chief occupation to-day, I think. Weather cloudy. Barometer 28·75; thermometer 60° at 5 p.m.

15*th*.—Rested at Alexander Spring. Went for

a walk to a flat-topped hill about S.S.E. 50 chains
from camp, which I have since named Mount
Allott, and placed a cairn on it; another hill close
by I named Mount Worsnop, after respectively
the Mayor and Town Clerk of Adelaide. Found
two natives' graves close to camp; they were
apparently about two feet deep, and covered with
boughs and wood; they are the first I have ever
seen in all my travels to the eastward in Australia,
and Windich says he has never come across one
before either. We also found about a dozen
pieces of wood, some six feet long and three to
seven inches wide, and carved and trimmed up.
All around were stones put up in the forked trees.
I believe it is the place where the rite of circum-
cision is performed. Barometer 28·84; thermometer 60° at 5 p.m.

16th.—Left Alexander Spring, in company with
Windich, to look for water ahead. Steered east for
twelve miles, over spinifex sand-hills with some
salt-marsh flats intervening. We then turned
S.E. for seven miles to some cliffs, and followed
them along east about one mile and a half, when
we saw a clear patch a little to the N.E., on reaching which we found a fine rock water-hole holding
over 100 gallons of water. We had a pannican
of tea, and gave our horses an hour and a half's
rest. Left a note for my brother, advising him to
camp here the first night. We continued on a
little to the south of east for about fifteen miles

over spinifex plains, when we camped on a small patch of feed. Saw a fire about three quarters of a mile south of our camp, and supposed that natives were camped there.

17*th*.—Early this morning we proceeded to where we saw the fire last night, but could not find any natives : it must have been some spinifex burning. We continued about east for two miles ; found a rock water-hole holding about fifty gallons, and had breakfast. After this, continued on a little south of east for twelve miles, when we turned more to the north, searching every spinifex rise that had a rocky face, first N. and then N.W. and W., all over the country, but not over any great extent, as my horse (Brick) was knocked up. About one o'clock we found enough to give the horses a drink, and to make some tea for ourselves. We saw some low cliffs to the north, and proceeding towards them we saw ahead about N.N.E. a remarkable high cliff. I therefore decided to make for it. I had to walk and drive my horse before me, and before we reached the cliff we had hard work to get him to move. When we got close we were rejoiced to see cliffs and gorges without end, and descending the first hollow found a fine rock hole containing at least 250 gallons. We therefore camped, as it was just sundown. I am very sanguine of finding more water to-morrow, as our horses will soon finish this hole. There was very little feed about the water.

18*th*.—This morning we began searching the ranges for water. First tried westerly, and searched some fine gullies and gorges, but without success. My horse soon gave in again, and I left him on a patch of feed and continued the search on foot. I had not walked a quarter of a mile before I found about 200 gallons in a gully, and, following down the gully, we found a fine pool in a sandy bed, enough to last a month. We were rejoiced at our good fortune, and, returning to where we left the horse, camped for the remainder of the day. There is not much feed anywhere about these cliffs and gullies, but as long as there is plenty of water the horses will do very well. To-morrow I intend going back to meet the party, as the way we came was very crooked, and I hope to save them many miles. It is certainly a wretched country we have been travelling through for the last two months, and, what makes it worse, the season is an exceptionally dry one; it is quite summer weather. However, we are now within 100 miles of Mr. Gosse's farthest west, and I hope soon to see a change for the better. We have been most fortunate in finding water, and I am indeed very thankful for it.

19*th* (*Sunday*).—Started back to meet the party, leaving old Brick hobbled, and my saddle, rug, &c., hidden in a tree. After travelling about twenty miles, met the party coming all right. Everything had gone on well during my absence.

They had slept last night at the rock hole, where
we stayed on the 16th, and found sufficient
water for the horses in it. The note I left
had been taken away by the natives, who were
very numerous about there. Many tracks were
seen, following mine and Windich's for several
miles. The party had not, however, seen any of
them. They were rejoiced to hear of the water
ahead, and we steered for it, keeping to the west
of our return route to search some cliffs on the
way for water. After travelling nine miles we
camped without water, on a grassy flat close to
some cliffs; most miserable spinifex country all
day; this is the first grass seen. Walked over
twenty miles to-day myself.

20th.—Steered N.E. straight for the water found
on the 18th for fourteen miles; reached it and
camped. Found the horse Brick I left behind,
and saddle, rug, &c., as we left them. Horses
were very thirsty, but there is plenty of water for
them. Feed is rather scarce. I named this creek
and pool after the Honourable Arthur Blyth, Chief
Secretary of South Australia.

21st.—Rested at camp. I took observations
for time, intending to take several sets of lunars,
but the day was cloudy, and I only managed to
get one. Intend going ahead to-morrow in search
of water.

22nd.—Started in company with Pierre to look
for water ahead, steered a little north of east for

about twelve miles to the points of the cliffs, and
ascended a peak to get a view ahead. The line of
cliff country ran N.E., and to the east, spinifex
undulating country; nevertheless, as I wished to
get a view of some of the hills shown on Mr.
Gosse's map, I bore E. and E.S.E. for over thirty
miles, but could not find a drop of water all day,
and we had come nearly fifty miles. Camped on
a small patch of feed. Very undulating spinifex
country, and no place that would hold water, even
after rain, for more than a day or two.

23rd.—Decided not to go any further, although
I much wished to get a view further to the east,
but our horses would have enough to do to carry
us back. Steered north for a few miles, and then
N.W. for twenty miles, thence W.S.W. to camp,
which we reached after dark, not having had any
water for ourselves or horses since we left it
yesterday morning. The weather was very warm,
and our horses were done up when they reached
camp. On our return we got a fine view to the
N.E., which looks more promising. My brother
and Windich intend going to-morrow in that
direction in search of water.

24th.—My brother and Windich started in
search of water. We rested at camp. Took lunar
observations, but did not get results which I care
much to rely on, owing to the distances being
too great.

25th.—Rested at camp. My brother and Windich did not return, so I have good hopes that they have found water ahead. Took several sets of lunars this evening. Barometer 28·80 at 5 p.m. ; warm weather.

26th (*Sunday*).—Rested at camp. My brother and Windich returned late this evening, having been over sixty miles to the E.N.E., and having found only one small rock water-hole with water in it. Many rock holes had been seen, but all dry. They had met several natives. One woman and child they had caught and talked to. She did not seem frightened, and ate readily the damper and sugar given her. The country appears more parched than it has been, which I had thought scarcely possible. A range and flat-topped hill were seen about fifteen miles to the east of their farthest point, but they were unable to reach it. Barometer 28·70; fine.

27th.—Rested at Blyth Pool. Intend going a flying trip to-morrow. Worked out several lunar observations, and the position of Blyth Pool is in latitude 26° 1′ 50″ S., longitude 125° 27′ E. Barometer 28·72; thermometer 67° at 5 p.m.

28th.—Left camp in company with Windich to look for water ahead, taking a pack-horse and ten gallons of water, besides two small tins for our own use. Steered N.E. nearly along my brother's tracks for twenty miles, and reached the water in the rock hole seen by him, and had dinner. In the afternoon continued on a little south of east for about seven miles. Camped without water for the horses on a small patch of old feed. The weather is dark and cloudy, and there is much thunder about. I expect rain this evening; if it comes it will be a great boon, and will enable us to travel on easily.

29*th*.—Rained lightly during the night ; my rug got wet. Thinking we could get plenty of water ahead, I left the drums and water, as the horses would not drink. We steered about east over miserable spinifex country, and cut my brother's return tracks. Passed a rock hole seen by him, and found only a few pints of water in it, proving to us that very little rain had fallen. We sighted the range and hill seen by my brother, and reached it at sundown. I have named it the Todd Range, and the highest hill, which is table-topped, I have named Mount Charles, after Mr. C. Todd, C.M.G., Postmaster-General of South Australia. No sign of water, and apparently very little rain has fallen here last night. Found an old natives' encampment, and two splendid rock holes quite dry; if full they would hold 700 or 800 gallons. Was very disappointed at this, and it being now after dark we camped without water for the horses, having travelled over forty miles. Before we reached the range we had most miserable spinifex sand-hills. Scarcely any feed in the range, and spinifex everywhere. What grass there is must be over two years old.

30th.—Very thick fog this morning. We bore north for four or five miles, and then S.E. for about five miles, when we got a fine view to the east, and could see some hills, which are no doubt near Mr. Gosse's farthest west. They bore S.E. about eighteen miles distant. I could not go on to them, as I was afraid the party would be following us, on the strength of the little rain we had the night before last. Reluctantly, therefore, we turned westward, and soon after came to an old native encampment with a rock hole quite dry, which would hold 1000 gallons if full. It must be a long while since there has been rain, or it would not have been dry. We continued on, searching up and down and through the Todd Ranges, finding enough for our horses from the rain. Late in the afternoon we found another camping-place with four rock holes quite empty, which, if full, would hold 3000 or 4000 gallons at least. This was very disheartening, and we felt it very much. It appeared to us that there was no water in this country at this season, and we felt it was useless looking for it. We now decided to make back towards the party; but being uncertain that my brother would not follow, on the strength of the rain, determined to bear S.W. until we struck our outward tracks. After going six miles, camped without water, and nothing but some old coarse scrub for the horses. One good shower of rain would enable us to get over this country easily; but in this season, without rain, it is quite impossible to move a number of horses.

31st.—Steering about S.E. towards our outward tracks, came across a native with his wife and two children, the youngest about two years old. As soon as they saw us, the man, who had a handful of spears, began talking at us and then ran off (the eldest child following him), leaving his wife and the youngest child to take care of themselves. The child was carried on its mother's back, and hung on without any assistance. Thus encumbered, the woman could not get away. She evidently preferred facing any danger to parting with her child. Windich spoke to her, and she talked away quietly, and did not seem much afraid. We could not understand anything she said, so allowed her to follow her husband, who certainly did not come up to our standard of gallantry. We continued on until we reached our outward tracks, and I was much relieved to find that the party had not gone on. We found a little water in a small rock hole, and rested two hours, as our pack-horse (Little Brown) was knocked up. We continued on about five miles, and camped on a patch of feed in a range, without water. Little Brown was so knocked up that we had great difficulty in getting him to walk.

August 1st.—Steering westerly for about eight miles, reached our bivouac of the 28th, and gave our horses the water from the drums. Continued

on, making straight for camp; stayed two hours
to give the horses a rest, and when within fifteen
miles of camp found a rock hole with about 100
gallons of water in it. Little Brown completely
gave in, and we were obliged to leave him. Pushed
on and reached the party a little after dark, and
found all well, having been absent five days, in
which time we had travelled about 200 miles.

2nd (*Sunday*).—My brother and Pierre went on
a flying trip to the S.E. in search of water. Kennedy and myself went and brought Little Brown
and pack-saddle, &c., to camp. Windich shot an
emu ; saw about twenty. Thermometer 95° in
sun during the day ; barometer 28·62 at 5 p.m.

I now began to be much troubled about our
position, although I did not communicate my fears
to any but my brother. We felt confident we
could return if the worst came, although we were
over 1000 miles from the settled districts of Western Australia. The water at our camp was fast
drying up, and would not last more than a fortnight. The next water was sixty miles back, and
there seemed no probability of getting eastward.
I knew we were now in the very country that had
driven Mr. Gosse back. I have since found it did
the same for Mr. Giles. No time was to be lost.
I was determined to make the best use of it if
only the water would last, and to keep on searching. (Even now, months after the time, sitting
down writing this journal, I cannot but recall my

feelings of anxiety at this camp.) Just when the goal of my ambition and my hopes for years past was almost within reach, it appeared that I might not even now be able to grasp it. The thought of having to return, however, brought every feeling of energy and determination to my rescue, and I felt that, with God's help, I would even now succeed. I gave instructions to allowance the party, so that the stores should last at least four months, and made every preparation for a last desperate struggle.

3rd.—Rested at camp. My brother and Pierre did not return this evening, so I concluded they must have found some water for their horses. Barometer falling slowly; getting cloudy towards evening.

4th.—A light shower of rain this morning. Rested at camp. My brother and Pierre returned this evening, having found a few small rock water-holes, but not sufficient to shift on. They had been about fifty miles E.S.E., and had passed over most miserable spinifex country the whole way. They had not had any rain, not even the light shower we had this morning. They had seen four natives, but did not get near enough to talk to them. I intend going with Windich ahead to-morrow, in the hope that rain may have fallen last night to the E.N.E. The weather, which had looked threatening all day, cleared off this evening. Barometer 28·56.

5th.—Thinking that rain might have fallen to the N.E., I left camp with Windich to ascertain, instructing my brother to follow on the 7th; before leaving to bury some flour and everything that could be dispensed with, and to carry all the drums full of water. He has since informed me that he buried on left bank of brook, seven yards north of a small tree with a tin plate nailed on it, on which is written, "DIG 7 yds. N.," two pack-bags, containing 135 lbs. flour, six leather water-bottles, two tomahawks, one pick, one water canteen, one broken telescope, three emu eggs, some girths and straps, one shoeing hammer, one pound of candles, and left a lantern hanging on a tree. A bottle was also buried, with a letter in it, giving the latitude and longitude of the camp, and a brief outline of our former and future intended movements. We reached the rock holes about N.E. twenty miles, and were delighted to see them full, besides plenty on the rocks. This was very èncouraging, and after resting two hours we pushed on E.N.E., to a range visited by my brother on his last flying trip, and which I named the Baker Range, and the highest point Mount Samuel, after Sir Samuel Baker, the great African Explorer, and could see that lately rain had fallen, although much more in some places than in others. Travelled till after dark through and over spinifex plains, wooded with acacia and mulga scrub, and camped without water and only a little scrub for the horses, having travelled nearly forty miles.

6th.—Our horses strayed during the night. After we had found them we proceeded to the Baker Range and found water in a gully on some rocks, and the rock holes seen by my brother and Windich on their former trip had also a good deal in them. I was greatly delighted at this; there must have been a good shower or two here. Before reaching water Windich shot a turkey, which we roasted and ate for breakfast, not having had any tea last night. We rested here about two hours. Continuing on E.N.E. for about sixteen miles, came to the four large rock holes seen by Windich and myself on our former trip. They were quite dry, but, as we suspected, there was a good deal of water in a rocky gully close by. About two miles before we reached here we passed a rock hole full of water, about sixty gallons. I left a note telling my brother to camp here on Sunday night, and to follow on our tracks on Monday. We continued on about five miles, and camped not far from Mount Charles, without water for the horses; but they were not thirsty. So far we have been most fortunate, although there is very little to fall back on should we be unable to proceed ; in fact, as soon as the surface water dries up it will be impossible. We are, however, three days in advance of the party, and if we can get enough for our two riding-horses we shall be able to stop them before there is any great danger, although we may lose some of the horses.

7th.—Steered S.S.E. for about four miles to two large rock holes seen by Windich and myself on our former trip, but found them quite dry, as before. Continued on S.E. towards the hills seen by us formerly, and, after travelling about ten miles, got a fine view of the country, which looked splendid. High hills and ranges as far as could be seen to the south and east, and we thought all our troubles were over. We pushed on about E.S.E. to a high hill about ten miles off, over red sand-hills covered with spinifex. Country of the most miserable description. We reached the hill, which I named Mount Harvest, after Colonel Harvest, the Acting-Governor of Western Australia at the time of our departure, and who took a great interest in the expedition. We ascended the hill; more ranges and hills were seen—in fact, the whole country was one mass of hills and ranges to the south, S.E., and east. We followed down gullies and over hills, passing two rock holes dry, until after dark, but could not find any water. The country is most beautifully grassed, and is a great relief after travelling over so many hundreds of miles of spinifex; but the season is very dry, and all the gullies are dry. We camped for the night without water for ourselves or horses. I have since learnt that these ranges were seen by Mr. Giles, and were named the Warburton Ranges.

8th.—Early this morning Windich and I went
on foot to search the hills and gullies close around,
as our horses were knocked up for want of water.
We returned unsuccessful about 8 o'clock. Close
to where we found our horses we found a tree
with the bark cut off one side of it with an *axe*
which was sharp. We were sure it was done by
a white man, as the axe, even if possessed by a
native (which is very improbable), would be blunt.
We are now in the country traversed by Mr.
Gosse, although I am unable to distinguish any of
the features of the country, not having a map
with me, and not knowing the latitude. Should
we find water, and the party reach here, there
will no doubt be little difficulty in distinguishing
the hills. The country certainly does not answer
the description given of his farther westward.
However, I will leave our position geographically
for the present, and treat of what is of much more
importance to us, viz., the finding of water. We
saddled our horses and continued our search about
S.E., over hills and along valleys—the distance or
direction I am unable to give—our horses scarcely
moving, and ourselves parched with thirst. The
sun was very hot. At about noon we found some
water in a gully by scratching a hole, but it was
quite salt. As our horses would not drink it, it
can be imagined how salt it was. We drank about
a pint of it, and Windich said it was the first time
he ever had to drink salt water. I washed myself

in it, which refreshed me a little. Our horses
could not go much further without water, but we
crawled along about north, and shortly afterwards
found a small rock hole in the side of a large rough
granite hill, with about five gallons of good water
in it. We had a good drink ourselves, put half a
gallon into a canteen, and gave the rest to the
horses. From here our usual good fortune returned. We had not gone far when Windich
called me back and said he had found horses'
tracks, and sure enough there were the tracks of
horses coming from the westward. Windich took
some of the old dung with him to convince our
companions that we had seen them. We followed
westward along the tracks for half a mile, when
we found two or three small rock holes with water
in them, which our horses drank. Still bearing
to the north we kept finding little drops in the
granite rocks,—our old friend the granite rock has
returned to us again, after having been absent for
several hundred miles. We satisfied our horses,
and rested a short time to have something to
eat, not having had anything for forty-eight hours.
We bore N.W., and soon afterwards found a fine
rock hole of water in granite rocks, sufficient to last
the party a day. Plenty of water on rocks, also,
from recent rain here. We were rejoiced, as we
now had a place to bring the party to. But our
good fortune did not end here: continuing on
westerly or a little north of it, we came on a

summer encampment of the natives, and found a native well or spring, which I believe would give water if dug out. This may make a good depôt if we require to stay long in this neighbourhood. We were overjoyed; and I need not add I was very thankful for this good fortune. When everything looked at its worst, then all seemed to change for our benefit. We camped two miles from the water.

9th (Sunday).—Took the horses back to the water, and on our way there found a clay-pan with a few hundred gallons of water in it. Started back to meet the party, intending to await their arrival at the first range we came to on our outward track. Steering a little north of west for fourteen miles, we camped on west side of Mount Harvest, not having seen a drop of water on our way. Luckily we brought nearly half a gallon with us, so shall be able to manage until the party overtake us to-morrow. Our horses will be very thirsty, but I will give them five gallons each out of the drums. Shot a wurrung on our way, which we had for dinner. Found two fine rock holes quite empty. There appears to have been no rain here, although fifteen miles east there has been a good deal. I hope the change of moon on the 11th will bring us some rain, as we shall then be able to travel along easily. My personal appearance contrasts most strikingly with town life—very dirty, and I may say ragged. I scarcely think my friends would know me. Washing, or brushing one's hair is out of the question, unless when resting at camp.

10th.—We stayed at our last night's bivouac until 12 o'clock, when we saddled up and followed back along our outward tracks to meet the party, which we expected to find this afternoon. About 3 o'clock met them coming on, all well. They were all rejoiced to hear of the water ahead. We gave the horses water out of the drums, and turned eastward with them. We reached Mount Harvest by sundown, the party having travelled thirty miles, and camped on grassy flat without water for the horses. Latitude 25° 55' 43" S. by Altair, longitude 126° 32' E. Everything had gone on first-rate with the party. They had nearly finished all the water at Mount Samuel, and in the Todd Range, so that we cannot now turn back, even if we wished, unless with the risk of having to go ninety or a hundred miles without water.

11th.—Continued on to the water found ahead, and on our way saw some clay-holes with water and satisfied the horses. When near the spring, saw natives' tracks, and shortly afterwards a fire with a whole kangaroo roasting in it. The natives had made off when they saw us, leaving their game cooking. Continuing on, and passing the native well, we reached the granite rocks, two miles from the spring, and camped. While having

dinner we saw two natives about a quarter of a
mile from us, watching us; we beckoned to them,
and Windich and I approached them. As we
neared them they began talking and moving off
slowly; we could not get close to them, although
they did not appear to be afraid of us. Some
fine ranges are visible from here S.E. Latitude
of camp 25° 54' 53'' S., by meridian altitude of
Altair. Marked a tree $\frac{F}{70}$, being the 70th camp
from Geraldton. Barometer 28·26 at 5 p.m.
We are not in the latitude of Mr. Gosse's track
by fifteen miles, yet there are tracks only about
two miles south of us! I cannot account for this.
The tracks may be Mr. Giles's, as I cannot think
Mr. Gosse could be out in his latitude.

12*th*.—Left camp with Tommy Windich to
find water ahead, instructing my brother to follow
on to-morrow. We bore E.S.E. for a few miles
over grassy flats towards some high hills, but,
seeing what we supposed a good spot for water,
we turned east towards it, over miserable spinifex
sand-hills, and found some splendid granite rocks
and holes, but not much water—enough, however,
to give the horses a drink. If there was rain, there
would be enough water here for a month or more.
Near these rocks found a tree resembling the figtree (*Ficus Platypoda*), with ripe fruit about the
size of a bullet, which tasted very much like a
fig. I ate some of the fruit, which was very good.
Fine hills and ranges to the eastward, and country

very promising, and in many places beautifully grassed. After resting two hours we pushed on about east, and, after going five miles over spinifex sand-hills, came to a granite range and found two fine rock holes, sufficient to satisfy the horses. Continuing on, we camped close to a peaked granite hill, which I named Mount Elvire. No water for the horses. Found the old horse-tracks, just before we camped, coming from eastward. I cannot make them out to be Mr. Gosse's; they must be Mr. Giles's. There appears to be a great number of horses', but am uncertain if there are any camel-tracks.

13th.—Found a rock hole with about forty gallons of water in it close to camp. After watering our horses we followed along the old tracks, going nearly N.E., and passed a gnow's nest, where they had apparently got out eggs. Shortly afterwards found where the party had camped without water, and continued on to some high hills and ranges; then we left them to follow some emu tracks, which, after following up a gully and over a hill, brought us to a fine spring of good water in a gully. We camped here, and intend waiting for our party, which will reach here to-morrow. We watched at the water for emus, and after waiting about four hours saw two coming, one of which Windich shot. Fine grass, although old and dry, down this gully. Ranges in every direction. The country con-

trasts strikingly with what we have been travelling through for the last three months. The
party whose tracks we followed this morning have
not been to this spring, so they must have missed
it. All my troubles were now over, inasmuch
as I felt sure we would accomplish our journey
and reach the settled districts of South Australia;
although, as it afterwards proved, we had many
days of hard work and some privation yet to
endure. Still the country was much improved,
and not altogether unknown. I then gave out
publicly to the party that we were now in safety,
and in all human probability in five or six weeks
would reach the telegraph line. I need not
add how pleased all were at having at last bridged
over that awful, desolate spinifex desert.

14th.—Went to a hill close to camp, the highest
in this neighbourhood, and erected a pile of
stones. About 1 o'clock the party arrived all
safe. They reported having seen three natives
the day we left, and had induced them to come to
camp, and had given them damper and sugar
and a red handkerchief each; they did not remain
long. Each had two spears, very long and thick,
and made out of three pieces spliced together,
with large barbs on them. The party had finished
all the water on their way, the horses yesterday
having drank over ten gallons each. This afternoon I took a round of angles and bearings from
a pile of stones on the hill. Marked a tree $\frac{F}{72}$,

near spring, which I named Barlee Spring, after
the Honourable F. P. Barlee, Colonial Secretary of
Western Australia, from whom I have ever received much kindness and assistance, and who
took a great interest in this expedition. A
remarkable hill bore S.S.W. from spring, which I
named Mount Palgrave. Barlee Spring is in
longitude about 127° 22′ E. Unable to get
latitude : too cloudy.

15th.—Left camp with Windich to look for
water ahead, instructing my brother to follow to-
morrow. Steered E. along the S. side of a rocky
range for ten miles, when we ascended a hill to
get a view ahead. About thirty miles to east
fine bold ranges are visible, also broken ranges
from N.E. and round to S.E. ; they are no doubt
the Cavanagh Ranges of Mr. Gosse. About
five miles ahead we saw some granite rocks, to
which we proceeded, and found a tremendous
rock hole full of water; it was in between two
large rocks and completely shaded from the sun.
As the country east to the ranges appears to be
all spinifex and red sand-hills, I decided to remain
here to-night and continue on in the morning.
Left a note telling my brother to camp here on
Sunday night. In the afternoon got a fine round
of angles from granite rocks. The country passed
over to-day was along and through ranges which
are no doubt the Barrow Ranges of Mr. Gosse.
The flats are very grassy, but the hills are covered

with spinifex. My brother marked a tree at this camp $\frac{F}{73}$, and observed the latitude to be about 26° 4', but was unable to get very good observation on account of clouds. The *Ficus Platypoda* was also found here, loaded with ripe fruit.

16*th (Sunday)*.—Steering about E.N.E. towards the ranges, we passed over very miserable spinifex plains and red sand-hills the whole way, about thirty miles. After reaching the ranges we followed up a fine grassy wide flat, splendidly grassed, although old; and on the flat were innumerable horse-tracks—unmistakable evidence of horses being camped for months in this neighbourhood. Kept on up the gully and flat for about a mile and a half, when Windich found a gum-tree marked E. GILES OCT. 7, 73. My former suspicions that Mr. Giles must have been in this neighbourhood were now confirmed. Soon after we came on a cart-track, which rather astonished us, and soon found that it must have belonged to Mr. Gosse, who also camped close here. A deep, well-beaten track went along up the gully, which we followed, knowing it was the daily track of the horses to the water, and soon after found their old camp at a beautiful spring running down the gully a quarter of a mile. A stock-yard had been built, and gardens made, besides a large bush hut to shelter the party from the sun as well as rain. Trenches were dug round the hut and tent, so that they must have had rain. I should say Mr.

Giles must have been camped here for two or
three months at least.   We camped half a mile
down the gully from the spring.   Mr. Gosse and
Mr. Giles were within a few miles of each other at
the same time, and did not meet.

17*th*.—Went for a walk to examine the cart-
tracks; found two tracks going east and west.
This convinced me that the cart belonged to Mr.
Gosse, who I knew had returned.   Went to the
top of a high hill to take angles, while Windich
tried to shoot a kangaroo.   After a hard
climb I reached the summit, and had just commenced taking angles when I heard three shots,
and shortly after Windich cooeying.   Looking
round, I saw a native running along about 300
yards from me.   He disappeared in a hollow.
Fearing that Windich had been attacked by the
natives I descended towards him as quickly as
possible, but could not see him.   I looked about,
keeping a sharp look-out, expecting to be attacked, but could not find Windich.   Sat down a
short time and finally made my way back to
the horses, and, after finding them, saddled one
and started back to look for Windich.   Found
him coming along with a kangaroo on his back,
having shot three, but had not seen any natives;
he had been waiting for me a good while.   After
dinner I went back to get my coat and a compass
left at the foot of the hill, and then again
ascended the hill and got a fine round of angles.

The rock is very magnetic, and the compass is quite useless. Could see the dust from the party coming across the spinifex sand-hills, and, descending, met them just before sundown. They reported having had an encounter with the natives on the 16th, and having been followed by a number of armed natives for a long way. Finally they had been compelled to fire on them, but had not killed any. They were glad to hear of the spring found, and, continuing on, reached it about half-past 6 o'clock. The spring is Fort Mueller of Mr. Giles, where he was camped for a long while, and his most westerly permanent water. By observation Fort Mueller is in latitude 26° 11′ 30″ S., and longitude by lunar observation 128° E., the variation being about 1° 25′ E. by azimuths.

18th.—Rested at spring. Marked a tree sixty yards south of camp $\frac{F}{74}$, being 74th camp from Geraldton. Also erected a pile of stones on peak, thirty chains W.S.W. of camp, with a pole in centre, on which is marked

"J. FORREST, AUGUST 17, '74."

Took four sets of lunars, which place spring in longitude 128° E. of Greenwich.

19th.—Steering E.S.E. along Mr. Gosse's track for about thirty-five miles, over most miserable sandy hills and plains of spinifex, with the exception of a few miles at first, along a grassy flat.

Two rock holes passed were quite dry. Camped
without water on a grassy flat not far from the
ranges; hope to find water early to-morrow, as
our horses are too poor to go long without it.
Was obliged to abandon police-horse Brick to-day,
as he was completely done up. Nothing but
downright poverty is the cause of his giving in;
and the same in the case of Fame and Little
Padbury, which we abandoned over a month ago.
They were poor when they left, and have only had
very dry grass ever since. It is a wonder to me
they all do not give in, as many are mere skeletons.
Poor old Brick held up as long as he could, but
was forced to give in, and we had to leave him
to his solitary fate; he will probably go back to
the spring (Fort Mueller). Barometer 28·30;
latitude 26° 22′ 30″ S.

20*th*.—Got a very early start, and continued
on. At one mile found a sandy soak in a gully,
and by digging it out got sufficient water for all
our horses. Still proceeding onwards, following
a gully for two miles, came to Mr. Gosse's
depôt No. 13, at Skirmish Hill. A bullock had
been killed here, and the flesh jerked. Found
a large white gum-tree marked $^{GOS.}_{13}$ at camp. All
the water was gone. I, however, camped, and
took our horses to a place a mile west, where, by
digging in the sand, we got enough for them.
Went with Pierre to the summit of Skirmish Hill,
and took angles. To the south, nothing but

sand-hills and spinifex; to the N.E. the Tomkinson Ranges showed up and looked very remarkable and promising.   Marked a tree $\frac{F}{76}$, being
76th camp from Geraldton.   Camp is in latitude
26° 23′ 28″, longitude about 128° 32′ E.

21*st*.—Left camp at Skirmish Hill in company
with Windich, instructing my brother to follow
to-morrow.   Found a fine rock hole two miles
from camp, and followed along Mr. Gosse's track
for twenty miles to the Tomkinson Ranges, over
most miserable sandy ridges, covered with spinifex.
Fine grassy flats along and through the ranges.
We left the track to examine a gully to the north,
but could not find any water.   Got on the track
just before dark and followed it along a few miles.
Camped without water for our horses on a fine
flat of very old grass.   Windich's horse completely knocked up, and we had to walk and
drive him before us this afternoon.   The day
was excessively hot, and the horses are very
thirsty.   We have only about a quart ourselves.

22*nd*.—Early this morning we continued on,
Windich's horse scarcely able to walk.   After
about ten miles, found a rock hole with three
gallons of water in it, which we gave to our
horses.   Followed Mr. Gosse's track to see if
there was any water about his depôt No. 12, but
we either missed it or had not reached it.   About
noon Windich's horse could go no farther, and
mine was not much better.   What was to be

done? We nearly finished what water we had
with us. The party were coming on to-day, and
were depending on us to find water. I determined
not to follow the track any farther, but to search
for water ourselves. The horses were unable to
move; we therefore decided to leave them and go
for a search on foot. Windich said he had seen
emu tracks, and he thought they were making
south. We therefore started on foot. The sun's
heat was excessive. About 3 o'clock returned
unsuccessful, and finished what water we had
with us. What next to do was the question; no
time was to be lost. Mr. Gosse's map showed
some gullies ahead, but whether there was any
water in them was questionable; he states, "Nearly
all the waters discovered in the Mann and Tomkinson Ranges were running when left, and from
a considerable height." It must have been a
good season, and not like this. We decided to
go on foot to a gully about two miles north, which
had white gums in it. We started off and saw
more emu tracks going and coming, also natives'
tracks. Windich shot a wurrung, which he said
had lately drunk water. When we reached the
gully, many tracks were seen ascending it, and
we felt sure we should find water, and surely
enough we soon reached a most splendid spring,
running down the gully half a mile. We were
elated and very thankful. Windich got a shot
at an emu, but missed it. After having a good

drink we went back and got our horses, reaching the spring with them after dark. They were very thirsty and completely done up. Mr. Gosse missed this spring; probably there was water on the flats when he was here, and he did not look much. Although his track is easily followed, we had nearly got into serious difficulty by following it. Had we not found this spring our position would be very critical, not having any water for ourselves or horses, and the party in the same predicament. I will be careful not to follow the track too far in future, but to trust to our own resources and look for ourselves. We feel sure we passed water this morning, as in one place we saw emu tracks and pigeons. The party will reach here to-morrow, and I feel very thankful and relieved to have such a fine spring to bring them to. The feed is good a mile down from the spring, although it is very old and dry. There has not been any rain to speak of since Mr. Gosse was here, nearly twelve months ago, as can be seen by the cart-tracks crossing the gullies. I named this spring the Elder Springs, after my friend the Honourable Thomas Elder, who has been such a great supporter of exploration, and from whom I received a great deal of kindness and attention.

23rd (*Sunday*).—Awaited the arrival of the party. Shot an emu; and, while skinning it, heard a gun-shot, and soon after saw Kennedy coming on, walking. Found that the party were only half a mile off. They had been very distressed for water, and had left 120lbs. of flour and a pack-saddle five miles back, Taylor's mare about three miles back, and Burges and his saddle two miles back. When they saw my note, directing them to the water, they had gone back and got Burges, and with great difficulty got him close to camp, when he lay down and they left him. Windich and I started back on foot at once with two buckets of water, and met Burges within a quarter of a mile of camp, crawling along; we gave him the water and he then went on to the spring. We went back and found Taylor's mare, and brought her slowly to camp. We are now safe again, and I must give the horses a few days' rest. The weather has been hot, and if we had not found this spring, not more than five horses would have lasted out the day. I will send back and get the flour, as it is only five miles off. The party were all very glad to see such a fine spring, as their position was very dangerous, having only three gallons of water with them altogether.

24th.—Rested at Elder Spring. Found the barometer had got broken, which I was very sorry for. Worked out several lunars taken on the 11th at Giles's camp.

25th.—Worked out the remainder of the lunars. Marked a large white gum-tree close to camp, on left bank of Elder Springs, $\frac{F}{78}$, being the 78th camp from Geraldton. Found camp to be in south latitude 26° 15' 10", and longitude about 129° 9' E. My brother and Pierre went back and brought up the flour left five miles back on the 23rd.

26th.—Went with Pierre to a high peak, which I named Mount Jane, about four miles S.S.E. from camp, and got a round of angles, and a fine view of the country. To the east high ranges and grassy flats, but to the south, and from S.E. to west, nothing but level country with a few low rises here and there, apparently sand-hills covered with spinifex—most miserable country.

27th.—Left camp with Tommy Windich to look for water ahead, instructing my brother to follow to-morrow. Steered east for four miles, when we struck Mr. Gosse's cart-track. Followed along it a few miles, when we bore more to the north; then in the direction of emu tracks, and passed along a fine grassy flat with hundreds of kangaroos in every direction; also many emu tracks. We were sure we were getting close to water. A little farther on saw about twenty-five emus, and soon reached a spring in the brook, and camped for dinner. Concluded to remain here the remainder of the day. Went for a walk higher up the brook and found another spring, about one mile from the first. Returned and took our horses up to it, as there was better feed there. Left a note, telling the party to camp there also. In a good season these flats must look magnificent; at this time they are very dry, but there is a good deal of old grass on them. My brother marked a tree at spring $\frac{F}{79}$, which he found to be in latitude 26° 13′. I named this spring Wilkie Spring, after the Honourable Dr. Wilkie, the honorary treasurer of the Burke and Wills Exploration Fund, who took such a lively interest in Australian Exploration.

28th.—Continued on eastward and soon struck Mr. Gosse's cart-track. Followed it along about seven miles, passing Mount Davies, when we bore more to the south. Following the direction of some natives' tracks, and after going about two miles, found a native well in a gully, where water could be procured by digging. Left a note telling my brother to dig it out and see if he could get enough for the horses. We continued on about E.N.E., and soon after shot a kangaroo and rested an hour for dinner, after which we bore about N.E. towards a gully and white gums, and found it to be Nilens Gully of Mr. Gosse. Found his camp and a white gum marked with a broad arrow, but no water. We followed along and through the ranges, twisting and turning about, and at last found a number of natives' tracks, making towards a gap, and, following along them, found they led to a gorge and white gum gully, ascending which we found water in some little springs. After watering our horses we returned towards the party three miles and camped, intending to bring the party to the spring to-morrow.

29th.—Returned about five miles and met the party coming on all right. They reported having met about twenty natives yesterday, who were friendly, and who came to them, first of all laying down their spears. They had given them damper and a handkerchief. Pierre gave them two kylies. They had three kangaroos roasting in their fire. When we were passing Nilens gully I saw a native running, and, calling Windich, we went over and saw five natives sitting on some rocks watching us. I went towards them; at first they appeared hostile, but after talking at them and making signs they began to be friendly and came down close to us. They were all armed with spears. One of them gave me his spear, which was very blunt, and I sharpened it for him. He made signs for me to give him the knife, but I could not, as we were very short of knives. They were afraid at first when I showed them how a horse could gallop, but soon were very pleased and laughed heartily. Windich shot a chockalot and gave it to them. They were amazed at seeing the bird drop, and were very pleased when it was given to them, as they much prize the feathers of these birds. After this we left them and continued on to the spring found yesterday, and camped. Got plenty of water by digging a

few holes in the springy places. Marked a tree
$\frac{F}{80}$ in gorge close to spring. Found spring to
be in latitude 26° 7' 28" S., longitude about 129°
39' east.

30*th* (*Sunday*).—Rested at spring. Took bearings from hill close to spring, Mount Hardy bearing north 117° east magnetic, and Mount Davies
north 253° east magnetic. The Mann Ranges
were also clearly visible about ten miles off. In
the afternoon Windich found a fine spring in a
gully about half a mile north of camp, at which he
shot an emu. I named these springs the Crowther
Springs, after my friend Mr. Charles Crowther, of
Geraldton. Emus and kangaroos very numerous
in these ranges.

31*st*.—Got an early start and took the horses to
the water found by Windich yesterday, where they
could help themselves. Steered E.N.E. about,
over level country; spinifex generally, studded
with desert oaks, with limestone and snail-shells
on surface for about twenty miles. Reached the
Mann Ranges. Before we reached the ranges we
struck Mr. Gosse's track, and followed it along,
and shortly came to a very large and recent encampment of the natives. There must have been
a hundred camped here about a week ago. Found
two small springs not far off, but not strong
enough to water all our horses; but we soon found
some fine springy pools in a gully about half a mile
further on, where Mr. Gosse also had been camped,

and marked a tree with a broad arrow. I marked on the same tree $_{81}^{F}$, being our 81st camp from Geraldton. Mr. Gosse's return track leaves his outward track at this spot. I intend following his return track and make in to the telegraph line, down the Alberga, and on to the Peake. There is abundance of water at this place, which I have no doubt is permanent, as there are four springs within half a mile of one another, but three are very small. Took bearings from a very high range close by; Mount Davies, Mount Edwin, and Mount Hardy being visible. The Mann Ranges are very high and rough, and are composed of reddish granite. They are the highest ranges met with since leaving Mount Hale and Mount Gould, on the Murchison. Found camp $_{81}^{F}$ to be in latitude 26° 3′ 20″ S. by meridian altitude of Altair and Vega, and longitude about 129° 53′ E.

Sept. 1*st.*—Continuing about east along the foot of the Mann Ranges for about fifteen miles, came to Mr. Gosse's bivouac of October 11th, but could find no water; a well that had been dug in the sand was dry. Followed up the gully about a mile, and came to a small spring, and camped. After draining it out, found there was no supply, but were fortunate enough to find some large rock holes with water—no doubt soakages from the rocks— but they were in an almost inaccessible spot, and it was with great difficulty we managed to water the horses. One horse fell and nearly lost his life.

Country passed over to-day was poorly grassed,
and spinifex patches here and there. Large and
recent native encampments seen in two places to-
day. Latitude 26° 4' 45" S. Marked a tree $\frac{F}{82}$, close
to our bivouac in bed of gully.

2nd.—Followed along south side of Mann Ranges
over country pretty well grassed for about sixteen
miles, and reached Mr. Gosse's bivouac of October
12th. Found a little water in a sandy hole, and a
small spring about half a mile higher up the gully.
We had to carry the water from the spring in
drums, which was slow and hard work. When we
had watered half of the horses, Windich came,
having found great pools of water in a large rocky
gully about a mile west; we therefore packed up
again and went over to the water. It was a very
rough and rocky gully, and the horses had hard
work in getting up to it, but there was abundance
when they reached it. Pools of water, rock bottom; in fact, rock reservoirs, and fed by springs.
It was nearly night when we had finished watering. Windich shot four ducks. Found camp to
be in latitude 28° 8' S. Marked a tree $\frac{F}{83}$, being
83rd camp from Geraldton.

3rd.—Got a late start, owing to the horses
rambling. We continued on easterly and reached
Day's Gully, Mr. Gosse's No. 15 depôt. The
water was all gone, and we had to proceed. Followed his track along two miles, when Windich
and I went in search of water, the party waiting

our return. After searching a gully to the west without success, we went east to a bare granite hill and, passing through a gorge, emerged into a small flat, and saw about 100 natives, all sitting down eating kangaroos. As soon as they saw us they all rose and shouted, and many ran towards us with their spears. One spear came close to me, and stuck fast in the ground. Windich and I fired our revolvers at them several times, and chased them up the hill. After this they appeared more friendly, and some came towards us and followed us back towards the party, keeping about 200 yards behind. We reached them and went back to the natives ; they were perched all over the hills, more than twenty on one rock. They were friendly now, and about thirty came to us who talked away and seemed very pleased. They were much afraid of the horses, and would not come near them.   We made the natives understand we wanted water, and about forty conducted us to a rock hole with nearly fifty gallons in it, which we gave the horses. The natives laughed heartily when they saw us watering the horses, but much more when we hit them to drive them away. They were also delighted that Windich and Pierre were black, and marked about the body, and also at Pierre having his nose bored. They would not come with us further, and pointed towards water westward. We did not follow their direction, and continuing on easterly, camped without water, and only very

old dried grass for our horses. We were obliged
to abandon the mare supplied by Mr. John Taylor
to-day, together with about 150 pounds of flour,
also the pack-saddle. She is very near foaling,
and is very weak; she has carried only the empty
bags for some time, and has been gradually failing.
She is a fine mare, and I am sorry to lose her, but
we cannot help it. We have more flour than we
require, so I decided to leave 150 pounds, as our
horses are not able to carry it easily. We have
over 3 cwt. still, which will be quite sufficient. To-
morrow I intend pushing on to try and reach the
spring in the Musgrave Range shown on Mr.
Gosse's chart. It is about forty miles from here,
and I have no doubt the horses will go there, although they are very weak. The natives met to-
day were all circumcised; they had long hair and
beards, which were all clotted and in strands.
The strands were covered with filth and dirt
for six inches from the end, and looked like greased
rope; it was as hard as rope, and dangled about
their necks, looking most disgustingly filthy.
The men were generally fine-looking fellows. The
natives are very numerous in this country, as
fires and camps are seen in many places, besides
well-beaten tracks. Pierre dropped his powder-
flask, and one of them picked it up and gave it to
him. They were very friendly and pleased, and
I think, after the first surprise was over, only a
few were hostile. They were much amused at

my watch ticking, and all wanted to put their ears
to hear it.

4th.—The horses would not feed last night, and
had to be watched.   At 4 o'clock we got up and
collected them, and got under way by half-past
5 o'clock, following on towards the Musgrave
Ranges.   The morning was cool, and the horses
went along very well.   After travelling about
twenty miles Padbury and Butcher began to show
signs of giving in.   We still pushed on, in hope of
finding water in Lungley's Gully; the sun shone
out very hot in the afternoon.   Passed a remarkable high peak, which I named Mount Mary.   My
brother, Sweeney, and Pierre were behind with
the knocked-up horses, trying to get them along.
Windich went on Hosken, the only horse that was
strong enough, to the north to scour some valleys.
Kennedy and I pushed along slowly with the
main lot of horses.   If we halted a minute, many
of the horses lay down, and we had great difficulty
in getting them up again.   After travelling about
thirty-one miles we reached a gully which I
supposed was Lungley's, and I left Kennedy
with the horses while I ascended it on foot.   I
soon saw many emu tracks, and therefore was
positive water was a little higher up.   Found
Windich was about 100 yards in advance of me,
having crossed over into the same gully.   I soon
heard him shout that there was abundance of
water, and fired the welcome gun-shots to acquaint

the party. Returned, and after lifting up some
of the horses that had lain down, and met my
brother with the knocked-up ones, we all proceeded
up to the water, which we found to be a beautiful
spring running down the gully about thirty chains.
We were all rejoiced at this good fortune, as we
never before wanted water more than at the present time. Mr. Gosse had camped here, his depôt
No. 16, and I wonder he does not show such a
fine spring on his map. We are now in perfect
safety, and I will give the horses two days' rest.

5th.—Rested at spring. Windich and Pierre shot
three emus ; a great many came to water. Being
nearly out of meat, we are glad to get them.

6th (Sunday).—Took bearings from a hill about
a mile east of camp, from which there was a very
extensive view. Far as the eye could reach to
south, level plains extended, with low hills rising
abruptly out of them here and there ; to the west
the Deering Hills and Mann Ranges ; while to the
east the high Musgrave Ranges soon stopped the
view. The whole country is level, the ranges
rising abruptly out of the plains, and is not
like the hilly country in the settled districts of
Western Australia. Marked a tree close to
the camp $_{85}^{F}$, being 85th camp from Geraldton.
Found camp to be in latitude 26° 13′ 25″ by
meridian altitude of Altair, and longitude about
131° 3′ east.

7th.—Left spring, and steering about east for

seven miles along foot of Musgrave Ranges, when we turned N.N.E. for four miles, and east one mile to Mr. Gosse's depôt No. 17, found spring in a brook, large white gums in gully; a very fine spring, but not running; any quantity of water. First-rate feed in gully and on flat. Weather cloudy. Intend resting here to-morrow, as one of our horses is very lame, and there is everything we want.

8th.—Rested at camp. Rained lightly last night, and very stormy. Blew a hurricane towards morning. Rained lightly until noon; more rain than we have had on the whole trip. We have not had a drop of rain since the light shower on the 4th August. Marked a tree $\frac{F}{86}$, being 86th camp from Geraldton. Shod two horses. Finished all our meat. We have now only flour enough for the remainder of our journey. As my friend Mr. Gosse did not name this splendid place, I take the liberty of naming it Gosse's Spring, as that is the name we always gave it in referring to it.

9th.—The horses rambled away last night, and were not collected till late. It was nearly eleven o'clock when we started. We travelled about fourteen miles over fine grassy country, and camped on a fine flat with a little water in a gully which appears springy; good feed, although chiefly old, all round camp. One of our horses is very lame, and we have a little trouble in getting him

along. It rained again last night. Latitude
26° 15′ 23″ south.

10*th*.—Steered N.N.E. for five miles, and then
N.E. and east to Beare's Creek, Mr. Gosse's
depôt No. 18, where we found a most beautiful
spring running strong down the gully for half a
mile. I wonder he did not mark it permanent
water on his map, as it is one of the best springs
I have ever seen. Poor place for feed. The
horses inclined to ramble. Shot two ducks which
were in one of the pools, and two wurrungs, which
were very acceptable, being now altogether without
meat. Latitude 26° 9′ 50″. Grassy gorge on
our route to-day.

11*th*.—We got up long before daylight, intending to get an early start, and reach Whittell's
Creek, but two of the horses were missing, and
it was after eight o'clock when Windich returned
with them. We, however, started, and steering
easterly through dense acacia thickets without
grass for about thirty miles, we reached the creek,
and found plenty of water by digging in the sand.
Rough low granite hills all along our route, but
very little feed. Passed many clay-pans with
water in them. The country was sandy and
stony, and is thickly wooded. Mount Woodroffe
bears north 208° east mag. from our camp, and a
remarkable granite hill bore north, which I named
Mount Elizabeth. Latitude 26° 13′ south. Marked
a tree $\frac{F}{89}$, being 89th camp from Geraldton.

12*th*.—Continued onwards about N.E. for ten miles, over saltbush flats with water in clay-pans in places, to the north part of a range, from which I got a view of Mount Connor, which rose abruptly out of the ocean of scrub. Rounding the mount, bore S.E. towards Harry's Reservoir, reaching which we camped. It is at the head of a rocky gully; it is very rough to reach, and no feed within a mile and a half of it. There was plenty of water in the hole, which is about six feet deep. A white gum-tree close to the pool is marked $^{GOS,}_{19}$, and I marked under it, on same tree, $^{F}_{90}$, being 90th camp from Geraldton. This being such a rough place, and no feed near, I will move on to-morrow towards or to Figtree Gully. Weather dark and cloudy.

13*th* (*Sunday*).—Continued on towards Figtree Gully, having to go a long way north in order to get round and through the ranges. Most beautifully-grassed country all the way; by far the best-grassed country we have seen for months. After travelling about nineteen miles we found water on some granite rocks, and camped on a very fine grassy flat. Windich shot a large kangaroo, which was very acceptable.

14*th*.—About 2 o'clock this afternoon we collected the horses, and travelled on to Figtree Gully about four miles, our horses first finishing all the water on the granite rocks. We got enough at Figtree Gully to satisfy them, although there is not a great supply. There is a small soakage from the rocks; we filled the drums to-night, so as to have sufficieut for them in the morning, as the water does not come in quickly. The view to the east is not very interesting. A few low hills, and generally level country—apparently thickly wooded with mulga and acacia.

15*th*.—Got an early start, and steering about east for six miles, crossed the Gum Creek, and followed it along about a mile and a half, when we steered more to the east, until we struck the head of the Marryatt, which we followed down N.E. and east, until we reached the salt native well marked on Mr. Gosse's map. We camped here, and dug out the well, which was very brackish; yet the horses drank it. There was a very poor supply of water, and we kept bailing it out into the drums all night, and managed to get out about sixty gallons. We travelled about thirty miles to-day; our horses were very thirsty, the weather oppressive. I found a small water-hole, with about twenty gallons in it, about one mile north, to which we will take the horses to-morrow morning.

16*th*.—Went over to the rock hole and gave our horses the water—about one bucket apiece, after which we struck S.E. to the river, and found two rock holes with sufficient water in them to satisfy all the horses. Continued on and reached Mr. Gosse's camp, where he marks on his map

"Water-hole dug." Found it quite dry; but after going a few hundred yards we found a nice clay-pan with water in it, and camped. There has been a little rain here a few weeks ago, and it has not all dried up yet. If it was not for the rain-water we should have much difficulty in getting down this river, as all the old native wells dug in the sand are dry.

17th.—Followed down the Marryatt, and at six miles passed a native well, which was quite dry. We continued on, and at about eight miles found a number of rock water-holes, all nearly full of water, about a quarter of a mile south of the river, and camped. Shod some of the horses. Took a set of lunar observations.

18th.—Two of the horses rambled away during the night, and delayed our start. At eight o'clock we got under way, and followed along the river. The day was excessively hot, and we had to walk in turns. At two o'clock crossed the gum creek shown on Mr. Gosse's map, and searched for the large clay-pan shown a short distance beyond it; hundreds of natives' tracks seen all along. Towards evening we found a rock water-hole with about two gallons in it, which refreshed us, as we were all very thirsty. Here we were obliged to abandon police-horse Champion, he being completely knocked up; he has had a very bad back for a long time, and has been running loose without any load. We pushed on, and I sent Windich to look for water. We travelled until eight o'clock, when we camped for the night without water. Shortly after we had camped, Windich overtook us, and reported having found some clay-pans about six miles back. After having something to eat I decided to return to the clay-pans, and therefore packed up three of the horses, and let the others go loose, leaving the packs until our return. Reached the water by midnight, and the horses finished it all, and were not half satisfied. I thought there was more, or would not have come back for it. We hobbled them out, and had a few hours' rest.

19th.—Early this morning we searched the flat for water, and found a rock water-hole with about fifty gallons in it, but could not find any more clay-pans. We therefore gave the horses the fifty gallons, and pushed on towards " Water near Table-Land " shown on Mr. Gosse's map, about twenty-one miles distant. The day was excessively hot again, and walking was most fatiguing. Men and horses moved along very slowly, but did not give in. Towards noon a hot wind began to blow. Onwards still we pressed, and crossed the large creek coming into the Alberga about two miles from the water. I told the party we were now close, and showed them the low table-land just ahead. Before we reached it we found a clay-hole with water, and gave the horses a good drink, after which we moved on a mile and camped at

Mr. Gosse's depôt No. 20, where we got plenty of
water by digging in the sandy bed of the river.
I was very glad to reach here, for the horses were
getting very weary, and Sweeney was also done
up, and looked very ill and swollen up about the
head.   The walking was most harassing, for,
besides the ground being soft, the sun was over-
powering, and most excessively hot.   We are now
in safety again, and to-morrow being Sunday we
will rest.

20th (Sunday).—Rested to-day.   Windich shot
an emu.   Worked out lunar observations.   Marked
a tree $\frac{F}{97}$, being 97th camp from Geraldton.   Latitude 26° 44′ 19″, longitude about 133° 47′ E.

21st.—Continued down the Alberga about S.E.
for about twenty miles, over sandy country thickly
wooded with mulya and acacia, to Mr. Gosse's
bivouac of December 1st, but there was scarcely
any water by digging.   We therefore pushed on
and found a native well, from which, by digging
out about five feet, we procured abundance of
water.   Sweeney still very unwell, unable to walk;
others walking in turns.   Distance twenty-five
miles.

22nd.—The horses rambled back on the tracks
about three miles, and it was eight o'clock before
we got started.   We followed down the Alberga
over stony plains, poorly grassed and thickly
wooded, for about eighteen miles.   Found sufficient water by digging in the sand; there was

only a very poor supply, and it took us a good
while to water all the horses. The river bed is
more than a quarter of a mile wide and very
shallow, and spreads out over the plains for many
miles in heavy winters.

23rd.—Watering the horses delayed us a little
this morning, as there was a very poor supply
coming into the well. We followed down the
river, and after travelling about nine miles heard
a native shouting, and soon saw him running after
us. He was quite friendly, but could not speak any
English; he came along with us, and shortly
afterwards we found a native well with sufficient
water by digging, then camped, as our horses were
very weak, and required a rest. We finished all
our tea and sugar to-day, and have now only flour
left; we will therefore have bread and water for
the next week, until we reach the Peake. The
native ate heartily of damper given to him, and
remained all day, and slept at our camp. Distance ten miles.

24th.—Travelled down river, the native still
accompanying us, and at about six miles met a
very old native, and a woman and a little girl. They
were quite friendly, and showed us water; and the
woman and girl came with us to Appatinna, Mr.
Gosse's depôt 21, where we camped at a fine pool
of water under right bank of river. Windich shot
three emus that were coming to the water, and
we all had plenty of them to eat. The natives

were very pleased, and went back and brought up
the old man and another woman and child.   There
were now six with us.   They have seen the telegraph line, as can be seen by signs they make,
but they cannot speak English.

25th.—The horses rambled off miles, and it
was nearly ten o'clock before we got under way.
There was no feed at all for them.   We followed
down the Alberga for about fifteen miles, about
east generally, and camped, with very little old
dried-up grass for our horses.   About half an
hour after we left Appatinna this morning we had
a very heavy shower of rain, and, although it only
lasted about a quarter of an hour, it literally
flooded the whole country, making it boggy.
It was the heaviest thunderstorm I have ever
seen.   We shall have no difficulty in procuring
water now all the way to the telegraph line,
which is not more than forty miles from here.   The
natives stayed at Appatinna, as they had too much
emu to leave.   We did not want them, and were
just as well pleased they did not come on.   Mr.
Gosse's track went N.N.E. to the Hamilton River
from Appatinna.

26th.—Got off early and followed the river
about two miles, when it took a bend to the north,
and as it was rather boggy near it we left it, and
steered about east and E.N.E. for twenty miles
over most miserable country without any grass.
We camped on a small gully with a little water in

it, and some old dry grass in a flat. The horses were very tired, not having had anything to eat for the last two or three days, and some showed signs of giving in; in fact, all weak and knocked-up, and we have to handle them very carefully. For the first thirteen miles we passed many clay-pans full of water—water nearly everywhere—after which there was very little; and the rain does not appear to have been heavy to the east. The river is about a mile and a half north of us, and we have not seen it for some miles. Latitude 27° 9′ south. Hope to reach the telegraph line to-morrow.

27th (*Sunday*).—Continuing E.N.E. for two miles, came to the Alberga, and following along its right bank over many clay-pans with water, about east for twelve miles, and then E.N.E. for three miles, and reached the telegraph line between Adelaide and Port Darwin, and camped. Long and continued cheers came from our little band as they beheld at last the goal to which we have been travelling for so long. I felt rejoiced and relieved from anxiety; and on reflecting on the long line of travel we had performed through an unknown country, almost a wilderness, felt very thankful to that good Providence that had guarded and guided us so safely through it.

The telegraph line is most substantially put up, and well wired, and is very creditable at this spot;

REACHING THE OVERLAND TELEGRAPH LINE.

large poles of bush timber, often rather crooked, and iron ones here and there. I now gave up keeping watch, having kept it regularly for the last six months. Marked a tree $_{104}^{F}$, being 104th camp from Geraldton. We had not much to refresh the inner man with, only damper and water, but we have been used to it now more than a month, and do not much feel it. The horses are all very tired, and many of them have sore backs. I hope to reach the Peake on Wednesday night, where we shall be able to get something to eat. We find making the damper with boiling water makes it much lighter and softer, and is a great improvement. Latitude 27° 7′ 50″ south.

28*th*.—We travelled down the telegraph line for about twenty-one miles, and camped on a branch of the Neales River, with a little grass. Level plains and small rocky rises all the way; very stony country; many clay-pans with water. A well-beaten road goes along near the telegraph line. We did not get on it till we had travelled along the line about fifteen miles. It crosses the Alberga east of the line.

29*th*.—When we were nearly ready to start, police-horse Butcher lay down and died in a few seconds; he appeared all right when we brought him in, and was saddled as usual. Old age, very severe hard work, and continual travelling, is no doubt the cause of death: we took off his shoes, and left him where he died. I was sorry for the poor old horse; he had been rather weak for a good while, but had borne up well to the very last. We only had four horses to ride to-day, and Sweeney being still lame really made but three horses between five of us. We travelled down the road for about thirty-three miles over stony plains; many clay-pans with water, but no feed. Camped on a gully with some old feed in the flat, in latitude 27° 49′. Miserable country for grass all day, but plenty of water from recent rains everywhere. Hope to reach the Peake by mid-day to-morrow. Damper and water as usual.

30th.—Got off early as usual, all in high glee at the prospect of meeting civilized habitations again. Travelled along the road and saw cattle, and shortly afterwards reached the Peake, and rather surprised the people. Mr. Bagot, the owner of the cattle station, was the first I met; and after telling him who we were, he said he had surmised it was so. He soon told us that Mr. Giles had returned, and also Mr. Ross, who had been despatched by the Honourable Thomas Elder with camels and a good equipment to find an overland route to Perth, but was unable to get over to Western Australia. We were soon introduced to Mr. Blood, the officer in charge of the telegraph station, and, after unloading, were soon engaged at dinner, — the roast beef and plum pudding being a striking contrast to our fare lately ! Both Mr. and Mrs. Blood, as well as Mr. Bagot, did all they could to make us comfortable during our four days' rest.

Immediately on reaching Peake, I despatched a telegram to his Excellency Mr. Musgrave, Governor of South Australia, at Adelaide, informing him of the save arrival of the party, and received the following reply from the private secretary :—

His Excellency has received your message with great satisfaction, and congratulates you heartily on your safe arrival.

This telegram was accompanied by another from the Hon. Arthur Blyth, the Chief Secretary of the Colony :—

Is there anything you want? Mail leaves on October 10th. Shall be happy to facilitate any despatch you may wish forwarded to your Government. Superintendent of Telegraphs has given instructions for every assistance to be rendered you at the various telegraph stations on your road down.

The instructions sent by Mr. Todd, the Superintendent of Telegraphs, to Mr. Blood, the officer in charge at Peake station, were to the following effect :—

Please give my hearty congratulations to Mr. Forrest on the successful completion of his great feat, which I have communicated to the Government and press; also Baron Von Mueller, who sends his congratulations. I shall be glad to have a few particulars as to route followed, if convenient to Mr. Forrest to supply them. Render his party every attention.

Mr. Ernest Giles, the explorer, also telegraphed, and I also received messages from the editors of the *Register* and *Advertiser*, Adelaide newspapers, congratulating me, and asking for a few particulars for publication in their papers. I complied with the request immediately, forwarding a brief narrative of the more remarkable incidents of our journey. On the 15th of October, the day after our arrival at Peake, I wrote, for the information of Governor Musgrave, a short account of the journey, and this, accompanied by a more detailed narrative, addressed to the Hon. Malcolm Fraser, Commissioner of Crown Lands at Perth, was, together with several private telegrams, forwarded free of charge by the South Australian Government, which also provided us with fresh horses and everything we required for our journey to Adelaide.

We left the Peake on the 4th of October, greatly refreshed by the rest and the kind treatment we had received from Mr. and Mrs. Blood, and Mr. Bagot, the owner of the cattle station.

Before I record the details of our journey and the receptions given us at every place on the route, I will quote the concluding remarks of my journal relative to the expedition :—

I now beg to make a few remarks with reference to the character and capability of the country traversed ; and through the kindness and courtesy of Baron Von Mueller, C.M.G., &c., Government Botanist of Victoria, and of Mr. R. Brough

Smyth, Secretary for Mines of Victoria, I am enabled to annex reports upon the botanical and geological specimens collected on our journey.

The whole of the country, from the settled districts near Champion Bay to the head of the Murchison, is admirably suited for pastoral settlement, and in a very short time will be taken up and stocked; indeed, some already has been occupied.

From the head of the Murchison to the 129th meridian, the boundary of our colony, I do not think will ever be settled. Of course there are many grassy patches, such as at Windich Springs, the Weld Springs, all round Mount Moore, and other places; but they are so isolated, and of such extent, that it would never pay to stock them. The general character of this immense tract is a gently undulating spinifex desert—*Festuca* (*Triodia*) *irritans*, the spinifex of the desert explorers, but not the spinifex of science. It is lightly wooded with acacia and other small trees, and, except in a few creeks, there is a great absence of any large timber.

The prevailing rock, which crops out on the rises and often forms low cliffs, in which are receptacles for holding water, is *light red sandstone* (desert sandstone, tertiary). The only game found in the spinifex is a kangaroo rat, commonly called the " wirrup ;" but in the grassy openings there are many kangaroos, and often emus, also a rat known as the " wurrung." These animals are very

good eating, and formed a valuable addition to our
store department. At the permanent waters
there were always myriads of bronze-winged
pigeons, and also the white cockatoo with scarlet
crest, called the " chockalott ; " also the "beaccoo,"
or slate-coloured parrot. Generally, however, with
the exception of the crow and hawk, birds were
not very numerous except round water. Whenever
a sheet of water was found we found ducks, and
in Lake Augusta swans and ducks were innumerable.

In bringing this report to a close it is not necessary to refer much to the reasons that induced me
to keep more to the south than I originally intended. It will readily be seen, after perusing
this journal, that it was a necessity, and that we
could not get further north. It is a marvel to me
that we got through at all ; the season was an
exceptionally dry one—in fact, a drought—our
horses were of a very ordinary kind, and the
country most wretched.

When it is remembered that a horse in poor
condition and in warm weather cannot go much
over a day without water, and when the sterility
of the country is considered, it will be readily seen
what a disadvantage one labours under without
camels, which can go ten days without water.
Well can I sympathize with Mr. Giles when he
states in his journal : " All I coveted from my
brother explorers was their camels, for what is a

horse in such a region as this? He is not physically capable of enduring the terrors of this
country." And so it is; horses are the noblest
and most useful animals in the world, but they
must have food and water regularly. The camel,
on the other hand, is physically formed to travel
over these desolate regions, and in Australia has
been known to go twelve and fourteen days
without water, carrying 300 lbs., and sometimes
400 lbs. weight.

From these few remarks it will be seen what a
great disadvantage Mr. Giles and myself laboured
under compared with Major Warburton and Mr.
Gosse; and what in similar circumstances might
have been easily performed by them was quite
impossible in our circumstances.

In reading this journal, it may be wondered
why we followed so much along Mr. Gosse's track,
when a new route for ourselves might have been
chosen more to the south. The reason is, I
had intended, as soon as I reached the 129th
meridian (the boundary of our colony), to make a
long trip to the south, near to Eucla, and thus
map that important locality; but on reaching
there I was prevented by the following causes :—
The weather was excessively warm; the country
to the south seemed most uninviting—sand-hills
as far as could be seen, covered with spinifex;
our horses were very poor; our rations were
running short, the meat and tea and sugar being

nearly gone; water was very scarce, and I could clearly see that, although Mr. Gosse had travelled the route last year, it did not follow that we should be able to do it easily this, as all the water thus far where he had camped was gone. I felt we were altogether on our own resources for water, and I concluded to push on towards the telegraph line as quickly as possible. It turned out, although we had considerable difficulty, that we reached the line sooner than I could have anticipated.

I have the very pleasant duty to record my thorough appreciation of the services of my companions. To my brother, Mr. Alexander Forrest, I am especially indebted for his assistance and advice on many occasions, also for his indomitable energy and perseverance. Every service entrusted to him was admirably carried out. He never disappointed me. When absent for a week, I knew to a few minutes when we should meet again. Whether horses or loads had to be abandoned, it mattered not to him, he always carried out the service; and I attribute much of the success to being supported by such an able and hopeful second in command. In addition to this, he bestowed great care on the stores of the expedition; collected all the botanical specimens, besides taking observations for laying down our route on many occasions during my absence.

To Tommy Windich (native) I am much indebted

for his services as a bushman, and his experience generally. Accompanying me on many occasions, often in circumstances of difficulty and privation, I ever found him a good, honest companion.

To James Kennedy, James Sweeney, and Tommy Pierre I am thankful for the ready obedience and entire confidence they placed in me. They ever conducted themselves in a proper manner, and on no occasion uttered a single murmur.

I take this opportunity of thanking all those gentlemen who so kindly subscribed to the Expedition Fund.

In conclusion, sir, I beg you will convey to his Excellency Governor Weld my sincere thanks for the kindness and support he has given me in this arduous enterprise. I can truthfully state, if it had not been for his zeal and assistance, I should not have been able to undertake and accomplish this exploration.

I have also to thank the Honourable F. P. Barlee, Colonial Secretary, and yourself, for your kind attention and consideration, and your desire that I should have everything that was necessary to bring the expedition to a successful termination.

CHAPTER VI.

WE reached Beltana on the 18th, where we were joined by Mr. Henry Gosse, brother and companion of the explorer, and arrived at Jamestown on the 28th of October. This was the first township on the route, and the inhabitants, although somewhat taken by surprise by our appearance, would not let the opportunity pass for giving us a warm welcome. On the following morning there was a good muster of the principal residents at Jureit's Hotel, and an address was presented to me. Our healths were then drunk and duly responded to, and we had every reason to be highly gratified with our first formal reception.

The next day we reached Kooringa, on the Burra, and there too our arrival excited considerable enthusiasm, and we were invited to a complimentary dinner at the Burra Hotel Assembly Rooms, Mr. Philip Lane, the Chairman of the District Council, presiding. An address was presented, and, my health having been proposed by Mr. W. H. Rosoman, Manager of the National Bank, in replying, I took the opportunity of expressing my thanks to my associates in the expedition for their unfailing co-operation under occasionally great difficulties and privations.

On Saturday, the 31st, having witnessed a cricket-match at Farrell's Flat, we visited the Burra Burra Mines, and there we received an address from the manager, accountant, captain, chief engineer, and storekeeper. We remained at Burra the next day (Sunday), and on Monday morning started by train for Salisbury with our fifteen horses in horse-boxes. Eleven of these were the survivors of the expedition, and we were desirous that our faithful and hard-worked four-footed companions should have their share of the attention of our South Australian friends. At Gawler we were received by a crowd of people, and flags were flying to do us honour. The Town Clerk and a considerable number of the principal residents were waiting for us in an open space near the railway station, and presented an address on behalf of the municipality. We were then invited to a luncheon at the Criterion Hotel, the chair being filled, in the absence of the Mayor, who was unwell, by Mr. James Morton. Here again I was called on to respond for my health being proposed; but I need not weary the reader by endeavouring to repeat all I said upon that and other similar occasions. I acknowledged and deeply felt the personal kindness of the receptions my party had experienced; and I fully shared with those who signed the addresses I received, or proposed my health at dinners, the hearty desire that the successful issue of my expedition might be the means of uniting still more closely the two colonies in bonds of mutual good-feeling and sympathy. I had been similarly welcomed at Gawler and other places in South Australia on the occasion of my previous visit, and I was, I trust, not unjustifiably proud and pleased that my old friends had recognized my recent services.

At Salisbury, which we reached on the 2nd of November, a very hearty reception awaited us, and we were entertained at a dinner given at the Salisbury Hotel under the presidency of the Rev. J. R. Ferguson. After dinner the chairman read a brief address, signed by the Chairman of the District Council; and as the speeches referred not only to my own expedition, but were interesting in relation to other explorations and the method of conducting them, I may be pardoned for quoting a portion of the report of the proceedings which appeared in the local newspapers :—

The Chairman then said he wished to express the great pleasure it was to him to meet Mr. Forrest, his brother, and party, after their triumphant accomplishment of the daring and arduous undertaking of crossing from the Australian shores of the Indian Ocean to the very interior of South Australia. We at all times felt constrained to value and honour men who in any way contributed to the progress and welfare of mankind. We esteemed those men whose lives were devoted to the explorations of science, and whose discoveries were rendered serviceable to the comfort and advancement of the race; and what were the achievements of travellers but contributions to the advancement and welfare of the race—contributions in which were involved the most magnificent heroism in penetrating the regions which had hitherto been untrodden by the foot of the white man? They obtained their contributions to the advancement and welfare of men by the manifestation of high moral endurance, which enabled them to submit to privations and discomforts of the most trying character; while withal they showed dauntless courage in going forward and meeting dangers of every possible kind, even to the loss of life itself. He was disposed to rank the achievements of their guests with those of the foremost of travellers of whom we read. He had sat enchanted with the perusal of the travels of John Franklin in the Arctic Regions; and, by the way, John Franklin accompanied Caplain Flinders in his expedition in the year 1800, which was sent out for the purpose of surveying the south coast of Australia. He had perused with intense interest the travels of Samuel Baker in the interior of Africa along the source of that wondrous Nile, as also those of Speke, Grant, Stanley, and that prince of men, the late Dr. Livingstone; and the name of their guest was entitled to rank along with such. (Cheers.) Let now our stockholders and men of capital take advantage of Mr. Forrest's explorations—let his well-earned honours be bestowed upon him—and let all representatives of intelligence and enterprise hail him. We who were here as Australians were proud of him and rejoiced over him, and would seek to send him back to his own home with our loud plaudits and our heartiest gratitude.

The Vice-Chairman, in proposing " The Health of Mr. John Forrest, the Leader of the Expedition," said he was sure they were all extremely glad to see Mr. Forrest and his party in their midst. When Mr. Forrest was amongst them before they

all thought he was a fine, jolly young fellow, and thought none
the less of him on that occasion. (Applause.) At any rate,
he was stouter than when he appeared on his first visit. He
thought the country would feel grateful to Mr. Forrest and his
companions for the benefits which would result from their
achievement. (Applause.)

Mr. John Forrest, who was received with loud cheers, said
he thanked them very heartily for the enthusiastic way in
which they had drunk his health, and for the very handsome
address they had presented to him. He felt altogether unable
to respond in the way he could wish to the many remarks that
had been made by their worthy chairman. If he could only
make himself believe that he was worthy of being placed in the
rank of the men whom he had mentioned, he certainly would
feel very proud indeed. It had always given him the greatest
pleasure to read the accounts of the travels of these great men.
He remembered being closely connected with Captain Flinders's
researches upon the south coast of Australia, and, after his
journey from Perth to Eucla, Mr. Eyre, the late Governor of
Jamaica, wrote to him that he risked his life upon the accuracy
of Captain Flinders's observations, and in no case had he the
least cause to regret it. Exploration in other parts of the
world, as in Africa, was carried on in a very different style to
the exploration in Australia. Even in the early times, exploration here was carried on in a very different way to what it
was at the present time. Large equipages, many waggons, and
that sort of thing were used in the time of Captain Sturt and
other early explorers, until Mr. Eyre took a light equipment,
with very few horses and very few men. Since then the work
had had to be done with very light turn-outs. In Western
Australia a good deal of exploration was done before his time,
and expeditions had been very common. They generally cost
very little indeed. The horses were generally given by the
settlers, the Government contributed a few hundred pounds,
and young settlers volunteered for the service. The cost was
sometimes 400*l.* or 500*l.*; and upon his expedition, up to the
time they left the settled districts of Western Australia, they
had only spent about 330*l.* He did not know that he could

say anything more. He had spoken several times on his journey down, and it seemed to him that he had said the same thing over and over again. His forte was not in public speaking, but he hoped they would take the will for the deed. They never could forget the very kind and hearty reception they had received in every place they had visited in South Australia. (Cheers.)

The Rev. J. G. Wright proposed "The Health of Mr. Alexander Forrest and the remainder of the Party." He remarked that they had heard a great deal about Mr. Forrest, the leader of the party, and whilst he had manifested a great deal of courage and perseverance, and they all felt indebted to him as the leader of the party, yet there was much praise due to his brother and the rest of his companions. He was gratified at having the opportunity of meeting them before they went down to the metropolis, and he was sure it was no small matter to Salisbury to have such a band remaining with them for a short time. It would be a source of pleasure to colonists generally to see them, and he trusted that the work which had been so nobly performed, and what had followed after it, would tend to link the colonies more closely together. He was glad to see that original holders of the land in their western colony —the natives—had been employed in the work of exploration and opening up the country. (Hear, hear.) They were expected to do honour to generals and warriors who had distinguished themselves and placed their names high on the roll of fame, but he thought that such could not claim greater honours than the explorer. His work was not one of bloodshed, but one which was undertaken in the interests and for the benefit of humanity. Civilization, agriculture, art, and science followed the explorations of those noble men who had taken their lives in their hands and faced difficulties and dangers for the advancement of their fellow-men. He proposed with the heartiest feelings the toast of Mr. Alexander Forrest and his companions.

The toast was very cordially drunk.

Mr. Alex. Forrest, on rising to respond, was greeted with hearty and continued cheering He said he thanked the company most heartily for the manner in which they had drunk his health and that of his companions. He could assure them they felt highly flattered at the reception which had been accorded them. It was more than they expected. When here four years ago, it was on a small trip compared with what they had accomplished this time. It would not be necessary for him to go over the same ground that his brother had remarked upon —in fact, his brother had quite taken the wind out of his sails; and public speaking certainly not being his forte, although he was quite at home round the camp-fire, he must ask them to excuse him making a lengthy speech. He could assure them they all thanked them very sincerely for their kindness, and deeply appreciated the honour which had been done them. (Cheers.)

Tommy Pierre, one of the aboriginals attached to the expedition, being called upon to respond, after some hesitation, said,—Well, gentlemen, I am not in good humour to-night. (Laughter.) I am very glad I got through. We got a capital gaffer that leaded us through; but it wasn't him that got us through, it isn't ourselves, but God who brought us through the place, and we ought to be very thankful to God for getting us through. (Laughter and cheers.) I am not in good humour to-night to speak (laughter), but I will speak when I get in Adelaide. (Prolonged cheering.)

Tommy Windich, the other aboriginal attached to the expedition, was also asked to respond, but he could not muster courage enough to do so.

The preparations for our reception at Adelaide were most elaborate. It seems to have been resolved that the capital of South Australia should appear as the representative of the satisfaction felt throughout the colony at the successful completion of an adventure, the result of which was so deeply interesting, and which had been several times attempted by explorers, not less ardent and determined, but less fortunate than ourselves. At an early hour on the morning of the 3rd of November, on which day it was known our party would arrive, the streets through which we were to pass were thronged with thousands eager to bid us welcome. Not only the city itself, but the suburban districts contributed to swell the crowd. Balconies and housetops were thronged, and all along the line of route were flags and decorations of flowers and evergreens, streamers with inscriptions of welcome, and arches adorned with large pictures representing incidents of bush life. The bells, too, rang out merry peals, and the day was observed as a general holiday at Adelaide.

We left Salisbury at twelve o'clock, escorted by a considerable number of the inhabitants. Before reaching Adelaide we were met by carriages containing the Mayors of Adelaide, Port Adelaide, Kensington, and Norwood, the town clerks, and members of the different corporations. A very interesting and characteristic compliment was paid to us by the presence of members of various exploring expeditions, who, from their own experience, could best estimate the value of the results we had achieved, and the difficulties we had encountered. Following the official personages, on horseback, was Mr. John Chambers, who, with his brother, the late Mr. James Chambers, and the late Mr. Finke, sent out in 1860 the

parties under the leadership of the intrepid Mr.
John McDonald Stewart, to explore the interior
lying between South Australia and the northern
shores of the continent. Three members of this
party—Messrs. A. J. Lawrence, D. Thompson,
and John Wall—followed on horseback, carrying
standards marked with the dates " January, 1862,"
and " July 25, 1862," when Stuart departed from
Adelaide, and when he planted his flag on the
northern shores. Then came representatives of
the various exploring parties—Messrs. F. G.
Waterhouse, F. Thring, W. P. Auld, S. King, J.
W. Billiatt, and H. Nash, of Stuart's party; Mr.
R. E. Warburton, Mr. Dennis White, and Charley,
the native boy, of Colonel Warburton's expedition;
Mr. William Gosse (leader), and Mr. Harry
Gosse, of the Gosse expedition; and Mr. Ernest
Giles, leader of the Giles expedition.

The reception committee and representatives
of the Oddfellows, Foresters, Druids, Rechabites,
Good Templars, German, and other friendly
societies, followed, after which came our party.
We wore the rough, weather-beaten, and, it may
be added, shockingly dilapidated garments in which
we had been clothed during our expedition, and
were mounted on the horses which had served us so
well. It was wished that we should represent to the
Adelaide public, as realistically as we could, the
actual appearance of our party while engaged on
the long journey, so we slung our rifles at our

sides, and each of us led a pack-horse carrying the kegs we had used for the conveyance of water. In one respect, no doubt, we failed to realize adequately the appearance of our party when struggling through the spinifex desert, or anxiously searching for rock holes and springs. The month of great hospitality we had experienced since reaching Peake station had considerably improved our own personal appearance, and the horses were very unlike the wretched, half-dying animals we had such difficulty to keep alive and moving. After us came, in long procession, bands of music, and the members of the various orders, the German Club, the Bushmen's Club, and a goodly number of horsemen and carriages. The bands played inspiring strains, the crowd shouted and cheered, and my brother and I were perpetually bowing acknowledgments. As for the two natives, Tommy Windich and Tommy Pierre, they appeared to be perfectly amazed by the novelty of the spectacle, and the enthusiasm of the vast throng which lined the streets.

On our arrival at the town hall we were received by the Ministry, the Hon. W. Milne (President of the Legislative Council), Sir G. S. Kingston (the Speaker), several members of both Houses of Parliament, and other gentlemen. Having alighted, we were conducted to a platform, and addresses were presented to us by the Mayor, on behalf of the citizens of Adelaide; from the Odd Fellows, the Foresters, the Rechabites, the Good Templars, and four German societies. In replying to these I did my best, but very inadequately, to express my feelings of gratitude for the reception we had met with, and of thanks for the generous manner in which our endeavours to successfully perform an arduous task had been recognized. The Mayors of Kensington, Norwood, and Port Adelaide, also offered a few words of congratulation to our party.

" By particular request," we showed ourselves on the balcony, and bowed our acknowledgments for the very hearty welcome we received. Then we remounted our horses, and took them to the police paddocks, after which my brother and I were introduced to the Adelaide Club.

I have mentioned that several distinguished Australian explorers took part in the reception, and I may add that among them were the whole of Stuart's last party, except the gallant leader and Mr. Kekwick, who were dead, Mr. Few, who was in a distant part of the colony, and the farrier, who had gone no one knew whither. It was also appropriate to the occasion that two horses, who were memorably connected with explorations, should be associated with the animals who had served one so well. The horse which had carried poor Burke on his ill-fated expedition from Melbourne was ridden by Mr. F. G. Waterhouse, and Mr. F. Thring was mounted on a

horse which had crossed the continent with
Stuart.

In the evening we were entertained at a banquet
in the town hall, the chair being occupied by the
Hon. Arthur Blyth, the Premier of the colony.
The proceedings were fully reported in the newspapers on the following day; and as so many
explorers were present, and addressed the company, I may be permitted, apart from personal
considerations, to quote the principal speeches
delivered on the occasion.

The chairman rose to propose the toast of the
evening, and was received with cheers. He said,—
" I think, for the last two or three days, that there
has been a general feeling that South Australians
were not very good at receptions and getting up
processions; but at all events to-day we have
showed that we can manage such things as well
as people of more importance probably than ourselves—at all events quite as well as countries
much more thickly populated than our own.
(Cheers.) We have all of us read something
about the old Roman triumphs—how the con-
querors, when they went forth and were successful, were granted a triumph, and in this triumph
were accompanied by the most beautiful of their
captives, and the most wonderful and singular of
the animals they had taken, and passed through
the cities of which they were citizens, and received
the plaudits of their inhabitants.   To-day we have

granted a triumph, not to a warrior who has killed thousands of his fellows, or added much to the landed property of the country, but to one who has been a warrior nevertheless, fighting many difficulties that many warriors had not to contend with, and carrying his life in his hands, as warriors have done of old, in leading those who are associated with him in the triumph here to-day. (Cheers.) There was no beautiful captive in his train, and no curious animals, as in the old Roman triumphs. All that we saw were some dusty pack-horses, and some well-worn pack-saddles; yet with these the explorer has to proceed on his journey, and conquer the difficulties of the desert, knowing that with such slender things to rely upon he must hope to overcome the dangers, and endure to the end. (Cheers.) Gentlemen, in the page of 'Australian Exploration,' which is the sentiment attached to my toast—in its pages there are to be read too many tragic stories. We cannot think of the history of exploration without thinking with regret of some of the names connected with it. What an extraordinary page is that of Leichardt, of whom it has been said no man

'—— knows his place of rest
Far in the cedar shade.'

And yet so great is the interest which is taken in his fate that the wildest stories of a convict in the gaols of a neighbouring colony have been of

interest to us, and have caused some of our fellow-
Australians to send out a party to see if something could not still be heard of that explorer.
Then think of Burke and Wills, and what a tragic
tale was theirs—so nearly saved, so closely arrived
to a place of safety, and yet to miss it after all!
I daresay there are hundreds here who, like myself,
saw their remains taken through our streets in
the gloomy hearse on the road to that colony
which they had served so well; and we know that
now the country where they laid down their lives
is brought under the hand of pastoral settlement.
They were the heroes of other lands; but have we
not heroes also of our own? (Loud cheering.)
Have we not here the likeness of a man who knew
not what fear was, because he never saw fear—
who carried out the thorough principle of the
Briton in that he always persevered to the end?
And then, coming nearer to our own time,
speaking by weeks and months, had we not our
opportunity of entertaining in the city the leader
of an expedition that successfully passed its way
through the desert to the shores of Western
Australia?—I refer to Colonel Warburton. When
speaking, upon that occasion, of the noble way in
which the people of Western Australia had received our explorer, I ventured to hope that before
many months we should have an opportunity of
welcoming some explorer from that colony. Gentlemen, the hour has come, and the man. (Loud

cheering.) For West Australia, though the least of the colonies in population, has its exploring heroes too. (Cheers.) I have no doubt you have read, within the last few days, all about the battle that Mr. Forrest has had to fight with the spinifex desert, with unknown regions, and hostile natives. While giving all praise to those Australian explorers connected with this Australian Empire that is to be, I ask you to join with me in drinking the health of the last and not the least, and I now give you the toast of 'Australian Exploration,' coupled with the name of Mr. John Forrest." (Cheers.)

The toast was enthusiastically received, and three hearty cheers given.

Band : " The Song of Australia."

Mr. John Forrest, who was received with loud cheers, said,—" Mr. Chairman and Gentlemen,—I feel very proud that my name should be coupled with the toast of Australian Exploration. I assure you I feel altogether unequal to the toast so aptly proposed by our worthy chairman, my forte not being public speaking; still, I will try to do as well as I can. (Cheers.) Since I arrived at years of discretion, I have always taken a very deep interest in exploration, and for the last five years I have been what is generally termed in Western Australia 'The Young Explorer,' as I have conducted all the explorations that have been undertaken by our Government. In the year 1869 I was instructed to accompany an expedition as navigator, which was intended to be commanded by Dr. Mueller, of Melbourne, to search for the remains of the late Dr. Leichardt, who started from near Moreton Bay in 1848, I think. Dr. Mueller not having arrived to take command as was anticipated, and the expedition having been got ready, I was deputed to the command, and we went out about 500 miles to the eastward of the settled districts of our colony, in order to find out whether the statements of the natives relative to the existence of white men or their remains in the locality were correct or not. We were out about five months. Although we did not suffer very much, as we had sufficient water and sufficient provisions, still it was a very dry season. We came back and settled that there were no remains —that, in fact, the reports of the natives were unfounded, and that they referred to the remains of horses lost by an explorer of our colony, Mr. Austin, not many miles to the eastward. This was the first attempt at exploration I had made, and, although I had been brought up to bush life, I knew very little about exploration, as I found when I went out. I was made aware of many things that I did not know about before, and I must say that I was a much better second than a commander. After this I undertook to conduct an exploration north-east from our colony to Sturt's Creek, where Mr. A. Gregory came down about 1855, and down the Victoria River. This fell to the ground; but our present Governor, Mr. Weld, had a great idea that we should organize an expedition to come to this colony overland along the coast—along the course which was previously taken by Mr. Eyre, I think in 1841—and he requested me to take command. Of course I readily acquiesced in his suggestion, and in 1870 we started on our journey; and although we did not experience the difficulties Mr. Eyre experienced, still we had some little difficulty, and we would have had a great deal more, I have no doubt, if we had not had Mr. Eyre's experience to guide us. Many people—in our colony, I mean—thought it was a very little thing indeed we had done, as we had only travelled along another man's tracks, although they gave us a very hearty and enthusiastic reception. We reported that there was good country along the coast, and I am glad to say that in the course of a year a telegraph line will be run across the route we travelled. (Cheers.) I hope it will tend to unite more closely than they are at present united the whole of the Australian colonies, and especially this colony with our own. (Cheers.) There is a very great deal of good country inland from the south coast; and if only water can be procured, I am quite certain it will be the finest pastoral district of West Australia. (Hear, hear.) I have no doubt the establishment of telegraphic communication will tend to the

settlement of that part of the country, and I am
very glad indeed that the Government of South
Australia have acted so liberally as to join with
our Government in erecting the line. (Cheers.)
After this my exploration experience still increased, and I tried very hard to get up another
expedition; but, not being a wealthy man, I had
to depend upon others. I often represented that
I would like to go, and people talked about the
matter, and then I thought I would make an offer
to the Government, which they might accept or
not as they liked. We have the good fortune to
have in our colony a Governor—who, I am sorry
to say, is leaving shortly—who takes a great
interest in exploration. He had been an explorer
himself, having, as he has often told me, travelled
across New Zealand with his swag on his back.
(Cheers.) He has always been a great supporter
of mine, and done all he could to forward exploration; and about two years ago I laid before him,
through the Commissioner of Crown Lands, a
project which I was willing to accomplish if he
would recommend the granting of the necessary
funds. In a very complimentary reply he quite
acquiesced with what I suggested, and promised
to lay it before the Legislative Council with the
support of the Government; and in 1873 the
matter was brought before the Council. All I
asked was that the Government of West Australia
would grant me some 400*l*., and I would from my

own private purse, and those of others who had
agreed to assist me, stand the remainder of the
cost. (Cheers.) If they granted me that sum, I
was willing to undertake an exploration from
Champion Bay up to the Murchison, the head of
which we did not know, and strike the telegraph
line or Port Darwin, it being left to my discretion
which course should be pursued. Four hundred
pounds seems a paltry sum, but there was some
bitter opposition to its being granted, although by
the aid of the Government and other members it
was voted. Last year was the year when I should
have undertaken the exploration, and I was, of
course, quite prepared to do so; but in the mean-
time a whole host of expeditions from South
Australia had come into the field. Mr. Giles, I
saw, had started from some part of the telegraph
line westward, and I heard afterwards that he had
through some misunderstanding—I do not know
what it was; I only know by what I read in the
papers—returned to Adelaide. Then we heard
that the South Australian Government had despatched Mr. Gosse, and that the Hon. Thomas
Elder—whom I have the pleasure of meeting
to-day—had despatched Colonel Warburton—
(cheers)—to explore towards the same direction
—as we judged from the despatches and newspapers—that I intended to start from. I belong
to the Survey Department of West Australia, and
was requested by the Commissioner of Crown

Lands and Surveyor-General, the Hon. Malcolm Fraser, to superintend some surveys he specially wished undertaken that season. I had an interview with the Governor, and he said very wisely he did not wish to order me in any way; that it was no use running a race with South Australia, and that as they were first in the field, although we were the first to suggest the exploration, we should wait till the next year, when, if the South Australian explorers were fortunate enough to reach this colony, we should have no necessity to send an expedition, and that if they did not, we should certainly profit by their experience. I, being engaged in another service in which I took great interest, was willing to wait for another year; and if, as Mr. Weld said, the South Australians did not succeed, I would undertake it the next year, and benefit by their experience. As it turned out, the expedition undertaken by the Government, commanded by Mr. Gosse, did not succeed in reaching the colony of Western Australia, and the expedition undertaken by Colonel Warburton, under the auspices of my recent friend, the Hon. Thomas Elder, reached our colony, but so far north that it did not add to the knowledge of the route we had laid out for ourselves. He came out between the 20th and 22nd degrees of latitude, whereas we started from the 26th, and did not intend to go more north than that. After we heard—his Excellency the

Governor was away on a visit to New Zealand at the time—that Mr. Gosse had turned back, although he had succeeded in reaching a very great distance from the telegraph line, I had instructions from the Colonial Secretary to equip an expedition at once. If Mr. Gosse had succeeded, I am sure I would not have been here to-day; but, as he did not succeed, I had orders to equip an expedition, and as I was starting news arrived from the north-west coast by a coaster that Colonel Warburton and his party had arrived. (Cheers.) This, of course, gave us very great pleasure, and steps were at once taken to give him a reception in Perth. (Cheers.) As soon as we heard that he had arrived, our whole colony rose up to give him a welcome; and although what we did did not come up with what you have given to us to-day—for our colony is only a small one, with little over 30,000 inhabitants—still I am sure that Colonel Warburton told you it was a kind reception. (Cheers.) I am sorry to say that I was not able to be present when he was received, though I waited some time in order to have that opportunity. The opportunities for transport from our north-west settlements to the capital are very few at a certain time of the year, and that was the time when Colonel Warburton arrived in our settlements; so that in a matter of 700 or 800 miles, from Nicol Bay to Perth, he was delayed unfortunately three or four months.

It was a very great pity that he should have been delayed so long. After receiving addresses at Roeburne and Fremantle, the colonel arrived just in time to be forwarded 250 miles to catch the mail, and therefore he had not time, I know, to receive the reception that would have been given him by the people of West Australia had he remained in our colony a little longer. (Cheers.) All I can say is, that though what has been done for Colonel Warburton cannot compare with what has been done for us to-day, it was done in the same spirit, and we did our best. (Cheers.) I am sure that I would have been very much pleased to have met Colonel Warburton here this evening; but I understand that he is gone upon a tour to his native land, and so I am deprived of the opportunity. I have, however, had the pleasure of meeting other explorers, and I must congratulate South Australia upon possessing so many explorers. I had no idea that she could assemble so many, and that so young a man as myself should be able to meet so many, all young men. I have read a great deal of early explorations, and could tell you a good deal about them; but I have no doubt you are just as well acquainted with their histories as I am. I have only gleaned their history from books written by able men on exploration; and I therefore need say little upon that subject, and will content myself with a short reference to explorations of recent date. I have

already referred to Colonel Warburton. Mr.
Gosse's is of more recent date. I have never
been able to read his journal to this day; but I
hope to be able to do so now. Through the
kindness of Mr. Phillipson, of Beltana, I was able
to see his map of the country he passed over, with
which I am very well pleased; and, in spite of
what some people have said, I think that Mr.
Gosse's exploration will be found of considerable
benefit to the colony, and that his action was one
for which he deserved very much credit. He
travelled for some time in bad country, but, going
on, he got into good country; and that which he
has described as the Musgrave and Mann and
Tomkinson Ranges I hope to see next year stocked
with South Australian sheep and cattle. (Cheers.)
The country which Mr. Gosse found is country
abounding with any quantity of grass, with many
springs; and there are, perhaps, many more than
I saw, for I kept along Mr. Gosse's track; but
I will say that I always found water where he
said that it would be found. (Cheers.) There is
but one fault that I have to find with him, and
that is, that he did not say that water would be
found where I sometimes found it; but doubtless this arose from a very laudable caution in an
explorer, for had he stated that water would be
found where it failed it might have cost men their
lives. One place he marked springs, and if he
had been mistaken there, we would have lost our

lives; but I am glad to say that we found there a very good spring indeed—(cheers)—enough to last all the sheep of South Australia, or at any rate a good spring; and I am glad on this occasion to be able to thank him for being so careful to mark permanent water where permanent water really existed. Mr. Giles's exploration would have been as useful to me as Mr. Gosse's, but unfortunately he did not return before I left the settled districts of West Australia, and therefore I did not benefit by his work. I am sure that my companions and myself feel very much the hearty reception you have given us on this occasion. I cannot find words to express my feelings on that point at all. I feel very deeply thankful, and that is about all that I can say. (Loud cheers.) Six weary travellers, travelling through the spinifex desert with about fifteen or sixteen nearly knocked-up horses, not knowing whether they should find water, or whether their lives were safe or not, I am sure that we could not imagine that, after all our travels were over, we should receive such a reception as we have received to-day. (Cheers.) I am sure that if any stimulus is required to induce persons to become explorers, those who witness our reception to-day ought to feel content. I am very proud of the hearty and enthusiastic reception my companions and myself have met with. I hope you will take the will for the deed, and, in the absence of better speaking on my

part, consider that we are deeply thankful." (Loud
cheers.)

Sir H. Ayers, K.C.M.G., had much pleasure in
proposing a toast that had been allotted to him,
and made no doubt that the company would have
equal pleasure in responding to it. The toast
was "Early Explorers," and he had been requested to associate with it the name of Mr. John
Chambers. (Cheers.) It seemed to be the lot
of poor human nature that whenever we met for
rejoicing there was always sure to be some little
mournful circumstance attending it, and we could
scarcely think of the early explorers without re-
membering with regret the noble leaders and brave
members of former expeditions who have now
passed to their eternal rest. There was the
name of Sturt that came first in the list of our
old explorers. There was the name and the likeness of a man far more familiar to many of them.
There was Kekwick, and more recently poor
McKinlay—all gone to their last account. But
still he was proud to see, and he was sure it
formed a source of gratification to that company,
and especially so to our guest, so many brave
men at the table who had been companions of
those leaders and others in the early expeditions
of this country. (Cheers.) He said it with pride,
that in no other Australian colony could be seen
such a group as sat at that table who had gone
through the hardships and dangers of exploration;

for with one or two exceptions all of them in the
row were explorers.   It was hardly possible for
us to estimate how much we had benefited by
those who had opened up the country for us.
We were few in numbers and could not appreciate
the work of the explorer; but generations yet
unborn would bless the names of those men who
had carried it out.   (Cheers).   He thought that
it was doing only a just tribute to associate the
name of Mr. John Chambers with this toast,
because it might not be known to all present that
Mr. Chambers, with his late brother James and
Mr. W. Finke, enabled Mr. Stuart to accomplish
the journeys that he made throughout the continent.   (Cheers.)   It was their capital and his
great skill, for in the face of so many explorers he
was not ashamed to say that Mr. McDouall Stuart
was the greatest explorer that ever lived.   It was
their capital that had enabled him to perform the
work which he had done, and for which his name
would remain as a monument for ever in the
memories of South Australians.   For not only
were we indebted to Stuart for the most valuable
discoveries he had made, but he thought Mr. Todd
would say that his indications had proved the
most accurate.   But he had also done a great thing
for exploration in changing the *modus operandi*.
He had been one of Sturt's party that went out
with bullock-drays; but he had had genius, and
had changed all that, starting upon exploring with

light parties, and thus being able to accomplish so much, and he was glad to say that explorers since had followed up the same plan with great success. (Cheers.) And they were still further indebted to the Messrs. Chambers. They had not only assisted in discovering far-off country, but had been the first to invest their capital in stocking it and making it useful. He was sorry to see that there were not more Messrs. Chambers to go and do likewise; but he thought he saw signs of the spread of settlement further, for the toe of the agriculturist was very near upon the heel of the sheep-farmer, and if the sheep-farmers did not look out and get fresh fields and pastures new, they would soon find that the agriculturist was all too near. That was a question that he enlarged upon, especially in another place; but as brevity seemed to be the order of the night, he would only ask them to drink the health of "The Early Explorers," coupled with the name of Mr. John Chambers.

The toast was received with three cheers.

Band: "Auld lang syne."

Mr. J. Chambers rose amid cheers, and said that he was proud to say that he had been connected with the earliest of our explorations, having been associated with the gallant Captain Sturt in his exploration of the Murray. After his arrival in the colony he had first travelled with him and the then Governor, the late Colonel Gawler, in

exploring the south. They had had no difficulties
and dangers to encounter then that some of the
explorers of the present had to go through, and,
although they travelled with heavy bullock-drays,
managed to have plenty of water and food.
Their principal difficulty lay in getting through
the ranges to the south, and the interminable
creeks and gullies which they got into and had to
retrace their steps from. This was a small matter
of exploration, and might at the present day
appear absurd; but then there were doubts where
the Angas was, and whether the Onkaparinga in
Mount Barker District was not the Angas, and
when beyond the hills they did not know whether
Mount Barker was not Mount Lofty, and whether
Mount Lofty was not some other mount. It was,
however, done, and, having settled these matters
by observation, they returned to Adelaide after an
exploration of three weeks. They were on their
return made small lions of, although they had not
had to fight the natives, and had had bullock-
drays with them, while their horses were in rather
better condition than when they went out. There
was no doubt that the subject of exploration was
one of the most important to be considered by
those who in the future would have to do with the
country, as it was always well to have information
beforehand; and, if Governor Gawler and Captain
Sturt had known more, there would have been a
different result to their exploration journey up the

Murray. The gallant Captain Sturt had made Cooper's Creek his depôt, and that place twelve months ago had been looked upon as a home by persons in search of country with a view of stocking it. His youngest son had been round there for five months, and had penetrated the country far and wide, and had often to retrace his steps there for water. They had heard from the young explorer, Mr Forrest, how it was said when he came here before that he had only traversed the tracks of Mr. Eyre. So be it, and often was it said that Mr. Eyre did no good because he kept to the coast; but they had heard from Mr. Forrest that the tracks and descriptions of Mr. Eyre were of vast assistance to him. (Cheers.) Therefore no man could tell what good he might do; the finding of a spring in a desert might eventually become of great service to the descendants of those who lived at the time. There were some whom he wished could have been there, but Providence had ordained the contrary, and therefore he stood before them to say that it was for no purpose of self-aggrandizement, but for the purpose of good to the nation, that the early expeditions were promoted and conducted—(cheers)— and that the object of James Chambers, Finke, Stuart, and himself was to span this colony for the purpose of allowing a telegraph line to be laid. (Cheers.) When we read of the many times that Stuart was driven back by the force of circumstances, it could easily be conceived that he possessed a very energetic spirit. It was not once or twice that Stuart was driven back, but he was determined to penetrate the continent for the purpose, he was proud to know, of paving the way for telegraphic communication; and had it not been for his brother, Mr. Stuart, and himself, he was proud to say, we should not this day have had the telegraph. It was often said that there never would be a telegraph line, but their answer was always "yes." (Cheers). He thanked them heartily for the position in which they had placed him and Mr. Stuart's companions, and which they all appreciated. (Cheers).

Mr. J. W. Billiat, who was imperfectly heard, also responded. He said that when he went out with Mr. Stuart he was only a new chum; but he went out and came back again, and there he was. He could not say much about Mr. Stuart's explorations, as all that needed to be said had been so ably put by Sir Henry Ayers. There was no country in the world that had so tried the endurance and perseverance of the men on exploring expeditions as South Australia had done, and explorers should receive all the credit that could be given. He knew the difficulty of travelling country like that Mr. Forrest had come across, as several of Mr. Stuart's party had travelled upon it trying to strike the Victoria River. If Mr. John Chambers's liberality were known, and the way he had entered into the question of exploration generally were known, his name would be brought into more prominence than it had. He had sat in the background, but he had found both money and energy.

The Hon. W. Everard (Commissioner of Crown Lands) said the toast he had to give was "The Government and People of Western Australia." Owing to a variety of circumstances, our relations with Western Australia had not been so intimate or close as those with the eastern colonies. That would be readily understood, because Western Australia, being a small colony, and self-reliant and independent, had troubled us very little— occasionally for a few tons of flour or a cargo of notions. Another reason was that it had not had telegraphic communication with us or the rest of the world, and it was separated from us by a large extent of country which till lately was considered little better than a howling wilderness. He was happy to say that by the enterprise of Western Australia the magic wire which annihilated time and distance would be laid between the two colonies before long; and he was happy to say the Legislature here had agreed to construct the South Australian part of the line, so that Western Australia would be placed in communication, not only with South Australia, but the world. (Cheers.) And again, with reference to that large tract of hitherto supposed desert country which lay between the two colonies, the experience of the gallant men he saw around him, and not only of the Messrs. Forrest, but of Warburton, Gosse, and Giles, had shown that it contained grassy valleys, mountain ranges, and permanent waters, and he believed that before long it would be occupied by squatters. We must remember that, in South Australia, close upon the heels of the explorer came the squatter with his flocks and herds, and he even was not long left in quiet enjoyment; and if his runs were good they were soon taken from him for agricultural purposes. Considering the progress that we were making in agriculture, it was high time we sought to enlarge our borders. Although it was true that the band of explorers who were now before them had only made a line through the country, we must remember that it would be a base-line for future operations. Their work was very different to making a forced march of two or three days when it was known there was permanent water ahead. The explorer had carefully and deliberately to feel his way into unknown country, and if he went a mile or two too far he could not retrace his steps, and we could not attach too much importance to the services of those individuals who had risked their lives in that way. It was said, when Edward John Eyre made that wonderful journey of his along the coast of Western Australia, that he had done nothing but gone along the coast; but along

that very line there would be a telegraph to connect this colony with Western Australia. (Cheers.)
It was true that Western Australia was the smallest
of the Australian group, and she had not perhaps
been so favoured as South Australia, as her country
was not so good; but he believed, from the enterprise of her Government, and the courage, perseverance, and endurance shown by some of her
sons, that she would yet take her place among the
Australian group, and that at some future date
she would be one of the provinces which would
form one united Australia.   (Cheers.)

The toast was drunk with cheers.

Mr. Alexander Forrest responded.   He said he
thanked them most cordially for having associated
his name with that of the Government and people
of Western Australia.   He had had the honour
for the last four years of being employed in the
service of the Western Australian Government,
and he could assure them that they had a very
good Government.   They had representative government, although not responsible government;
but since they had been on their trip they had
heard that it was proposed to establish constitu-
tional government.   He did not believe it would
make much difference, but personally he was glad
to see it.   The people would have the management of their own money, and that he considered
a good thing, for they were never satisfied till they
had the control over it.   When the party left, all

the people of Western Australia were longing to do honour to and entertain Colonel Warburton ; and, although they were a small people, they did their best, and what they did they did heartily. (Cheers.) If Mr. Gosse had got over they would have given him also a good reception. He had not expected to see as many people as he had seen that day. The streets were crowded, and, wherever he looked, some one seemed to be looking in that direction. (Laughter.) The toast included the people of Western Australia, and he could assure them that, as he had travelled through the length and breadth of the land, he knew every man in it, every squatter, every farmer, every rich man, every poor man, and every magistrate. This was not the first time that he had been exploring, as he accompanied his brother to this colony four years ago, and in 1871 the Government sent him out in command of a party to find new land, when he went out about 600 miles. He thanked them for the very kind way in which they had spoken of his companions. Since they came to this colony they had been fed and clothed, and no one would take any money. (Cheers.) In the city he expected something great, but in the Burra, Gawler, and other places where they did not expect it, they had met with a hearty reception. He saw a great improvement in Adelaide. When he came here four years ago, the colony was not in such a good state, and a great many men were out of work ;

but now everything was in good order, and he believed South Australia would be one of the first colonies of Australia. (Cheers).

Mr. William Gosse rose, and was received with loud cheers. He said he felt honoured by being invited on the present occasion, and had much pleasure in taking part in the reception of Mr. John Forrest and party. He would take that opportunity of making a few remarks. His instructions, when he was sent out, were to find a route as nearly as possible in a direct line from his starting-point upon the telegraph line to Perth, only deviating when obliged to do so for water. He had to feel his way as he advanced, form depôts to secure his retreat if necessary, and accurately fix all points on his track. The last words the Hon. T. Reynolds had said to him were, "You fully understand that Perth is your destination, and not any other point on the western coast," or words to that effect. They would see by that, that had he been fortunate enough to discover the country by which Mr. Forrest got across, he should scarcely have been justified in proceeding. His farthest point west was between 500 and 600 miles from the explored portion of the Murchison, and 360 miles from the sources of the same. Copies of his diary and map had been forwarded to Mr. Forrest by Mr. Goyder on the 27th of February, 1874, the originals of which had been ready for publication on his arrival on the telegraph line, and had not

been compiled after their return to Adelaide, as
some people supposed from the delay in their publication.   He made these statements partly in
self-defence, as remarks had been made by members in the House to the effect that the Government had fitted out an expedition at an enormous
expense which had done comparatively nothing,
though his map showed 50,000 square miles of
country.

Sir John Morphett had been asked to propose
the toast of " The Australian Colonies."   It was
a very large toast indeed at the present time even,
and what it might be in the future it was impossible to say.   He hoped that it would be something wonderful.   (Cheers.)   At the present time
the immense country was occupied by 2,000,000
people, and we could not with that number get on.
What we wanted was more population.   What
were the products which Australia could produce ?
First of all was wheat—the best in the world.
Then there were wine and wool, and lead, and
gold, and copper, tin, and sugar.   These were all
products that the world wanted, and all that we
required to make our production of these a success
was federation.   We should have greater individual
strength and prosperity, and greater universal
strength and prosperity if we were federated, and
we would in time become what we wanted to be—
a nation.   (Cheers.)   Let them come to West Australia, which was the birth-place of their esteemed

and energetic friend Mr. Forrest. He was glad to see that she had at last freed herself from the shackles of that curse of convictism, and could now go hand in hand with the other colonies in the march of progress. He gave them the toast of the Colonies of Australia, coupling with it the name of Mr. Ernest Giles.

The toast having been duly honoured,—

Mr. Ernest Giles rose to respond, and was met with cheers. He had been called upon to respond to this toast, which, as Sir John Morphett had told them, was a very comprehensive one—so comprehensive that he was sure that he would fail to do it justice. What he had to say therefore on the subject would not detain them long. Sir John Morphett had touched upon the progress and prosperity of the colonies, and there was no doubt that at the present time the colonies were in a far more prosperous state than they had ever been in before. With regard to federation, a gentleman high in the service here, speaking to him, had said that if that was carried out exploration should not be forgotten, but that fresh lines should be taken with the co-operation of all the colonies. The splendid success which had attended Mr. Forrest would, he had no doubt, tend greatly to promote the ultimate prosperity of the colonies. (Applause.)

Mr. John Forrest, in a few complimentary words, proposed the health of the Chairman, which was well received and acknowledged.

A few days afterwards I was honoured by an invitation from Gawler to lay the first stone of a monument to commemorate the achievements of the late Mr. John McKinlay, the intrepid leader of the Burke Relief Expedition, and the explorer, under great difficulties, of the northern territory. Mr. McKinlay died at Gawler in December, 1874, and it was resolved to perpetuate his memory by the erection of an obelisk in the cemetery. The 14th of November was the day appointed for the ceremony, and after I had laid the stone with the customary forms, there was a luncheon, presided over by Mr. W. F. Wincey, the Mayor of Gawler. He delivered a really eloquent address, describing the character and heroic labours of the distinguished explorer, whose achievements we were celebrating. My own health and that of my brother was proposed, and in responding (my brother not being present) I once more took occasion to express the deep sense, on the part of all my associates, of the kindness with which we had been received.

After this my brother and I paid a flying visit to Melbourne, where we remained a few days, and received much attention from the Governor, Sir George Bowen, the Mayor of Melbourne, and others; and then, on the 5th of December, we bade farewell to our South Australian friends and started on our homeward voyage. On the 10th we reached King George's Sound, where we were heartily welcomed and presented with a congratulatory address. At Banbury and Fremantle we were received with kindness and enthusiastic demonstrations. At Banbury we met Mr. Weld. He was on his way to King George's Sound, *en route* for his new Government in Tasmania. He welcomed us very heartily, and expressed his regret that he was unable to receive us at Perth. The popular air, " When Johnny comes marching home again," was selected as extremely appropriate to the occasion, and after a champagne breakfast at the residence of the Chairman of the Municipal Council, Mr. Marmion, at Fremantle, we left for Perth in a carriage and six, Tommy Windich and Tommy Pierre riding on gaily-decked horses immediately behind us.

On reaching Perth we were met by the Commandant, Colonel Harvest, the chairman and members of the Reception Committee, and representatives of the Friendly Societies. The streets were crowded, and on our way to the Town Hall we were enthusiastically cheered. Mr. Randell, the Chairman of the Perth Municipality, read an address of welcome. I need not repeat what I said in reply; my words were but the expression of what has been felt ever since our perilous journey was completed,—thankfulness that I had been preserved and strengthened to do my duty, and that I had been so well supported by brave and faithful companions. But I will quote the characteristic speech of Tommy Pierre, who returned thanks on behalf of the party,—Windich was called on, but could not summon courage to say a word. Tommy said, " Well, gentlemen, I am very thankful to come back to Swan River, and Banbury, Fremantle, and Perth. I thought we was never to get back. (Laughter.) Many a time I go into camp in the morning, going through desert place, and swear and curse and say, ' Master, where the deuce are you going to take us ? ' I say to him, ' I'll give you a pound to take us back.' (Cheers and laughter.) Master say, ' Hush ! what are you talking about ? I will take you all right through to Adelaide ; ' and I always obey him. Gentlemen, I am thankful to you that I am in the Town Hall. That's all I got to say." (Cheers.)

No doubt we all shared Tommy's thankfulness, and I am sure his homely language very fairly expressed the spirit in which all my associates had shown their confidence in me during our long journey.

A banquet and ball were given in the Town Hall. Mr. Randell presided at the former, supported by the Bishop of Perth ; Sir Archibald P. Burt, the Chief Justice ; the Hon. the Commandant ; Mr. L. S. Leake, Speaker of the Legislative Council ; the Hon. A. O'Grady Lefroy, Colonial Treasurer, and other gentlemen of high position. The newspapers

published the following report of the principal
speeches delivered :—

The Chairman gave " His Excellency the Governor," whose
unavoidable absence he, in common with every one present,
deeply regretted, knowing full well the deep interest his Excellency had always evinced in connexion with exploration,
and especially in connexion with the expedition so successfully
carried through by their guests that evening.

The toast was drunk amid loud cheering.

The Chairman next gave " The Army, Navy, and Volunteers," which was duly honoured.

The Hon. the Commandant, in responding for the Army and
the Navy, heartily thanked the assembly for the loyal manner
in which the toast had been received. The toast of the British
Army and Navy, always appropriate at a banquet where Britons
were assembled, was particularly appropriate on the present
occasion, gathered together as they were to do honour to
valour. (Cheers.) It was needless for him to state that—all
knew it—British soldiers, well equipped, properly provided in
every way, and properly led, would go anywhere, and face any
mortal thing; and so, it appeared, would West Australians,
true sons of Great Britain. The other day, at the presentation
of the address given to Mr. Forrest by the citizens of Perth,
he (the Commandant), alluding to the young explorer's gallant
and truly heroic services in the field of exploration, had said
that, were he a soldier, the distinguished feat he had accomplished would have entitled him to be decorated with the soldier's most honourable mark of distinction—the Victoria Cross.
(Cheers.) Now he had no desire to accord Mr. Forrest the
least particle of credit beyond what he honestly believed he
was entitled to, but he meant to say this—that Mr. Forrest had
displayed all the noblest characteristics of a British soldier
under circumstances by no means as favourable for arousing a
spirit of intrepidity, and for stimulating bravery, as was in
operation on a battle-field, amidst the all-powerful excitement
of an engagement with the enemy, urged on to deeds of valour
by the examples of comrades. Who or what had Mr. Forrest

and his little band of followers to cheer them on, to urge them forward on their perilous and dreary enterprise ? What surrounding circumstances encouraged them to face unknown dangers ? He should think that many a wearisome day and night in crossing the arid, trackless desert-path he was traversing, he would, on laying down his head to rest, say, "Would for bedtime in Perth, and all well!" Nothing daunted, however, by perils, privations, and difficulties, he carried his enterprise successfully through; and although there were no Victoria Crosses for distinguished services of that nature, there, nevertheless, was an order of merit for rewarding exploits such as Mr. Forrest had performed, and he most heartily and sincerely trusted that the decoration of honour conferred upon the gallant Warburton would be likewise conferred on Mr. Forrest. (Applause.)

Captain Birch briefly responded on behalf of the Volunteers.

The Chairman then said the pleasing duty devolved upon him to propose the toast which was in reality the toast of the evening, and to ask them to drink with him "The Health and Prosperity of Mr. John Forrest and his Party." (Cheers.) Nine months ago, within a day, they had undertaken a perilous journey across an unknown country, to accomplish what was believed by many to be an impossible task on account of the terrible nature of that country. What dangers, what difficulties, what privations they had suffered in carrying out their daring enterprise, and what the result of their arduous labours had been, was already known to most if not all of those now present, a succinct chronicle of their journey having been published in the South Australian and in the local newspapers. To-night they were amongst them safe and sound, having been saved by Almighty Providence from dangers which they could not have contended with, and surmounted difficulties which but for such Divine help must have been insuperable. All honour to them ; all honour to the brave men who had assisted to achieve such a victory, of which even Mr. Forrest and his companions might well be proud, and the advantages of which he felt that we could not yet fully appreciate. (Cheers.) The

Hon. the Commandant had spoken so ably of their victory that little remained for him to add. He, however, ventured to differ from the gallant Commandant on one point, namely, that, when compassed on all sides by difficulties, far from aid, succour, or assistance of any kind, Mr. Forrest must have wished himself back in Perth, all well. He (Mr. Randell) did not believe that such a thought ever entered Mr. Forrest's head, fully determined as he was to cross the continent, or perish in the attempt. He was sure that not even the golden reward offered by Tommy Pierre, for turning back, exerted any influence on his gallant leader's mind; on the contrary, they found him quietly rebuking Tommy's failing courage with a " hush " and a promise to take him right through to Adelaide. Mr. Forrest's courage never failed him on the way, nor had they any reason to believe that the courage of any member of his party had really failed in the face of the terrible difficulties they had encountered, and, by God's help, surmounted. (Applause.) They all had read of the Olympic games of the ancient Greeks, and the kindred sports indulged in by the Romans of old. Their athletic contests being conducted in the presence of immense crowds of spectators naturally stimulated the athletes to distinguish themselves; the applause of their fellow-citizens urged them on to strive with might and main to win the crown of laurel or ivy leaves with which the brow of the victor was decked. He well remembered an incident recorded in Grecian history, where two brothers had been engaged in an athletic contest and been victorious. When they came forth to receive the crown which rewarded their victory, their aged father—who himself, in his younger days, had been an athlete—was present, and the sons placed their crown on his venerable head. He was sorry that the father of the young heroes whom they were then entertaining was not present to witness the reward freely bestowed upon his sons by their fellow-countrymen. (Cheers.) Our South Australian neighbours, in their magnificent reception of Mr. Forrest and his party, had given us a good example of how to appreciate and reward noble deeds, and it must be pleasing to every Western Australian to reflect on the cordiality of that reception. (Applause.) He thought the colony would be neglecting its duty if it did not, as one man, recognize the extreme kindness which had been shown our gallant explorers by the people and by the Government of our sister colony—South Australia. (Cheers.) It was a pleasing trait in Mr. Forrest's character that he had not been at all spoilt by the enthusiastic and really splendid ovation he and his party had received at the hands of our southern neighbours; nothing could be more admirable than his unaffected modesty and unassuming deportment in the face of such a reception. The life of a lion did not spoil their young hero, nor, as the *Inquirer* had said that morning, did he think it would suit him long; for however tempting it might be to some people to live upon laurels well earned, such men as Mr. Forrest had no difficulty in overcoming the temptation to ease and repose, however deserving and indisputable his claims thereto. (Cheers.) He believed with the *Inquirer* that it was Mr. Forrest's natural instinct to lead a hard life in the cause of exploration. He belonged—not by birth it was true, but through his parents—to a country that had produced such men as Mungo Park; Bruce, who explored the sources of the Nile; and Campbell, who, labouring in the same cause, traversed the wilds of Africa; and that greatest and noblest of all explorers, the dead but immortal Livingstone. (Cheers.) Mr. Forrest's achievements had entitled his name to stand side by side in the page of history with men of that stamp and others who had placed the human family under such great obligations by their undaunted and self-denying efforts in the cause of exploration. (Cheers.) It would not perhaps be right on his part to refer to the pecuniary reward which the Legislature had voted as an honorarium to Mr. Forrest and his party, but he would say this much—and he believed every one in the colony would be in accord with him —that the public would not have grumbled, on the contrary, would have been glad if the grant had been 1000*l.* and not 500*l.* (Hear, hear.) He did not think for a moment that the Legislative Council thought that 500*l.* was the measure of the value of Mr. Forrest's services; they were rather influenced by the extent of the public revenue and the ability of the country to pay a larger amount; nevertheless, he would have been pleased, and the public would have been pleased, had the vote been more commensurate with the value of those services. (Cheers.) In asking the present assembly to join him in drinking the toast of Mr. Forrest's health and that of his party, he considered it was as if he moved a vote of thanks on behalf of the colony for the labours in which they had been associated, for the honour they had conferred on their country, and he would ask them to join him in heartily drinking the toast. (Cheers.)

The toast was received with several rounds of cheering.

The Commandant rose in explanation, and said he never for a moment meant to infer that in the midst of his greatest difficulties Mr. Forrest ever thought of giving up his task. What he said was that he must have often, in lying down his head after a wearisome day's journey, wished himself at home in Perth all well, with his enterprise accomplished, but not otherwise (cheers). He did not believe that Mr. Forrest ever winced at danger, ever swerved from the path he had laid out for himself to traverse.

Mr. John Forrest, on rising, was received with applause, which rose to ringing cheers. Upon the subsiding of the applause, Mr. Forrest said—Mr. Chairman and gentlemen, I feel that I ought to say a great deal on this occasion, but I really hardly know what to say. I can, of course, say that I sincerely thank you for your kindness in inviting myself and companions to this great banquet, and when I say that, I trust you will give me credit for saying what I feel in my heart of hearts. But I feel I have much more than this to say this evening, knowing as I do that I would disappoint you if I did not address you at some length. I will endeavour to muster the words and the courage to do so; as you know, public speaking is not my forte, and if I fail in satisfying your expectations, you must accept the will for the deed (cheers). When I had the honour of being entertained at a public banquet at Adelaide, I had a good deal to say there of my career up to the present; but here I need not say a word about my antecedents, for most of you have known me from my childhood (cheers). For the last few years you all know I have had some little to do with exploration, and for me to tell you anything of my past experience would be simply waste of time and waste of words. You will, however, expect me to say something of our latest enterprise. I had been for some time animated by a desire to explore the untrodden interior of our island continent. I had, as you know, been twice before in the field; once in an east-ward direction, and once along the south sea-board to Adelaide —the latter, I was told, being considered a very small under-taking, quite a coasting trip, and one on account of which we could not lay claim to much credit. I therefore was desirous of penetrating the mystery that shrouded the interior, and, with that object in view, I used my utmost endeavours to organize an expedition in that direction. Without the support and co-operation of one who I am sorry not to see here this evening, he having quitted the metropolis—his Excellency Governor Weld—my endeavours, I may safely say, would not have re-sulted in the organization of the expedition I had at heart, and I should not have been here to-night, occupying the proud position which I do. (Cheers.) My proposition to his Ex-cellency, through the Commissioner of Crown Lands, was warmly received, and cordially espoused by the Executive. Any one can see it on application, together with his Excellency's minute, which was very complimentary to me. The proposition was carried through the Legislative Council, and a small sum of money was voted for the expedition, without which it could not probably have been organized and fitted out. I am happy to say that our trip is not likely to cost much more than the amount voted (400*l.*). Possibly the expense may reach 600*l.* or so; if it does, I have no doubt the Legislature will willingly vote the extra amount. (Hear, hear.) If it does not, of course we keep to the original proposition, and we shall only ask for the 400*l.* I am quite prepared to abide by the original arrangement; but I think that every man in the colony is satis-fied that the expedition was conducted at the least possible expense, and that we all tried to do our very best. (Cheers.) I scarcely think it is necessary for me to enter into any details of our journey; I have already given the most salient points in my published telegraphic despatch to the Government. We

experienced some difficulties, no doubt, and some few privations, but I can assure you none of us ever thought of turning
back. (Cheers.)   On one occasion, I admit, the thought did
enter my head that, possibly, we might have to turn back, but
I did not tell any member of the party a word about it.   The
thought haunted me at night, and I could not sleep; and had
we to carry it into execution we should have probably found
ourselves coming out somewhere near Victoria Plains, and it
struck me that I should be greeted with such expressions as
" Well, old man, I am glad to see you back, but I am sorry you
could not get through."   I knew people would be glad to see
us back, but their satisfaction at our safe return would be
alloyed with regret at our failure to get right across; so I said
to myself, " I never can face that ; I must try again," and try
again we did, and you know the result. (Cheers.)   I candidly
tell you that the thought struck me that if we were baffled in
our efforts to penetrate through, it might be all the better for
this colony, inasmuch as there would be a saving of expense
thereby, although the credit due to me would be considerably
diminished.   But I did not care so much for that.   When, however, I reached the settled portions of South Australia, I was
very anxious to get right through to the telegraph line, just to
show our neighbours that we could get across.   From the date
of our arrival at Peake Station, you know how cordially we
were received throughout the rest of our journey, and with
what kindness we were treated.   Probably all of you have read
of our enthusiastic reception at Adelaide.   I never saw so
many people in my life before, nor such a demonstration. They
say there were 20,000 persons present.   I thought there were
100,000 present. (Laughter.)   As for my brother, he seemed
enchanted with the sight, and especially with the ladies.   He
has said he thought they were all looking at him.   On the
contrary, gentlemen, I thought they were all looking at me.
(Laughter.)   Every one we came in contact with, both high
and low, treated us most kindly.   The same again in Melbourne. (Cheers.)   Now, I must say a word or two about my
first impressions on visiting Melbourne.   The first object of
interest that caught my attention was the splendid monument

erected to the memory of the gallant explorers, Burke and
Wills. Baron von Mueller kindly met me on the jetty when
we landed, and I accompanied him in a cab to have an interview with the Governor. When we came in sight of this monument I asked the Baron to stop while I alighted to inspect
it. He courteously did so. Gentlemen, a thrilling feeling
came over me on looking on that memorial of two brave men
who sacrificed their lives in the cause of exploration. The
monument represents poor Burke standing over Wills, who is
kneeling down. The first relief represents the party leaving
Melbourne, and the popular demonstration accorded them ; in
the next place the return from Carpentaria is depicted, and the
discovery of a depôt where some provisions had been deposited.
There is King in the act of holding a candle, Burke reading a
letter, and Wills's head is peering over his shoulder. Further
on there is a relief representing the death of the brave leader
with his revolver grasped in his hand. On the other side there
is Howitt and his party finding King, the sole survivor of Burke's
party, among a number of black fellows, with whom he had
been living for several weeks—the black fellows looking aghast
at the relief party. Several times afterwards, during my stay
in Melbourne, I went to look at this monument, and it always
sent a thrill through my very soul. (Cheers.) Gentlemen,
in conclusion, I must again express my gratitude for the kind
manner in which you have received me and the members of
my party back amongst you. My only consolation, in the face
of the ovations I have received, is that we all tried to do our
very best. (Cheers.) As to the vote of the Legislature,
alluded to by your chairman, while I thank him heartily for
his liberal spirit, I assure you I am very well satisfied indeed.
(Applause.) When I started on the expedition I never expected one farthing of honorarium from the public funds; but
though I am modest I am not altogether unselfish, and I did
expect what I think every Briton expects from his countrymen
when he does his best—but what he does not always get—the
thanks of my fellow-colonists. (Cheers.) That I *have* received
most abundantly, and I am quite satisfied with it, and so I
think are all the members of my party. We are also quite content

with, and thankful for, the provision made for us by the Legislative Council. I don't know whether I shall again appear before you as an explorer, or whether I shall rest on my laurels, as the *Inquirer* said to-day. I can only say that if my services are required I shall be found ready and willing. (Cheers.) In the toast you have so enthusiastically drank my companions are very properly associated with myself, for I am much indebted to them for their hearty co-operation. They always endeavoured to do what I desired, and the most friendly feelings existed amongst us throughout the journey. (Cheers.) I never withheld from them any information as to our whereabouts or our movements ; the maps, route, and the observations taken during the expedition were always open for their inspection, so that they could see our exact position from day to day. I had no secrets from them (hear, hear), and this confidence was reciprocated on their part. I never had occasion to check or to use an angry word to one of my party. They one and all always showed readiness and willingness to obey my instructions—in fact, I seldom had any occasion to instruct them: and I gladly avail myself of this opportuity to thank them publicly for their exemplary conduct. (Cheers.) On their behalf, as well as on my own behalf, I once more also thank you most sincerely for the honour you have done us and the kindness you have shown us. I hope that our future career will show that we are not altogether unworthy of that kindness. (Loud cheers.)

Tommy Pierre, one of the aboriginals attached to the expedition, then stepped forward, and, addressing the assembly, said: I only black fellow, you know; nothing at all but just a few words. I ought to give you good lecture. (Laughter.) Well, gentlemen, I am very thankful that I got into the city of Perth; that people give me welcome and everything. I am always thankful to any person that brought me into city of Perth. (Laughter.) When I speak so of city of Perth I don't speak wrong at all; what I speak is true and true. Well, gentlemen, I am very thankful to the people in Perth at the Town Hall; I am very thankful to every one that welcome me. I am always very glad to see white fellows around me. In

Bunbury, Governor Weld spoke to me and say he left me a
present in city of Perth, and I hope I will get it too. (Cheers
and laughter.) Governor Weld is a splendid fellow; splendid
governor. Well, gentlemen, I am all thankful; my last word is
—I am thankful to you all. (Cheers.)

Mr. Randell: In consequence of the absence of the Surveyor-
General—from what cause I am unable to state—his lordship
Bishop Hale has kindly consented to propose the next toast.
(Cheers.)

His Lordship, on rising, was received most cordially. He
said that the toast which had just been entrusted to him was
one that would have been better proposed by the Surveyor-
General. The sentiment was—" Australian Exploration." It
so happened that ever since he had arrived in Australia he had
been very much interested in exploration, and much mixed up
with persons engaged in that work. He had known the veteran
explorer Sturt, the discoverer of South Australia; and he had
also been acquainted with his brave companion, John McDougal
Stuart, who had marked out the route subsequently followed
by the trans-continental telegraph line from Adelaide to Port
Darwin, for, wonderful to say, no better route could afterwards
be discovered; the map of Stuart's journey and the map of the
telegraph line were almost identical. With regard to Mr.
Forrest's exploratory labours, referred to with unaffected and
characteristic modesty by the young explorer himself, his lordship believed that great and practical results would follow, and
that, even as Stuart's track from south to north of the continent
had become the line of communication between those two
extreme points, so would the path traversed by Mr. Forrest
become, some day or other, the line of communication through
the central portion of the continent from West to South Australia. (Cheers.) With respect to the necessity for exploration,
no doubt it was a very essential work to be carried out.
Whenever he had gone to distant and sequestered parts of the
colony in the exercise of his ecclesiastical functions, and was
called upon to console people so situated as to be cut off from
the blessings of regular ministration, he was in the habit of
saying to them, " Although you are at present cut off, yet you

may believe that God in His providence has designed that His world shall be inhabited, and ordained that pioneers shall go forth into desert places in order to accomplish that end." Explorers, therefore, like Mr. Forrest, might well feel that in devoting themselves to the work of exploration they were doing their duty to God and to their country in seeking to discover new fields, likely to be of practical use as new settlements for the ever-increasing human family. Their efforts in that direction, often purchased with much suffering and privation, entitled explorers to be classed in the front rank of benefactors to mankind. (Applause.) The population of the world was continuously increasing, and new settlements became a necessity. In London alone it was said there was a birth every five minutes. What, then, must be the population of the British empire if the increase in one city was at that rate? It was but due to Mr. Forrest and to all such explorers that they should receive the thanks of their fellow-men for devoting their lives to so desirable a work as the discovery of new country, fitted for the habitation of civilized men. (Applause.) He would not trespass any further on the patience of the assembly: he was present in order to join in that general feeling of admiration which Mr. Forrest's exploit had evokep. Cooler courage and greater heroism could not be displayed under any circumstances than were displayed by his young friend on his right, circumstanced as he had been on divers occasions during his journey, with his life and the lives of his brave companions frequently in imminent peril. (Cheers.) Mr. Forrest had just told them that he did not think it necessary to enter into the details of that journey, inasmuch as the most important particulars connected therewith had already appeared in his telegraphic despatch to the Government, published in the local newspapers. That telegram was certainly one of the most explicit and distinct records of the kind that his lordship had ever perused. He had paid but a moderate degree of attention to it, but had experienced no difficulty whatever in pricking out Mr. Forrest's track on a map, and in forming a distinct conception of his journey. (Cheers.) It only remained for his lordship to ask them to join him in drinking the sentiment of

"Australian Exploration," and at the same to drink the health of Mr. Alexander Forrest, whose name was coupled with it. (Cheers.)

The toast was enthusiastically honoured, the band playing "The Song of Australia."

Mr. A. Forrest, on rising, was received with applause. He was indistinctly heard at the reporter's table, owing to the distance which separated him from it, and the constant hum of conversation, which by this time was becoming general. He was understood to express the proud satisfaction he felt at being present that evening, and more especially as his name had been associated with the toast of Australian Exploration. The sentiment was a wide one, and they need not suppose that he was going to enter into the history of all Australian explorations that had taken place. He was sure that time would not admit of his making even cursory remarks upon these events. Mr. Forrest then alluded to the exploratory labours of Stuart—perhaps the greatest of Australian explorers—of McKinlay, of Burke and Wills, of Captain Roe, and the Gregorys, and of the veteran Warburton. The hospitality shown by this colony to the last-named gallant explorer had produced a lasting feeling of gratitude throughout South Australia. The manner in which our southern neighbours spoke of the kind treatment extended by the inhabitants of this colony to that aged explorer, from the day he reached our north-west settlements to the hour he embarked on board steamer for Adelaide, reflected honourably upon the hospitable nature of West Australian people. Mr. Elder, one of the enterprising gentlemen at whose expense the expedition was organized and equipped, had told him (Mr. Forrest) that he never heard of such kindness. The South Australians, however, were not long before an opportunity was afforded them of returning that hospitality, and they certainly had not neglected the opportunity. Than the treatment which the party to which he had the honour of belonging had received at the hands of the people of South Australia nothing could be kinder—nothing could possibly be more hospitable. Every house was thrown open to them; their horses were fed free of charge; it did not cost them a single penny in travelling; everywhere they were met with the most cordial reception. Their triumphal entry into Adelaide was a demonstration worthy of a prince. (Cheers.) Having thanked his fellow-colonists for the very hearty reception accorded them on their return, Mr. Forrest spoke in very complimentary terms of the other members of the expedition. The two natives were first-rate fellows, and, as for Sweeney and Kennedy, he would never wish to have better companions in the bush. They were always for going ahead; no thought of turning back ever entered their heads; in their greatest privations not a murmur escaped their lips. (Loud cheers.)

Mr. L. S. Leake said: The toast I have to propose is " South Australia and the Sister Colonies "—a sentiment which I think might most appropriately have immediately followed on the speech of my noble friend, Mr. John Forrest, who by his remarks paved the way to the few words I have to say. Why South Australia should be placed before the other colonies on this occasion it is not difficult to conjecture. She has, above all others, gained our affection by her kind and hospitable treatment of our fellow-colonists, our respected guests this evening, who were received in Adelaide with even greater honour than the son of our beloved Queen. (Cheers.) With reference to Mr. Forrest himself, Western Australia should be proud of having produced such a man; and I only wish I had arrived in the colony four years and a half earlier, so that I might lay claim to having been born here. Many of those around me are natives of Western Australia; and although I am proud of Old England, my native country, I should have been glad to boast of having been born in the same colony as John Forrest. All of his fellow-colonists should be proud that Mr. Forrest has accomplished a feat which the whole civilized world must admire. (Cheers.) I did think that the Surveyor-General would have considered it worthy of his coming here to-night to join us in doing honour to Mr. Forrest, and that he would have introduced you to a gentleman connected with the Government of Victoria, now in this colony— Mr. Wardell, the Inspector-General of Public Works, for

whose services we are under deep obligation. I believe him to
be an excellent engineer, and in examining our harbour at
Fremantle he will be the right man in the right place. Had
he, however, been in his right place to-night, he would have
been here amongst us, introduced by the Surveyor-General,
and we should thus have an opportunity of publicly thanking
the Victorian Government for granting us the benefit of his
services. (Hear, hear.) But, though Victoria is not represented at this festive gathering, South Australia is, and that
by a gentleman whose name it affords me great pleasure to
connect with the toast which has been entrusted to me. This
colony was established in the year 1829, and in 1830 there
arrived amongst us one of our pioneer settlers, a good, worthy,
honest—I cannot say English, but Scotch—gentleman, Mr.
Walter Boyd Andrews, than whom a more upright man
never landed on our shores. He is represented here to-
night by his eldest son, with whom I spent the greater
portion of my younger days, and who for the last ten
years has been Registrar-General of the colony of South
Australia. I have, therefore, much pleasure in associating
his name with the toast which I now ask you to join me
in drinking, " Prosperity to South Australia and the Sister
Colonies." (Cheers.)

The toast was drunk with loud cheering, the band playing,
" Pull, pull together."

Mr. Andrews, in response, said: Mr. Chairman and gentlemen, I rise at once to return thanks, because I always fancy
that words spoken on the spur of the moment come from the
very heart. I will first of all dispose of myself, having been
taken completely by surprise in finding my name associated with
the sentiment proposed by my old friend, Mr. Leake. I thank
you most heartily for the honour you have done me, and the
kind manner in which you have responded to the toast. As
regards " South Australia and the Sister Colonies," you have
done South Australia the proud honour of giving her pre-
cedence over her sisters of the group, thereby showing, as Mr.
Leake has said, the warmth of your affection towards her,
which kindly feeling, I sincerely believe, is reciprocated on her

part. The cordial reception accorded to your gallant explorers is an earnest of that feeling, and I think I may venture to say that the colony which I have the honour to serve will at all times extend a hearty welcome to any West Australian colonist. There is, I assure you, a very affectionate feeling entertained by South Australians towards this colony—a feeling that has been in existence for a long time, and which is growing deeper and deeper every day. She is not only willing to extend the right hand of friendship to you, but, as you know, has expressed her readiness to meet you half way across the desert that separates you from each other by means of the telegraph. (Cheers.) She does not feel jealous that you should receive telegraphic intelligence from the outside world earlier than she does; on the contrary, she is anxious that you should be placed in the same advantageous position as regards telegraphic communication as your other sisters are. (Applause.) Gentlemen, on her behalf, and on my own behalf, I thank you most heartily for the kind manner in which this toast has been received.

Since then, in the summer of 1875, I have visited Europe and received many proofs of the interest felt by Englishmen in Australian exploration. In the colonies, too, I find that the spirit of adventure which stimulates settlers to follow eagerly in the steps of the pioneer has been active. Already stations are being advanced on each side along the shores of the Great Bight, and a telegraph line is being constructed from King George's Sound to Adelaide, along my route of 1870, which will connect Western Australia with the telegraph systems of the world. Farther north, towards the head waters of the Murchison, advances have been made, and I and

other explorers must feel a gratification, which
gives ample reward for all our toil, in knowing
that we have made some advance at least towards a more complete knowledge of the interior
of vast and wonderful Australia.·

APPENDIX TO JOURNAL.

I.

DESCRIPTION OF THE PLANTS, ETC., COLLECTED ON EXPEDITION;

SHOWING ALSO THE LOCALITY FROM WHICH THEY WERE TAKEN:

BY BARON VON MUELLER, C.M.G., ETC.

CAMP 21.—Latitude 25° 57′ 32″ S.; longitude 117° 20′ E. :—
Cassia desolata. Trichodesma Zeilonicum. Stylobasium spatulatum. Psoralea Cucantha. Scaevola spiniscens. Sida petrophila. Codonocarpus cotinifolius. Adriana tomentosa. Sàlsola Kali.

CAMP 31.—Latitude 26° 8′ 31″ S.; longitude 119° 18′ E. :—
Acacia aneura. Œschynomene Indica. Eremophila longifola. Cassia Sturtii. Plectronia latifolia.

CAMP 33.—Latitude 26° 13′ S.; longitude 119° 32′ E. :—
Santalum Preissianum. Plectronia latifolia.

CAMP 36.—Latitude 26° 17′ 12″ S.; longitude 119° 53′ E. :—
Brachychiton Gregorii. Dodonaea petiolaris. Cassia artemisioides. Eremophila latifolia. Hakea lorea. Acacia aneura. Eremophila longifolia.

CAMP 40.—Latitude 25° 38′ 44″ S.; longitude 120° 38′ E. :—
Cassia eremophila. Eremophila longifolia.

CAMP 46.—Latitude 25° 0′ 46″ S.; longitude 121° 22′ E. :—
Stemodia viscosa. Eremophila longifolia. Sida petrophila. Adriana tomentosa. Convolvulus erubescens. Cassia Sturtii. Hakea lorea.

CAMP 48.—Latitude 25° 22′ 50″ S.; longitude 121° 57′ E. :—
Acacia aneura. Eremophila longifolia. Cassia eremophila. Cassia desolata. Eremophila Brownii. Loranthus Exocarpi.

CAMP 52.—Latitude 25° 41′ 23″ S. ; longitude 122° 53′ E. : —
　　　*Pappophorum commune. Cassia eremophila. Acacia
　　　salicina. Santalum lanceolatum. Senecio
　　　lantus. Eremophila Duttoni. Ptilotus alo-
　　　pecuroides. Brunonia Australis. Hakea lorea.
　　　Cassia eremophila. Eremophila longifolia.*

CAMP 59.—Latitude 25° 43′ 8″ S.; longitude 124° 10′ E. : —
　　　Cassia notabilis. Cassia artemisioides.

CAMP 61.—Latitude 25° 53′ 23″ S.; longitude 124° 31′ E. : —
　　　Eremophila Latrobei. Dodonaea petiolaris.

CAMP 62.—Latitude 26° 5′ 10″ S. ; longitude 124° 46″ E. : —
　　　*Crotalaria Cunninghami. Indigofera brevidens.
　　　Sida petrophila. Acacia salicina. Dodonaea
　　　petriolaris. Condonocarpus cotinifolius. Cassia
　　　Sturtii. Cassia artemisioides. Kochiá Brownii.
　　　Eremophila longifolia. Loranthus Exocarpi.*

CAMP 70.—Latitude 25° 54′ 53″ S.; longitude 126° 48′ E. : —
　　　*Hakea lorea. Cassia desolata. Eremophila longi-
　　　folia. Abutilon Fraseri. Acacia salicina.
　　　Cassia platypoda. Ficus platypoda (the native
　　　fig).*

CAMP 71.—Latitude 26° 1′ S. ; longitude 127° 7′ E. : —
　　　*Crotolaria Cunninghami. Indigofera brevidens.
　　　Cassia Eremophila. Trichodesma Zeilanicum.
　　　Cassia artemisioides.*

CAMP 72.—Latitude 26° 2′ S.; longitude 127° 22′ E. : —
　　　*Abutilon Fraseri. Trichodesma Zeilanicum. Acacia
　　　salicina.*

CAMP 78.—Latitude 26° 15′ 10″ S. ; longitude 122° 9′ E. : —
　　　*Gossypium Sturtii. Hibiscus Farragei. Ptero-
　　　caulon Sphacelatus. Salsola Kali. Condono-
　　　carpus cotinifolius. Heliotropium undulatum.
　　　Scaevola spiniscens. Stylobasium spatulatum
　　　Adriana tomentosa. Tecoma Australis. Ficus
　　　platypoda. Trichodesma Zeilanicum. Sida
　　　virgata. Dodonaea viscosa. Helichrysum api-
　　　culatum. Jasminum lineare. Adriana tomen-
　　　tosa. Indigofera Australis. Petalostylis
　　　labicheoides. Scaevola Aemula. Pterocaulon
　　　Sphacelatus. Santalum Preissianum. Festuca
　　　(Triodia) irritans.*

The *Santalum Preissianum*, the so-called native peach, with edible fruit, is found generally on the whole route.

The *Spinifex* so often mentioned is the *Festuca* (*Triodia*) *irritans*, the Spinifex of the Desert Explorers, but not of Science.

Latitude 25° 46′ S.; longitude 118° E. :—
> *Marsdenia Leichardti*, the climber with edible pods and milky sap, the seeds with a downy top, called by the natives " Carcular."

Latitude 26° 4′ S.; longitude 129° 50′ E. :—
> The *Casuarina Decaisneana*, the Shea-oak or Desert Oak peculiar to Central Australia.

II.

REPORT FROM R. BROUGH SMYTH, ESQ.,

SECRETARY FOR MINES OF VICTORIA,

ON THE GEOLOGICAL SPECIMENS COLLECTED ON THE EXPEDITION.

sition of locality ere the specimen was collected	Remarks by Mr. John Forrest on the specimens forwarded.	Mr. R. Brough Smyth's report on specimens.
t. 26° S. ng. 117° 20′ E.	Taken from Mount Hale on the Murchison River. This formation extends to long. 120° E , and is very magnetic, also very heavy. There must be a great deal of iron in it The hills are very high, and the echo very remarkable. I have seen the same kinds of hills in lat. 29°, long. 120°. Bare granite rocks sometimes in the vicinity, though not attached. (May 4th.)	Two small specimens of Micaceous Iron-ore with brown Hæmatite. Impossible to state the age. Similar ore occurs in Victoria, in Elvans in Porphyry, but it also occurs in Tertiary rocks.
. 26° 17′ S. ng. 119° 54′ E.	The water-shed of the Murchison, after crossing which we entered the Triodia desert. Found oozing out of rock in the water-shed of the Murchison.	Brown Hæmatite, decomposing to yellow. (Tertiary.) Bituminous material. Mr. Cosmo Newbery reports that it is probably the result of the decomposition of the excrement of bats. It contains fragments of the wing cases of insects, and gives reactions similar to the bituminous mineral or substanc found in Victoria.

Position of locality where the specimen was collected.	Remarks by Mr. John Forrest on the specimens forwarded.	Mr. R. Brough Smyth's report on specimens.
Lat. 25° 14′ S. Long. 121° E.	Peaks rising out of sandy Triodia desert (May 29th.)	5, Quartz; 6, Chalcedony; 7, Quartz; 8, Silky Shale (Silurian); 9, very Micaceous Schist (Silurian).
Lat. 25° 40′ S. Long. 120° 35′ E	Found in the Frere Ranges.	10, Ferruginous rock (Tertiary); 11, portion of a seam or joint of a rock; 12, very fine soft purple slightly micaceous rock (Silurian); 13, white micaceous slaty sandstone (Silurian).
Lat. 25° 39′ S. Long. 120° 40′ E	This rock was broken off the face of the side of a bank of brook. It is rather soft, and would split; it is all in layers. I cut my initials in it with a chisel.	Purple brown slate (Silurian).
Lat. 25° 40′ S. Long 122° 20′ E. Mount Moore.	Many ranges and some grassy country running from long. 122° to long. 124°, generally composed of this description of rock.	15, Rough quartzite (conglomeritic) Tertiary; 16, rough quartzite with white band, brown and purple (Tertiary).
Lat. 25° 32′ S. Long. 124° 17′ E	Taken from rough range rising out of gently undulating desert. (July 5th.)	White flinty rock; consists in the main of Silica, with Magnesia and Alumina; it also contains water and traces of the Alkalies. It is probably derived from the decomposition of granite The "rough ranges" are perhaps granitic.
Lat. 26° 6′ S. Long. 124° 46′ E.	From a low table hill (Alexander Spring).	Translucent greenish quartz. Impossible to state the probable age.
Lat. 26° 2′ S. Long. 125° 27′ E	This sandstone is the usual rock found in all the country from long. 122° to 126° 30′. In it are receptacles for water, and all the rising ground is composed of it. Very often one side of the rise forms a cliff. Where this is taken from there is a long line of cliffs with many creeks running from them, and low cliff-hills all about.	Light red sandstone (desert sandstone, Tertiary).
Lat. 26° S. Long. 126° 30′ E.	From the farthest ranges westward from telegraph line; good grassy country in flats. The dark piece from a salt gully. (Aug. 8th.)	20, Silico felspathic rock impreg nated with Micaceous iron (probabl; from a dyke); 21, 22, green schis (Silurian).
Lat. 26° 12′ S. Long. 128° E.	In the Cavanagh Ranges. Many ranges. (Aug. 17th.)	Greenstone (Diabase ?).
Lat. 26° 18′ S. Long. 129° 9′ E.	Tomkinson Ranges. Many ranges running E. and W., and grassy flats between them. (Aug. 26th.) Mount Jane.	Aphanite.

NOTE BY THE EDITOR.

The publication of the preceding Journal affords an appropriate occasion for inviting attention to the remarkable progress of Western Australia within the last few years. Mr. John Forrest is proud to acknowledge himself as belonging to that colony—indeed native-born—and his fellow-colonists have invariably supported and encouraged his explorations. Belonging to the public service, he has recognized as his main object the discovery of new and good country with the view of extending colonization, while within his ideas of duty there has been a steadfast regard for those objects which promote the welfare of young settlements. It has long been observed that Western Australia requires to be thoroughly understood in its great capacities for carrying a large population. There are vast resources yet to be developed, and what has been accomplished in sheep and cattle stations, in copper and lead mining, in wine-growing, in pearl fisheries, besides other important operations, prove that the country has scarcely been "tapped," and will be sure to reward those who have the enterprise and industry to become settlers. It is only necessary to substantiate these statements by official documents, and, in the hope that this volume will do good service to Western Australia, the following papers are reprinted.

GOVERNOR WELD'S REPORT TO THE EARL OF CARNARVON.

Government House, Perth,
September 30, 1874.

My Lord,—It has appeared to me that your lordship may think it desirable that, before I leave, I should, so far as the limits of a despatch may enable me to do so, place before you the present state of this colony, review the progress it has made within the last five years, and indicate its future prospects·

2. When I was appointed to the Government of Western Australia I was aware that from various causes the colony had made but little progress; and on my arrival in September, 1869, I found chronic despondency and discontent, heightened by failure of the wheat crop, by the prospect of the gradual reduction of convict expenditure and labour on which the settlers had been accustomed to depend, by the refusal of the Home Government to continue to send out free immigrants, and by that vague dread of being thrown on their own resources so natural to men who have been accustomed to take no part in their own affairs, and who have consequently learned to rely entirely upon the Government, and not at all upon themselves. One healthy symptom there was, and that was a desire, not very strong perhaps, or even generally founded upon a just appreciation of the past, or political foresight of the future; but still a very wide-spread desire, and to many a reasonable and intelligent desire, for a form of representative institutions which might give the colonists some real voice in the management of their own affairs.

3. At the earliest possible moment I commenced work by travelling over as much as possible of the settled and partially settled districts of the colony; an old colonist bushman and explorer myself, travelling on horseback and " camping out " were but natural to me, and I wished to judge for myself of the capabilities of the colony; and before I had been six months in the country I had ridden considerably over 2000

(two thousand) miles, some part of the distance unfortunately, owing to an accident, with a fractured rib and other injuries. I had made acquaintance with settlers of all classes, and was able to form an opinion so accurate, both of the people and of the country I have since had to deal with, and of their capabilities, that I have never altered that opinion, nor have my many subsequent journeys done more than supplement the knowledge I then gained.

4. My first political aim was to promote local self-government in local affairs by establishing or giving real power to road boards and municipalities (a policy I afterwards carried into effect with school boards also); and, so soon as I had obtained the sanction of her Majesty's Government, I introduced that modified form of representative institutions provided by 13 and 14 Vic., chap. 59, and then passed the Municipal Acts I have mentioned above. This policy has fulfilled not only my expectations but my hopes, and should the Council that is about to meet wish to take the ultimate step of entering into complete self-government by adopting the "responsible" system, the preparation afforded by the last five years will admittedly be of the greatest value.

5. It fell to me to carry into effect the ecclesiastical policy indicated by Lord Granville in a despatch, No. 80, of July 10, 1869, held over for my arrival, in which his lordship suggested that grants (regard being had to the number in the community of each denomination) should be equal in substance and alike in form, and asked if there were any difficulties in applying to Western Australia "that principle of religious equality which had long been recognized in the Australian Colonies." Lord Kimberley, in an enclosure to his despatch, No. 78, of December 19, 1870, expressed similar views. To this on March 1, 1871, in my despatch, No. 37, I was enable to reply that I had already carried the policy recommended into practice, that the grants had been equalized by "levelling up," that the vote for the Church of England was "now handed over to the Bishop of Perth, the Government reserving the right to satisfy itself that it is applied to those purposes of religious ministration and instruction for which it

is voted, and that all vested interests are maintained intact and claims on the Government respected." Since then I have supported such measures as were thought desirable to promote self-organization, and I have moreover made liberal grants of land for glebes, churches, schools, and institutions to the various religious bodies in proportion to their numbers. I have reason to know that on all sides satisfaction is felt at the position in which I shall leave ecclesiastical affairs so far as the action of Government may effect them.

6. The elementary educational question, on my arrival, was a source of much contention and ill-feeling, which came prominently into play, when in the second session of 1871 I caused a Bill, drafted by myself, and the general provisions of which I was subsequently informed were "entirely approved of" by your lordship's predecessor, to be introduced into the Legislature, and carried it—not, however, quite in its original form. Though the alterations are unquestionably defects, and may somewhat mar its success, it has hitherto worked very well, and has proved itself not only effective but economical : it has received praise from its former opponents and from the most opposite quarters, and old bitternesses are now (I hope for ever) things of the past.

7. I have not failed to give the utmost support in my power—a support unfortunately much needed in a colony like this—to the Chief Justice, and it has been a great gratification to me that, on my recommendation, the long and valuable services of Sir Archibald Paull Burt have been recognized by her Majesty, and that he has received the honour of knighthood—a rank which none of her Majesty's servants will more fitly adorn. I have suggested to the Legislature that a small increase of salary should be given to uphold the dignity of the Supreme Court ; and the question, to which I have already drawn the attention of the Legislature, of the appointment of two Puisne Judges and constitution of a Court of Appeal ought to be taken into consideration at no distant period. One new resident magistracy has been established in a district where it was very much needed, and 2 (two) Local Courts have been constituted. There is some difficulty in finding a

sufficiency of fit persons for the commission of the peace who are willing to exert themselves, and the pay of the "resident magistrates" is in too many cases insufficient to enable them properly to support their position as representatives of the Government in their districts.

8. In the Military Department I have enabled successive commandments to make reductions in the enrolled Pensioner Force. By withdrawing the guard from Rottnest Island, and by concurring in the reductions at out-stations, a very considerable saving has thus been effected. I have given all the encouragement in my power to the Volunteer movement, and I may confidently state that the Volunteer Force was never before in so good a state, either so far as regards numbers or efficiency. To this result the efforts of successive commandants and liberality of the Legislature have mainly contributed.

9. It has been for me to preside over the latter stages of the existence of the Imperial convict establishment in Western Australia, as a large and important department; henceforth it will be confined in narrow limits, and I may state with confidence that the great reductions and concentrations that it has been my duty to effect have not been attended with those disastrous effects to the colony that were so confidently predicted, and also that although the residue of convicts are, many of them, men of the doubly reconvicted class and long-sentence men, discipline is well kept, serious prison offences are rare, the health of the men is excellent, whilst severe punishments are seldom needful. I here beg leave to make favourable mention of Mr. W. R. Fauntleroy, Acting Comptroller-General of Convicts, who has proved himself to be a most valuable officer.

10. Much remains to be done in the Survey and Lands Department. When Mr. Fraser in December, 1870, took charge of the department, the greatest economy was needed to make the revenue of the colony meet the expediture, and consequently it was necessary to reduce and lay upon our oars; Mr. Fraser reorganized his department, putting it on a new system, letting out work by contract instead of keeping up a large permanent staff, and thereby effected a considerable

annual saving ; at the same time he has been steadily working, as time and means have permitted, towards certain definite objects, namely, in the direction of a trigonometrical survey, by fixing points, by making sketch and reconnaissance surveys of new and important districts, and by accurately fixing by survey main lines of road : this will give a connexion to the records in the Survey Office which has been hitherto wanting, and will contribute to enable him to construct that great desideratum—a large and accurate map of Western Australia, so far as it is settled or partially settled. I concur with Mr. Fraser in thinking that, so soon as means will admit, a considerably increased annual expenditure should be devoted to surveys.

11. The joint survey of the coast will also aid in this work. The Admiralty, in assenting to my proposal to undertake a joint coast survey, which has been placed under a highly meritorious officer, Navigating Lieutenant Archdeacon, R.N., have conferred a great benefit on this colony, and promoted the interests of British commerce and navigation, much valuable work having already been done.

12. In close connexion with the Survey and Lands Department is the topic of exploration. So soon as possible after my first arrival, I took upon myself to send Mr. John Forrest overland to Adelaide, along the shores of the Great Bight, nearly on the line of Mr. Eyre's route in 1841. I did this before the introduction of representative government, and it is right to say that I knew that I could not have got a vote for it. I felt that this was the last act of an expiring autocratic régime, and I believe it was one of the least popular of my acts; but certainly no small sum of public money has been expended with greater results—for, as I hoped, Mr. Forrest's expedition has bridged the gap that separated West Australia from the other colonies, has led to settlement on the shores of the Great Bight, and to the connexion of this colony with the rest of the word by electric telegraph. I never doubted of the future of West Australia from the day when the news of Mr. Forrest's success reached Perth. Since then more interest has been taken in exploration. A second expedition was sent out

to the eastward under Mr. Alexander Forrest in 1871, with the support of the Legislature and some of the settlers, and at present under the same auspices Mr. John Forrest is again exploring to the northward and estward. His route will be guided by circumstances, but it is not improbable that he may aim for the Central Australian telegraph line, and I am already anxiously expecting tidings of him.

13. In 1870, with a vote I obtained from the Council, I engaged Mr. Henry Y. Brown as Government Geologist. His geological sketch map and his researches, which he pushed in one instance far into the interior, have been of the greatest value; and it was with much regret that in 1872, owing to the disinclination evinced in the Legislature in the then straitened circumstances of the colony to expend money on a scientific department, that I was obliged to forego my desire of making it a permanent part of the establishment.

14. As Colonel Warburton's journey from the Central South Australian telegraph line to our north-west coast was set on foot and its expenses defrayed by private colonists of South Australia, I only allude to it to acknowledge the obligation that this colony lies under to those public-spirited gentlemen and to the gallant leader and his followers. Parties headed by Mr. Gosse, by Mr. Giles, and by Mr. Ross have all within the last two years penetrated from the eastern colonies to within the boundary of our unexplored territory, but, beyond a certain extension of geographical knowledge, without effecting any material results.

15. Under the head of Survey and Lands Department, it will be proper to glance at the alterations in the Land and Mineral Regulations, which have offered increased inducements and facilities for cultivation and occupation, and which have considerably promoted mining enterprise. Gold Mining Regulations have been also prepared and are ready for issue, should occasion, as is likely, render them requisite. I willingly acknowledge the assistance I have received from Mr. M. Fraser, the Surveyor-General and Commissioner of Crown Lands, who has had much experience in New Zealand, for the services he has rendered in all these matters.

16. The mineral riches of this colony are very great. I have never doubted but that they would ultimately bec me a main source of its advancement. All the different kinds of auriferous quartz known in other colonies are found abundantly in various parts of this—the question of payable gold is, as I have long since reported, simply a question of time. After many efforts, I at last, in 1873, obtained a vote for prospecting, and the results are most promising, the fact of the existence of rich auriferous quartz being now established. We shall immediately be in a position to crush specimen consignments of quartz by a Government steam-crusher, and I doubt not but that, if followed up, the results will be most important. But gold is not the only nor perhaps the most important of the minerals possessed by West Australia. The colony is extraordinarily rich in lead, silver, copper, iron, plumbago, and many other minerals are found in various localities, and indications of coal and petroleum are not wanting—what *is* wanting, is energy and enterprise to develop these riches, and that energy and enterprise is being attracted chiefly from Victoria, first by means of concessions that I was enabled to make, and now by the reports of the new comers to their friends. I made a small concession to a smelting company : and another, and also an iron mining company, is in the field.

17. When on my arrival I turned around me to see what was to be looked for to supply the place of Imperial expenditure, only second to our minerals, our forests attracted my attention. They could not fail to do so, because just before I came there was an outcry for the development of this industry by Government aid. With Lord Granville's assent I made liberal concessions, and thereby induced a pioneer company, shortly followed by others from Victoria, to embark capital in the enterprise. The public ardour here had, however, cooled, and an ignorant cry was raised against " foreigners," and the prospects of the trade were systematically decried. Several causes besides this militated against it, but it is surmounting them, and at the present moment not only are the companies largely employing labour and expending money, but their own success is becoming an established fact, and the export is

enormously increasing, and with good management must continue to increase indefinitely. Whilst on this subject I may allude to the question of the preservation of our forests, but as I am treating it more fully in a separate despatch I will only say that this and the kindred question of planting ought, at no distant period, to occupy the attention of our Legislature.

18. The pearl shell and pearl fishery may be said to have sprung into existence within the last few years. It employs a fleet of cutters and schooners, chiefly of small size, on the north-west coast, Port Cossack being the head-quarters. At Sharks Bay also there are a number of smaller boats. A licence fee on boats and a tax on shells has been imposed by the Legislature ; laws for the protection of aboriginal divers and Malays have been enacted. I shall immediately have a Government cutter on the north-west coast for police and customs purposes, which will also be useful in cases of shipwreck amongst the islands and inlets, and in searching for and reporting the position of reefs, of anchorages, and of new banks of pearl oysters. It will probably hereafter become advisable to let areas for pearling under certain regulations as in Ceylon, but this could not well be done with our present means and knowledge.

19. To turn now to the more settled industries, first in importance is that of agriculture. It is chiefly in the hands of men of little capital, and is carried on in a very slovenly way by the greater part of them. Bad seasons, an over-great reliance on cereals, which have for several successive years been seriously affected by the " red rust," and a neglect of other products suitable to the soil and climate, added in too many cases to careless and intemperate habits, have until lately rendered the position of many of the small farmers a very precarious one. Last year, however, was more favourable, and they to a great extent recovered themselves. The lesson of the past has not been altogether lost; they have also been much assisted by the new Land Regulations, and a few prosperous seasons will, I sincerely trust, put this class, which ought to be a mainstay of the colony, into a really prosperous condition.

20. The cultivation of the vine is a profitable pursuit, and

the quantity of land fitted for that purpose is very great; both soil and climate are eminently favourable to the growth of the grape. Recent legislation has given some encouragement to wine-growers by facilitating the sale of home-grown pure wine. The quantity of land laid down in vineyards is slightly increased, but the class of settlers that are most numerous in Western Australia do not readily take to industries that are new to them, however profitable they may be, nor can they afford to wait for returns, nor have many of them the knowledge necessary to make good wine : still this industry will become one of the most important in the colony.

21. The pastoral interest is the pioneer interest of a new colony. Western Australia has been somewhat less favoured than some other parts of Australia in its pastoral lands, but it has, nevertheless, a good deal of very good pastoral country, and under the extremely liberal concessions lately offered to those who will devote capital to the eradication of poison plants much more may be made available, whilst fresh country is being largely occupied inland.

The progress, however, of the pastoral interest, considering the age of the colony, though latterly great, is not *so* great as might have been expected; the comparatively good prices obtainable and anticipated for meat have kept down the increase of stock, and consequently the yield of wool; and as yet very little or nothing has been done to supplement natural resources by growing artificial grasses and fodder plants. No country presents greater capabilities for horse breeding, and cattle do exceeding well and are very profitable.

22. The sandal-wood trade is in a flourishing condition, and has brought money into the colony, and enabled many of the poorer classes to obtain a livelihood by cutting that aromatic wood for export. It is, however, doubted by some whether the labour employed in this trade does not withdraw many from more steady and permanently useful labour on their farms and small holdings.

23. In the matter of minor industries, sericulture holds a first rank. I look to it in the future as a source of employment for paupers on the hands of the Government, and also for

women and children. I have taken much interest in this pursuit, and have caused a mulberry plantation to be made and plants distributed, and have published much information on the subject. The Report of the Chamber of Commerce of Como (Italy), alluded to in my despatch, No. 61, of 20th May, 1873, conclusively shows that this colony is remarkably well adapted for the cultivation of silk. The cultivation of the olive and the castor-oil plant are industries for which this soil and climate are extraordinarily well adapted. Tobacco, hops, and dried and preserved fruits might largely add to the riches of the colony. In great part at my own expense, I have introduced and distributed hop plants and various kinds of fruits of great utility, and have, in fact, in the absence of any botanic garden (in which I have vainly endeavoured to get the settlers to take an active interest), made my own garden a kind of nursery for acclimatization and distribution of useful and ornamental plants, and I have also given a small concession for the culti- vation of the cocoa-nut on the north-west coast, where, in the absence of vegetables, it would be invaluable. And, thanks to the Government of the Mauritius, I have been able to introduce various kinds of sugar-cane, for which part of this territory is well adapted. The growth of coffee has been also attempted on a Government plantation, but without success. Cotton had already been proved to thrive admirably, and to be excellent in quality, but is not considered likely to pay without cheap labour. I may here note that, with an eye to the future, I have made reserves for the purposes of public parks and re- creation grounds in several places.

Deer, Angora goats, hares, and trout have been also introduced.

24. I will now proceed to another branch of my subject— public works and undertakings; and first in the category of public works and undertakings I put those which relate to communications, and under that subdivision immeasurably the most important are such means of communication as, by ter- minating the isolation which has been the great bar to the advancement of this colony, may make it a living part of the system of life and progress which has been growing and pros- pering around it.

On this end was my mind set when I was appointed to the Governorship, to this end have I worked steadily ever since, and this end is partially accomplished, and its complete fulfilment is not distant.

The vote for the construction of the telegraph line viâ Eucla to South Australia, passed last session, and the proposal of Messrs. Siemens Brothers regarding a submarine cable to Madras, fitly close an administration which found Western Australia within twelve miles, and has already placed her in possession of a complete telegraphic system, consisting of about 900 (nine hundred) miles of wire, worked at a remarkably small cost, in efficient order, already remunerative, and affording the greatest advantages both to the public service and to private business. It is noteworthy that four or five years ago there was a strong feeling that the construction of telegraph lines was a waste of public money, and only a few months ago a prominent member of the Legislature publicly objected to the line which is to connect this colony with the rest of the world, that it would only benefit a few individuals! Such ideas, however, are rapidly becoming obsolete even in Western Australia.

I will here note that, under a power given me by law to fix and alter rates, I, in January, 1873, reduced the charges to a uniform rate of 1s. (one shilling) per ten words, and 1d. (one penny) for each additional word (press messages at quarter price), and was the first to do so in the Australian colonies.

25. After much and persistent opposition, the Legislature was at length induced to vote a subsidy for steam on the coast, connecting our western ports and all this part of the colony with Albany, King George's Sound, the port of call of the Royal mail steamers from Europe and the eastern colonies. This has done much to throw open this colony, rendering access to it no longer difficult and uncertain, and greatly facilitating intercommunication. A very Chinese objection to steam communication has been publicly made by the same gentleman to whose opinion on telegraphic communication I have already alluded ; namely, that it enabled people to *leave* the colony. I am, on the contrary, of opinion that it is

certainly conducing to progress and the promotion of commerce.

The steamer we have at present is, however, insufficient, but I doubt not but that a second and more powerful boat will shortly be procured, as it is already required : I understand, however, that no West Australian capital is as yet forthcoming for the purpose, nor for steam communication with India, than which nothing could be more important, as it would render available the magnificent geographical position of the colony, and open a market close at hand for its products. I have long ago and frequently stated my willingness to give all possible Government support to such an undertaking.

26. I am immediately about, by invitation, to proceed to Champion Bay, and to cut the first sod of the first West Australian railway, on the Geraldton and Northampton line. I have already fully indicated the advantage that there is good reason to anticipate will result from the opening of that line, which will, I do not hesitate to say, be the parent of future and greater undertakings.

When the colony arrives at a position safely to borrow a million or a million and a quarter, a railway from Fremantle and Perth, probably up the Helena valley, into the York district, and thence down the country eastward of the present Sound road, to the fine harbour of King George's Sound, would do more than anything else to give an outlet to the resources of the country and supply its wants ; such a line would ultimately be extended through the eastern districts and Victoria plains northward to the Irwin, Greenough, and Geraldton.

But I will recall myself from these and other speculations of the yet more distant future, and look back upon the modest past. Two tramways with locomotives now bring timber to the coast from the Garrah forests, and there are also two other tramways for the same purpose, of less extent, but still of some importance. I have made concessions to the companies constructing them.

27. With regard to ordinary roads, I can very confidently say that, considering the extent of the country and its scattered

population, no colony that I have ever seen is in a better position regarding roads. Occasionally, owing to the loss of convict labour, the scarcity of free labour, the disinclination of the people to tax themselves locally, and the great extent of the roads themselves, parts of the roads already made fall out of repair whilst other parts are being formed; but on the whole, having perhaps traversed more of Western Australia than any one man in the colony, I very confidently assert that, taking all in all throughout the country, the roads are in a better condition than they have ever been before. Large bridges have been constructed over the Upper Swan, Moore River, Blackwood, Capel, and Preston, besides 12 (twelve) smaller bridges, and a large one completed at the Upper Canning.

28. "Bushing" the Geraldton sand-hills has been a very useful and successful work; the experiment was first tried by Lieutenant-Colonel Bruce. Part of the work has been done by convict labour, and part by farmers and settlers in payment for a loan advanced to them for seed-wheat before my arrival. It is not too much to say that this work has saved the town of Geraldton and its harbour from destruction by sand.

29. A little has been done in the way of improving the Swan River navigation by means of a dredge imported by Governor Hampton, and worked by prison labour and by an appropriation in the Loan Act of 1872. A work has also been constructed, from funds provided out of the same loan, at Mandurah, by which the entrance to the Murray River has been improved.

30. Harbour improvements have occupied much of the attention of Government. A fine and substantial open-piled jetty at Fremantle, 750 (seven hundred and fifty) feet long, has been constructed, and answers all the purposes for which it was designed; but the larger and extremely difficult question of the construction of a really safe harbour at or near Fremantle is yet undecided. Various plans have been proposed, and great pressure has been put on the Government to commence works hastily and without engineering advice. At one

time one scheme has found favour, and another at another, and
the merits of the rival schemes of our amateurs have been
popularly judged upon the principle of opposing most strongly
anything that was supposed to find favour with the Government.   Last session a strong wish to do *something* caused
the Legislature to advocate a scheme which many persons
think would cause the mouth of the River Swan to silt up, and
expose the town of Fremantle to danger, lest the river in
flood should burst out (as no doubt it did formerly) into the
South Bay over the town site.   The question, however, is referred to the Victorian Government engineer, and the Melbourne
Government have been asked to allow him to visit this colony,
but I fear that the people will not accept his decision ; and unless
the members of the new Legislature will agree to do so, or, in
the event of his not coming, do what I have long since recommended, namely, ask your Lordship to refer the whole
question to the decision of Sir John Coode, or some other great
authority, and undertake beforehand to abide by it, I see no
chance of anything being carried into effect until the warmth
and personal feeling which, strangely enough, is always evoked
by this question, shall be succeeded by a more reasonable and
business-like mood.   One of my first acts on reaching this colony
was, in accordance with the previously expressed wish of the Council and colonists, to send for an engineer of high repute to report.
His report only raised a tempest of objurgations, and I must
frankly confess failure in my efforts to leave Fremantle with a
harbour ; and, indeed, I am far from being convinced that
anything under an enormous outlay will avail to give an
anchorage and approaches, safe in all weathers, for large ships,
though I, with the Melbourne engineers, think that the plan
of cutting a ship channel into Freshwater Bay, in the Swan
River, advocated by the Rev. Charles Grenfel Nicholay, is
worthy of consideration.   Jetties at Albany, King George's
Sound, the Vasse, Bunbury, and Geraldton, have been
lengthened, one at Dongarra constructed, and money has been
voted for the construction of one at Port Cossack.   Moorings
have been procured from England, and are being laid down at
Fremantle and other ports.

31. With respect to public buildings, the Perth Town Hall—a very large and conspicuous building, commenced by Governor Hampton—was completed not long after my arrival, and handed over by me to the City Council and Municipality on June 1, 1870; attached to it I caused the Legislative Chamber to be built, and so arranged that at no great cost this colony possesses a council-room more convenient and in better taste than many I have seen of far greater pretensions. It is, however, proposed hereafter to build legislative chambers in the new block of Government buildings, of which the Registration Offices now about to be commenced will form a wing, for which the contract is 2502*l.* (two thousand five hundred and two pounds). The public offices at Albany were finished shortly after my arrival. I may mention, among a number of less important buildings, the harbour-master's house, Albany; school-houses there and in various other places; large addition to Government Boys' School, Fremantle; court-house and police-station, and post and telegraphic offices at Greenough and at Dongarra; police-station, Gingin; addition to court-house, York; post and telegraphic offices at Guildford, York; and Northam Bonded Store, Government offices, and police-station, Roebourne. Considerable additions have been made, which add to the convenience and capabilities of the Fremantle Lunatic Asylum, and alterations and adaptations and additions have been made to several other buildings; for instance, at Albany a resident magistrate's house and also a convenient prison have been formed at no great outlay. At Perth a building has been erected to which I call attention, the Government printing-house; this new department has been of immense service during the four years in which it has been in existence—in fact, it would have been impossible to have gone on without it; and the Government printing work is most creditably done at a very reasonable cost. A handsome stone sea-wall has been commenced by convict labour at the new jetty at Fremantle, which will reclaim much valuable land, and greatly improve the appearance of the place. Harbour lights have been erected at several places. A large lighthouse is in the course of erection at Point Moore, at Geraldton,

which will be of much importance; and it is proposed, with the co-operation of other colonies, to erect one near Cape Lecrowin, as recommended at an intercolonial conference on that subject.

32. Postal facilities have been increased, several new offices opened, and postages (under powers vested in me by law) considerably reduced, on both letters to the colonies and newspapers, from the tariff I found in force. In this a step in advance of some of our neighbours was taken.

33. I have reduced several police-stations on the recommendation of Captain Smith, the superintendent, which appeared to be no longer necessary; but, on the other hand, I have extended police protection into outlying districts, both for the benefit of European settlers and of the aboriginal inhabitants. These latter have gained little and lost much by the occupation of their country by settlement. I have fought their battle against cruel wrong and oppression, holding, I trust, the hand of justice with an even balance, and I rejoice to say not without effect and benefit to both races. Their services as stockmen, shepherds, and pearlers are invaluable; and when they die out, as shortly no doubt they will, their disappearance will be universally acknowledged as a great loss to the colonists.

34. The Legislature, I am happy to say, have latterly seconded my efforts by encouraging industrial institutions for their benefit. Similarly they have in the last session turned their attention to the condition of the destitute and criminal children of our own race; and, in my own sphere, I have done what was possible for the encouragement of the (denominational) orphanages which have been long established and are in full working order. This colony is, for its size and means, well supplied with hospitals, asylums, and establishments for paupers, in which I have taken great personal interest.

35. In legislation I have endeavoured to avoid over-legislation and premature legislation. I have considered that free-trade principles are especially in place in a colony situated as this is. The *ad valorem* duty, and that on wines, spirits, and a few other articles, has been raised for revenue purposes; some others have been put on the free list. I successfully resisted

the imposition of a duty on flour; I should have simplified the
tariff still further than I have done, and admitted free many
more articles—some of food, others used in our industries—
had the Legislature not objected; the tariff as it stands is
inconsistent. The English bankruptcy system has been
introduced, and an Act passed regarding fraudulent debtors;
distillation has been permitted under proper safeguards; Sunday
closing of public-houses has been rendered compulsory with
good effect; a Lunacy Bill on the English model has become
law; the "Torrens" Land Registration system has been
adopted, and will shortly be put into force. Many equally
important measures are alluded to in their places in the pages
of this despatch, and I will not inflict upon your lordship a list
of many minor Acts, some not unimportant, which have proved
beneficial in their degree.

36. Among lesser but not unimportant matters, I may
mention that I have extended the system of taking security
from Government officers in receipt of public moneys.

The commencement of a law and parliamentary library has
been made.

37. Immigration from England has, on a small scale, been
set on foot lately, and families are now expected from
nighbouring colonies, but our population from obvious causes
has increased but slightly during the last five years; on
my arrival it was said to be actually decreasing, and there
were many reasons why such an opinion was not unreasonable
—reduction of the convict establishment threw some out of
employment, expirees also desired to quit a country which to
them had been a land of bondage, and the prospects of the
country were gloomy; now there is a great want of labour,
any that comes is at once absorbed, and every effort should be
made to attract a constant stream of immigrants.

38. It will be observed that when the whole authorized loan
is raised, the colony will be only in debt to the extent of a
little over one year's income, or 5*l*. 16*s*. 5¼*d*. a head, whilst
Victoria is indebted 15*l*. 14*s*. 10¾*d*., New South Wales 19*l*. 7*s*.,
South Australia 10*l*. 19*s*. 5*d*., Queensland 32*l*. 12*l*. 7¾*d*.,
Tasmania 14*l*. 3*s*. 6¾*d*., New Zealand 40*l*. 5*s*. 11*d*. I beg also

to call your lordship's attention to the fact that Western Australia has only yet spent the 35,000*l.* (thirty-five thousand pounds) loan, and has now only begun to spend that of 100,000*l.* (one hundred thousand pounds). I also would point out that the last annual increase of revenue has about equalled the whole capital amount which has been expended out of loans.

39. I have caused the following statistics to be furnished me from the Treasury and Customs Departments for six years, ending on the 30th September of each year. The first year given, that ending on the 30th September, 1869, is the year immediately preceding my arrival, I having been sworn in on that very day.

	1869.			1870.			1871.			1872.			1873.			1874.		
	£	s.	d.	£	s.	d.	£	s.	d.	£	s.	d.	£	s.	d.	£	s.	d.
*Imports .	232,830	0	11	232,590	18	8	201,070	3	4	224,396	10	0	253,680	16	2	367,417	15	0
+Exports .	178,860	15	2	204,447	2	2	194,934	9	3	228,807	12	9	278,502	16	0	398,900	8	6
‡Customsduties	48,157	8	9	45,270	14	6	43,464	2	3	53,556	4	5	60,022	1	1	82,016	12	0
§Revenue .	108,600	1	0	109,978	6	3	102,128	3	4	107,828	5	10	120,937	14	8	161,443	8	10
§Expenditure .	107,213	1	10	119,478	8	4	112,285	10	7	103,205	16	0	120,259	11	9	131,334	18	5

OBSERVATIONS.

* Ships now expected will greatly swell the items of Imports and Customs.

+ This is exclusive of re-exported articles, and the valuations are very moderate. In round numbers, the Exports may be said to be over £400,000.

‡ Part of the increase of Customs duties is owing to increase of duties on spirits, wines, and some other items; and ad valorem, on the other hand, credit should be given for some articles which have been admitted free. Taking the balance as the amount accruing from increase of duties, it may be put at £12,000 on the last year.

§ It will be observed that for some time, until better seasons returned and measures bore fruit, I had to a slight extent to rely on the surplus found in the chest to make Revenue and Expenditure meet. To have starved the Expenditure at that time would have been to have damaged the future progress of the colony, and the Legislative Council opposed several reductions that I thought might have been effected.

On the 30th September, 1874, there was a sum of 36,616*l.* 3*s.* 5*d.* (thirty-six thousand six hundred and sixteen pounds three shillings and fivepence) in the chest, and something like this sum will be at the disposal of the Legislature at their meeting, beyond current revenue.

40. I need hardly say that the commercial state of the colony is admittedly sound, and I am informed in a more prosperous condition than at any previous period of its existence. Landed property, especially about Perth, has lately risen immensely in value, and the rise is, I hope, spreading and will reach the outlying districts. Perth has lost its dilapidated appearance, and neat cottages and houses are springing up in all directions, and the same progress to some extent is noticeable in Fremantle and elsewhere.

41. I will not conclude this Report without recalling the success which attended the efforts made by the Government, to which my private secretary Mr. Henry Weld Blundell largely contributed, to represent the products of Western Australia at the Sydney Exhibition of 1873. Much of this success was attributable to the exertions of Mr. F. P. Barlee, Colonial Secretary, then representing at Sydney this colony in the intercolonial conference.

In that conference, the first to which a representative of this colony was admitted, and which therefore marked an epoch in its political existence, Mr. F. P. Barlee took a prominent part, ably upheld the trust I placed in him, and received a most marked and cordial reception from our colonists on his return.

41. I have further to express my obligations to that officer for the assistance he has ever given me; were it not for his fearless and loyal support, for the confidence which is placed in him by the very great majority of the colonists, and for his fidelity in following my instructions and carrying out my policy, it would have been impossible for me, under a form of government most difficult to work, to have carried to a successful issue the trust that has been imposed upon me, and to have left this colony prosperous and self-reliant.

42. Should your lordship, considering the position in which I found Western Australia,—the reduction of imperial expendi-

ture it has been my duty to effect, the failure of the wheat crop for four successive seasons and consequent depression, the inexperience of a new Legislature, the absence of any propositions for the benefit of the colony from the opposition, the obstacles thrown at first in the way of all measures which have eventuated in good,—should you, considering these things and the present state of the colony, be of opinion that the administration of its affairs during the last five years has not been unsatisfactory or unfruitful, I beg that you will award a due share of credit to the Colonial Secretary, who, as my mouthpiece in the Legislature, has carried on singe-handed all parliamentary business, and also to those gentlemen who are now, or have at various times been, members of my executive, and who have ever united to support me; to the nominated members of the Legislature who have steadily voted for all the measures which have led to the present progress of the colony, and whose merits the constituencies have fully recognized by electing them as representatives on vacancies in every case where they have stood; to the elected members, who every session have given me increased support, and who, forming two-thirds of the Legislature, had it in their power entirely to have reversed my policy; and lastly, to the people of Western Australia, who on each election have increased my strength, on whose ultimate good sense, I—knowing colonists, myself an old colonist—put my reliance, a reliance which has not been disappointed.

I have, &c.,

(Signed)   FRED. A. WELD,

Governor.

The Earl of Carnarvon,
    &c.   &c.   &c.

STATISTICS.

Value of Imports and Exports from 1861 to 1873.

1861	...	£147,912	...	£95,789
1862	...	172,991	...	119,313
1863	...	157,136	...	143,105
1864	...	169,856	...	132,738
1865	...	168,413	...	178,487
1866	...	251,907	...	150,066
1867	...	204,613	...	174,080
1868	...	225,614	...	192,636
1869	...	127,977	...	101,359
1870	...	213,258	...	200,984
1871	...	198,011	...	199,288
1872	...	226,656	...	209,107
1873	...	297,328	...	265,217

Value of Imports and Exports for 1874.

COUNTRIES.	IMPORTS.			EXPORTS.		
United Kingdom .	£188,243	10	8	£268,726	4	0
British Colonies :						
Victoria. . . .	75,588	7	0	8,038	1	0
South Australia .	44,021	9	2	41,004	11	0
New South Wales	1,236	4	9			
New Zealand . .	2,065	1	6	12,768	6	0
Mauritius . . .	23,247	7	4	3,435	1	0
Singapore . . .	11,346	19	2	53,648	16	0
Ceylon	1,135	2	0	437	0	0
British India . .	20	10	0	1,345	0	0
All other British Possessions . .	20	10	0	130	3	7
Foreign Countries :						
China	11,461	18	0	36,133	17	0
Java	5,646	2	6	2,934	19	6
Timor	246	14	4			
U. S. of America .	3	15	0	101	0	0
Macassar . . .	...	...		118	0	0
Whaling Ground.	...	...		16	0	0
Total . .	£364,262	15	0	£428,836	19	1

Revenue and Expenditure from 1861 to 1873.

1861	...	£67,261	...	£81,087
1862	...	69,406	...	72,267
1863	...	71,708	...	71,073
1864	...	71,910	...	70,714
1865	...	77,942	...	74,985
1866	...	89,382	...	84,652
1867	...	90,430	...	89,501
1868	...	99,496	...	89,726
1869	...	103,661	...	103,124
1870	...	98,131	...	113,046
1871	...	97,606	...	107,146
1872	...	105,301	...	98,248
1873	...	134,832	...	114,270

Revenue and Expenditure for 1874.

Revenue.	£	s.	d.
Customs	82,275	7	3
Land Sales	7,679	2	4
Land Revenue	19,806	0	5
Money Orders	5,888	12	0
Telegrams	1,784	17	8
Fines, Forfeitures, and Fees of Court	2,022	13	3
Reimbursements in aid of expenses incurred	1,482	12	3
Special Revenue (North District) .	2,133	12	0
Miscellaneous Revenues . .	11,152	18	11
Total Revenue . .	£134,225	16	1

Expenditure.	£	s.	d.
Civil Establishment . . .	58,745	9	9
Miscellaneous Disbursements .	53,111	8	6
Parliamentary Salaries . .	3,910	15	8
Judicial Establishment . .	6,098	18	10
Customs ,, . . .	2,045	1	3
Police ,, . . .	12,923	16	2
Medical ,, . . .	2,377	3	4
Postal and Telegraph Department	4,053	13	3
Total Expenditure .	£143,266	6	8

PUBLIC DEBT £100,000

POPULATION OF WESTERN AUSTRALIA.

1850	. .	5886	1859	. .	14,837	1868	. .	22,733
1853	. .	9334	1862	. .	17,246	1871	. .	25,724
1856	. .	13,391	1865	. .	20,260	1874	. .	26,209

SUCCESSION OF GOVERNORS OF WESTERN AUSTRALIA.

NAME AND TITLE.	APPOINTMENT.	RETIREMENT.
Captain James Stirling, Lieutenant-Governor.	June, 1829.	Sept. 1832.
Captain Irwin, Acting Lieut.-Gov.	Sept. 1832.	Sept. 1833.
Captain Daniell, Acting Lieut.-Gov.	Sept. 1833.	May 11, 1834.
Captain Beete, Acting Lieut.-Gov.	May 11, 1834.	May 24, 1834.
Sir James Stirling (formerly Capt. Stirling), Governor.	Aug. 1834.	Dec. 1838.
John Hutt, Esq., Governor.	Jan. 1839.	Dec. 1845.
Lieut.-Col. Clarke, Governor.	Feb. 1846.	Feb. 1847.
Lieut.-Col. Irwin (formerly Captain Irwin), Governor.	Feb. 1847.	July, 1848.
Captain Charles Fitzgerald, Governor.	Aug. 1848.	June, 1855.
A. E. Kennedy, Esq., Governor.	June, 1855.	Feb. 1862.
Lieut.-Col. John Bruce, Acting Governor.	Feb. 17, 1862.	Feb. 27, 1862.
J. S. Hampton, Esq., Governor.	Feb. 27, 1862.	Nov. 1868.
Lieut.-Col. John Bruce, Acting Governor.	Nov. 1868.	Sept. 1869.
F. A. Weld, Esq., Governor.	Sept. 1869.	Sept. 1874.
W. C. F. Robinson, Esq., C.M.G.	Sept. 1874.	

GILBERT AND RIVINGTON, PRINTERS, ST. JOHN'S SQUARE, LONDON.